Chinatown

In the series

Conflicts in Urban and Regional Development

edited by John R. Logan and Todd Swanstrom

CHINATOWN

The Socioeconomic Potential

of an Urban Enclave

MIN ZHOU

Foreword by

Alejandro Portes

 Temple University Press

Philadelphia

Temple University Press, Philadelphia 19122
Copyright © 1992 by Temple University. All rights reserved
Published 1992
Printed in the United States of America

The paper used in this publication meets the minimum
requirements of American National Standard for Information
Sciences—Permanence of Paper for Printed Library Materials,
ANSI Z39.48-1984

Library of Congress Cataloging-in-Publication Data
Zhou, Min, 1956–
    Chinatown : the socioeconomic potential of an urban enclave /
Min Zhou ; foreword by Alejandro Portes.
        p.   cm. — (Conflicts in urban and regional development)
    Includes bibliographical references and index.
    ISBN 0-87722-934-1 (cl.)
        1. Chinese Americans—New York (N.Y.)—Economic conditions.
2. Chinatown (New York, N.Y.)—Economic conditions.   3. New York
(N.Y.)—Economic conditions.   I. Title.   II. Series.
F128.9.C5Z46   1992
305.895′107471—dc20   91-28649

To Mother and Father

Contents

List of Figures

List of Tables

Foreword
by Alejandro Portes

Chinatown: The name evokes images of an exotic world where people different from the rest of us lead secretive, mysterious lives. The excitement one experiences in stepping into these patches of urban territory comes from the paradox of finding oneself in a wholly foreign land without ever leaving home—the Orient a bus ride away. And yet these extraordinary social entities have been the subject of remarkably little sociological inquiry. Perhaps their very foreignness, their vast distance from the everyday realities of American urban life, has ruled them out as serious subjects of investigation. Chinatown is in the city, but not really of it. One might as well study a foreign country.

Most of what has been written about these areas takes two distinct tacks. The first portrays them as dark recesses of capitalism where poor newcomers, ignorant of the language and their labor rights, are mercilessly exploited by fellow nationals for the ultimate benefit of large concerns in the mainstream economy. The Chinatown sweatshop has become a familiar buzzword as an example of what capitalist greed can do to defenseless foreign workers. Even darker practices are adumbrated as common features of this ethnic economy: drug trafficking, illegal gambling, and prostitution. In the final analysis, these uniformly negative writings represent the continuation, in modern academic garb, of the anti-Chinese literature of the turn of the century. Then as now, Chinatown is portrayed as an unruly den of exploitation and iniquity. If the intention has changed—from excluding the foreigners to unionizing them —the consequence is the same, as these portrayals consistently reinforce the bad image of the place. Journalistic and academic critics have had a hard time explaining how it is that, despite all these shortcomings, these ethnic areas have continued to survive and prosper with nary a word of protest from most of the participants. You have never heard of a Chinatown going up in flames.

The second tack is to assimilate these areas into the broader category of early reception areas for recent immigrants. Most large-scale migrations have developed similar staging centers, where new arrivals can be protected for a while from cultural shock and provided with the necessary information to navigate their new social surroundings. The Chinese are no different. In the end, these reception areas are left behind by successful immigrants to decay into ethnic ghettos or to host a new wave of migrants from another country. The average sociology professor out for a casual stroll in Chinatown exudes an air of confident knowledge and understanding. He has read his Robert Park, knows everything about the theory of ethnic transitions, and what he is seeing is a typical immigrant neighborhood sheltering newcomers prior to their certain assimilation into the American mainstream.

Wrong. The area was indeed a place of refuge in its early years, but it has evolved since then to become a large ethnic economy of considerable resilience and vigor. It is not only a residential area, as most immigrant neighborhoods or current inner-city ghettos are, but a veritable enterprise zone. It is the place where Chinese immigrants and their descendants have founded a host of independent small businesses which converted them into one of the most economically successful groups in the history of American immigration. The agglomeration of these ethnic businesses gives Chinatown a bustling ambiance, a thrilling sense of purpose and ambition absent from the inert look of inner-city storefronts. More than anything, this ethnic economy is characterized by giving newcomers an alternative to wage labor in the mainstream labor market—an alternative that may exploit some but gives others their only chance of someday launching their own enterprises.

Understanding the inner dynamics of the Chinese enclave is no easy task because, in addition to the theoretical blinders that have defined it as a lumpen zone or as just another immigrant neighborhood, there is the question of overcoming the barriers of language, local reserve, and custom. Min Zhou has accomplished this task admirably by making use of her knowledge of the culture, while avoiding the influence of widely accepted but erroneous tales about what Chinatown is like. Instead, she painstakingly assembled census and historical data about the Chinese in New York and went into the area to talk to the people in their own language. The results are novel and persuasive. Zhou portrays Chinatown as an old but constantly renewed immigrant community that has gone through many phases before reaching its mature identity. Chinatown today is not only a place where impoverished immigrants live but an area with which residents, business owners, and workers alike can identify. It possesses all the characteristics of a well-knit community and, as such, offers to its members a clear sense of place, a source of local pride, and some unique economic opportunities.

The unschooled visitor, unfamiliar with sociological theories, may think of the area instead as a foreign intrusion. Present-day Chinatown gives indeed the impression of an ethnic tour de force, a deliberate foreign creation in America. Zhou's analysis makes clear that the opposite is actually the case: Chinatown is a unique American creation. The original settlers were not profit-oriented capitalists, nor did they plan to settle down in America. They came as miners and railroad workers, recruited in Chinese ports and planning to return to their villages once they had saved enough gold. Few succeeded in this goal because of the relentless exploitation to which they were subjected and the implacable enmity of white workers. The Chinese went to New York to escape xenophobic persecution in California and became small entrepreneurs by default. Barred from regular wage labor by nativist agitation, they took to hand laundries and cheap ethnic restaurants, economic niches that no one else wanted, as a means of survival.

The fact that Chinatowns were not the outgrowth of deliberate entrepreneurial initiative but an adaptive response to harsh realities in the host society had a decisive effect in their subsequent development. The notorious reserve of Chinese entrepreneurs, their "clannishness," and the readiness of community representatives to adopt a "minority" discourse despite the obvious economic progress of the group in recent years can all be related, in part, to an earlier history of persecution. But because Chinatown was an American creation, it also facilitated the adaptation of the small entrepreneurs to the American system and the successful entry of their children into U.S. colleges and universities. Today, the typical Chinatown restaurant owner is probably more knowledgeable about American business practices than most of his patrons. He probably can outbuy and outsell most of them.

More than an outpost of a foreign country in America, the Chinese enclave is a unique American phenomenon, which today plays a significant role as a conduit of modern culture and modern aspirations to the original communities to which it is linked by sentiment and family obligations. An entity suspended in midair between two countries, Chinatown is certainly not. A growing American ethnic economy reaching out to its historical roots for both family reasons and material gain, it clearly is. Zhou's work has made our understanding of this complex community and its historical origins much clearer than it has been so far. In the future, theory will have to accommodate to the peculiar realities of this unique immigrant group rather than the other way around.

Preface

My focus in this book is on the experience of recent immigrant Chinese in Chinatown's enclave economy and how networks of the ethnic community facilitate their social mobility. Instead of approaching Chinatown as an urban ghetto where poverty and urban diseases prevail, I view it as an immigrant enclave with strong socioeconomic potential for channeling immigrant Chinese into the mainstream U.S. society.

Since the reform of the U.S. immigration law in 1965, which abolished the national-origins quota system favoring European immigrants, the Chinese have entered the United States in unprecedentedly large numbers. As a result, many urban centers and suburban cities have developed visible Chinese populations and satellite Chinatowns. Meanwhile, as a sizable minority group, Chinese-Americans have successfully made headway into the mainstream, exhibiting remarkable socioeconomic achievements. According to the 1980 census, the average levels of educational attainment and median household income for persons of Chinese descent were higher than the national average. For the first time, Chinese-Americans were applauded as a great "success story" and celebrated as a "model minority."

Behind the applause and celebrations, however, little attention has been paid to the socioeconomic potential of Chinatown in helping immigrants fight a general struggle to "make it" in America without losing their ethnic identity and solidarity. Paradoxically, the desire of immigrant Chinese for economic incorporation and security seems in conflict with cultural assimilation. Past studies of American Chinatowns have been limited. Many historians and anthropologists have tended to portray Chinatown as a survival strategy or as a first stop along a unilinear assimilation path by which immigrants enter at the bottom of the socioeconomic hierarchy to begin a process of acculturation and social mobility. Political scientists have tended to view Chinatown as a site facilitating capital exploitation of cheap and nonunionized labor. These studies uniformly lament a failure of assimilation. In this book, I have tried to uncover Chinatown's socioeconomic potential for serving as a positive alternative for immigrant incorporation.

I have selected New York City's Chinatown for a number of reasons. First, it is one of the nation's largest Chinatowns, concentrating a sizable number of Chinese-Americans and recent Chinese immigrants. Results generated from this study are expected to bear significant import for Chinatowns in other metropolitan cities despite substantial differences that may exist among Chinatowns across the nation. Second, New York City's Chinatown is, after San Francisco's, the oldest Chinatown in the United States. The enclave economy has a long history and has hosted several successive first-generation and some second-generation immigrant entrepreneurs. Although data are cross-sectional, implications can be made intergenerationally. Third, New York City's original Chinatown has experienced rapid decentralization, with satellite Chinatowns being established in outer boroughs, such as Queens and Brooklyn, and with outlets of its economy spreading all over the city. While recent immigrant Chinese tend to be more residentially dispersed, they are still predominantly concentrated in jobs generated in the enclave economy—a pattern prevailing in other major Chinatowns. Finally, New York City's Chinatown is more accessible to me, for there I can benefit not only from my own ethnicity but also from a close-knit social network comprising my immigrant relatives and family friends. Chinatown is my community. My attachment to the community and my personal experience as an immigrant, shared with many immigrant Chinese, give me rapport with the community. During my fieldwork research in Chinatown, I have been able to conduct most of my planned interviews with informants who talked to me as if they were talking to their daughter, sister, or close friend.

Research on Chinatown's enclave economy is a relatively new area. My conclusions are based on qualitative case studies as well as on quantitative data. I rely mainly on the following sources of data, obtained from the U.S. census, documentary accounts, and extensive fieldwork interviews.

A. U.S. Census Data
  1. *Census of Population and Housing*, 1980 PUMS—the 5 percent Public-Use Microdata Sample A file. This data set is extracted to include only the Asians and non-Hispanic whites in the New York metropolitan area, that is, New York City

and counties adjacent to the city in New York (Nassau, Rockland, Suffolk, Westchester) and New Jersey (Bergen, Essex, Hudson, Mercer, Middlesex, Monmouth, Morris, Passaic, Somerset, and Union).

2. *Census of Population and Housing,* 1980 STF3A—Summary Tape File 3A. This data set is extracted to include the same set of county groups in New York and New Jersey as specified above. The census tract data contain smaller geographical units and are used to supplement the PUMS data, whose smallest geographical unit is the county. It is used to measure the degree of segregation in decentralized groups of Chinese across the New York metropolitan area.

3. *Survey of Minority-Owned Business Enterprises: Asian and Pacific Islander, 1972, 1977, 1982, and 1987.* The data provide information on growth and changes in development of Chinese-owned firms.

B. Other Statistical Data

   1. *Statistical Yearbook of the Immigration and Naturalization Service.* Immigration statistics provide accurate and more recent data on the socioeconomic characteristics of immigrants. This kind of information updates, to some extent, some of the census data.

   2. *Manhattan Real Estate Transactions, 1988.* These data are collected annually by the New York City Real Estate Corporation. The data show the property transactions, ownership, payment patterns, and the location of property for sale. I am particularly interested in observing whether properties in Chinatown have changed hands among the Chinese or between Chinese and non-Chinese owners. The data are used to examine patterns of neighborhood take-over and geographical expansion of Chinatown.

C. Documentary and Historical Data

   Quantitative data are sometimes misleading and deceptive, since the immigrant Chinese have a tendency to feel intimidated by census personnel and research workers in surveys. Thus, I have supplemented those data by careful examination of historical and other documentary records and by extensive fieldwork.

   1. Newspaper files. Old newspapers contain invaluable historical accounts of Chinatown and the settlement patterns of Chi-

nese immigrants. Newspapers also provide clues and sources of a wide range of community data, such as follow-up stories on different issues of interest, the exact dates of events, names of informants, community interviews, and frequencies of Chinatown publicity. I mainly focus on the *New York Times*, and three of the major local Chinese newspapers—*World Journal, Central Daily* (*Zhong Bao*), and *Overseas Chinese Daily*.

2. Government records, study reports, and community files. New York City's Department of City Planning has conducted studies on the Chinatown area over the last fifteen years. Also studies on a wide range of broader issues—immigration, racial discrimination, ethnic business development— have been conducted by various government agencies and organizations. Moreover, because many businesses are government regulated for tax purposes, they are required to provide regular reports for the government and the public. These study reports and files help in understanding many community issues.

3. Telephone directories. Those published in Chinatown list most of the Chinese firms in the New York metropolitan area. They provide information on the types and locations of Chinese firms in and out of Chinatown and the changes over an extended period of time. Simple frequency counts display the distribution of Chinatown's economic activities; comparison of the two directories—1958 and 1988—shows changes and development trends over time.

D. Fieldwork

I collected fieldwork data during 1988 and 1989 by periodic observations in Chinatown and extensive interviews with city government officials, local leaders, community organizers, investors and bankers, real estate agents, business owners, enclave workers, and nonenclave Chinese immigrant workers, longtime residents, and finally, American-born Chinese.

I used a snowball sampling method in selecting fifty informants of various occupations. Questions directed to government officials and local community leaders covered the overall perception of Chinatown, the changing policies targeted at community planning, government-community relations, zoning, and revitalization projects. Questions directed to business leaders covered locational decisions, return on monetary and human-capital investments, previous jobs, advantages and disadvantages of self-employment, sources of financing for business start-up and expansion, and possible upward mobility within the enclave or mobility into the larger economy. Questions for both enclave and nonenclave workers involved the immigration process, education before and after immigration, English proficiency, family relations, ethnic identity, past employment, experience of racial discrimination, inter- or intraethnic labor-market experiences, job satisfaction, and experience with labor unions. I personally conducted all the face-to-face and telephone interviews with my informants and some of their families in Cantonese, Mandarin, and English. The interviewees were informed of the research purpose before interviewing. All the interview information was taped and is either translated or quoted directly from the original, with grammatical modifications in the English quotations. For the sake of confidentiality, pseudonyms are used for the interviewees throughout the book, unless a full name is given.

The Pinyin system of romanization is used for most of the Chinese names unless otherwise specified, that is, Taishan replaces Toishan, Guangdong replaces Kwang-tung, and so on, but Canton remains to refer to a specific area of Guangzhou.

This book does not contend that the Chinese constitute a model minority whose success illustrates the openness of the American society. Rather, I believe their experience shows that there are alternative paths to social mobility in spite of the many obstacles to assimilation, possibly including participation in Chinatown.

Acknowledgments

This book is a result of the contributions, help, and support of many people and agencies, both in the academic field and in the Chinese community in New York City.

Throughout this study, John R. Logan, my adviser and friend, was always ready to offer advice, criticism, and encouragement but was never interfering and prodding. I am deeply indebted to him for his sympathetic and persistent help and support. Many thanks are also due to Richard Alba, Nan Lin, and Todd Swanstrom, not only for their encouragement and support, but also for their kind forbearance with my innumerable requests for advice and discussion at various stages of the study.

As always, I have benefited greatly from the advice and discussions of many scholars in the field—Sucheta Mazumdar, Victor Nee, Alejandro Portes, Glenna Spitze, Betty Lee Sung, Roger Waldinger, Walter Zenner, and many others.

I am particularly grateful to the Center for Social and Demographic Analysis at SUNY-Albany for making the census data available to me, and many thanks to Brian Fisher, whose help was significant in my data analysis.

This study involves many discussions and interviews with city planners, community organizers, business leaders and entrepreneurs, immigrant workers and their families, and retired old-timers—all of whom were more than generous with their time and knowledge. I would have difficulty singling out every name of these individuals, but I cannot allow the opportunity to pass without thanking Hsuan-tsun Kuo of New York City's Department of City Planning; William David Chin of the Chinatown History Project; Ping Kee Chan of the Chinese Consolidated Benevolence Association; Jonn Wang of the Chinatown Planning Council; Schuman S. Tu of Great Eastern Bank; Suen Heong Chiu of the Bayard Street Restaurant; Frank S. P. Chu of EastBank; Henry Cheng of the

Flushing Chinese Business Association; May Chan, Katty Quan, and others from the International Ladies' Garment Workers' Union—Local 23-25. Many thanks also to my relatives and friends Qi-huan Qiu, Pei-qing Liu, Kwock Choi Chow, Melvin Fung, and Shuyang Zhou, who provided me with room and board and helped me build community connections while I was doing research in New York City.

I am especially grateful to Russell Wise, Joanne Ebihara, and Nan Guo for their time and effort in proofreading and editing the earlier draft of the manuscript.

Finally, I owe many thanks to my family, whose love, support, and understanding were indispensable.

Chinatown

1

Introduction

Strolling along the Lower East Side of Manhattan, New York City, one cannot possibly miss Chinatown, one of the many old ethnic neighborhoods that has formed part of the city's social mosaic. In Chinatown shops of all kinds are marked with signs written in Chinese characters, narrow sidewalks are crowded with vegetable stands and vendor carts, restaurant windows show rows of barbecued ribs and roast chickens and ducklings, and the air is filled with smells of dim sum[1] and other delicacies. Every day camera-toting tourists jam the busy streets, wandering about restaurants, shops, and vendor stands to try to get the sensation of an exotic culture.

The local residents of Chinatown cling to old values and traditional ways to keep alive bits and pieces of a culture that are not meant for display. The community's cloistered inwardness, its preoccupation with concerns that mean little elsewhere in the larger society, and the language barrier seem to keep the outside world from understanding much about the inner workings and dramatic changes of this unique community.

This book focuses on the lives and experiences of immigrant Chinese and their relationship with Chinatown for the past two decades. It explains how an immigrant enclave has successfully channeled its group members into the American mainstream and guarded itself against social dislocation, ghettoization, and degradation.

Immigrant Enclaves and Assimilation

The United States is a nation of immigrants. This land is often perceived as a "melting pot," where peoples of different national origins or racial and ethnic backgrounds will all eventually assimilate into a unified identity and become Americanized with the passage of time.

Immigrant or ethnic enclaves are often seen as a form of segregation, an obstacle to assimilation. Prior research has often treated residential segregation as an indicator of general shifts in the relative positions of the groups.[2] Why have thousands of immigrants, upon arrival in the United States, isolated themselves in enclaves, and why have some enclaves been more persistent than others? The assimilation model, perhaps the most influential perspective on ethnic segregation, posits that all ethnic groups, regardless of national origin or racial and ethnic background, tend to be drawn into the economic mainstream and to gain social acceptance through their educational and occupational achievements. It hypothesizes an inverse relationship between residential segregation and socioeconomic status. Because of the initial disadvantages associated with immigrant status, such as lack of knowledge of English, information about the larger society, transferable skills, and employment networks, new immigrants often confront various obstacles in crossing the threshold to the larger society.[3] Therefore, upon arrival, they usually form their own ethnic enclaves and cluster around those communities.

Following a universal law of natural selection, the majority of the new immigrants have to settle temporarily in less-desirable areas, depend on each other for survival, and take whatever jobs are available in order to survive in their new country. Most of the time, they are limited to jobs that are located at the narrow margins of the larger economy or to small-scale, family-based, low-wage businesses developed by ethnic subeconomies. Yet, they slowly learn as they go. As members of ethnic groups climb up the socioeconomic ladder, they tend to convert their status attainments into contacts with the majority group by moving out of their original ethnic community and into places with higher status and greater advantages. In time, immigrant communities disperse as interethnic contacts become more frequent and ethnic group members become acculturated and establish themselves socioeconomically in the larger society. Therefore, segregation is only temporary. Distinctive ethnic traits disappear and residential dispersion occurs as natural and inevitable outcomes of race contact or as a function of length of residence and occupational achievement.[4] An ethnic subeconomy, according to the same logic, is significant only in serving the short-term survival needs of the newcomers. The possible fate of the ethnic enclave, following the assimilationist reasoning, is twofold. It may diminish as group members, having improved their labor-market position and absorbed mainstream values, choose residences in more affluent white middle-class neighborhoods, retaining only a "symbolic" ethnicity. Or it may remain as a continuously declining ghetto made up of only the least successful group members.[5]

These hypotheses have gained credibility from research on European ethnic minority groups such as Italian-Americans.[6] However, the persistence of ethnicity and race, both as important facets of personal identity and as triggers for prejudice and discrimination, has led to a reconceptualization by social scientists of the process of absorbing group members. Contrary to the melting-pot assumption that immigrants should lose their cultural uniqueness and acquire mainstream values to become assimilated into U.S. society, the ethnic-cultural model adopts a pluralistic approach. This model proposes a "salad-bowl" thesis, suggesting that there exists an acceptance or tolerance of the diversity of various immigrant groups in their modes of adaptation to their new country. It assumes that ecological factors do produce significant effects upon segregation of ethnic communities in the urban environment, precisely by supporting the vitality of distinctive cultures. Though segregated, people in cities live in meaningful social worlds. These worlds are inhabited by different groups, based on ethnic culture, religion, shared values, beliefs, and behaviors, or other common traits.[7] Ethnicity often represents a shared lifestyle, similar needs in daily life, and social boundaries for interpersonal interaction and support. Sociologists who use this approach consider ethnic segregation a result of exposure to a dominant culture.[8] Segregated ethnic communities provide the sense of physical and psychic security that comes from the familiar and dependable environment. Although, over time, the immigrants and their descendants may move to newer and better neighborhoods, the original area of settlement often remains a center for ethnic stores and services and thereby a symbol of common ethnic identity.[9]

The ethnic-cultural model asserts that communal solidarity helps immigrant groups respond to the specificity of the immigrant situation, by organizing the collective resources needed to exploit economic opportunities and, thus, providing an "elective affinity" with the requirements of an ethnic subeconomy.[10] The development of ethnic subeconomies necessarily depends upon a combination of ethnic and class resources. Unlike any bourgeois in the larger economy, who presumably utilizes only his or her class resources—human capital and physical capital—to prosper in business, the ethnic bourgeois has a unique access to ethnic resources.[11] He or she is able to draw upon traditional values and solidarities in business establishments. These ethnic resources enable ethnic entrepreneurs to widen their profit margins, and support them in the competitive environment of the larger economy. In doing so, the ethnic subeconomy provides a means of social mobility for the entrepreneurs themselves and a means of survival for their co-ethnics who are denied entry into the larger labor market because of initial disadvantages.

The ethnic-cultural model does not completely deny the possibility of eventual assimilation. However, it depicts the path as much more difficult for immigrants, especially for those who have been deeply socialized and rooted in their original culture before entering the new world and who have directly benefited from the ethnic community. Over the course of several generations, ethnic enclaves have a tendency to decay.[12] The second and later generations more readily turn away from the enclave's traditional institutions and some of its cultural values, adopt a white, middle-class lifestyle, and become fully Americanized. But this process is not necessarily preceded by a loss of individual ethnic traits and cultural identity.

The experience of adaptation for some immigrant groups suggests contrasting paths that do not agree with the unilinear process of assimilation offered by the assimilation model and implied by the ethnic-cultural model. Alejandro Portes and his colleagues have put forward the enclave-economy model to describe an alternative mode of incorporation of ethnic minority groups, especially immigrant groups, into the mainstream society.[13] This model emphasizes the crucial role that an ethnic economy and ethnic social networks can play in the social mobility and status attainment of ethnic group members.

The enclave-economy model contains both an economic and a cultural component. The ethnic enclave is understood as a segmented sector of the larger economy, a partially autonomous enclave economic structure constituting a distinct labor market. The enclave economy, as well as its related labor market, is structured in a way similar to the larger economy, but it functions to support ethnic businesses and to help them compete more successfully in the larger economic system. With the existence of such an alternative, immigrants do not necessarily start from the secondary economy or at the lowest rung of the societal ladder. Instead, they can organize themselves to trade exclusively or primarily within the enclave.

Portes specifically argues that the enclave does not necessarily block the upward social mobility of its members. Evidence from the Cuban enclave in Miami has shown that immigrant businesses are able to capture the positive characteristics and advantages of the primary sector of the larger economy better within the enclave than outside it. The most apparent advantage has been a substantial return on past human-capital investment, such as education and labor-market experience. The Miami study has concluded that although most immigrant firms are small, competitive enterprises, enclave workers can get significant earning returns for human-capital characteristics. Such returns are absent among immigrant workers in the open secondary labor market.[14]

The enclave economy also benefits from the positive cultural identity of the group through such communal institutions as the family, kinship networks, and other ethnic social institutions. Ethnic solidarities, in the long run, help immigrant entrepreneurs mobilize the collective resources needed to exploit the opportunities for small-scale enterprises and provide immigrant workers with work conditions and return on past human-capital investment that replicate the primary economy. Within the highly differentiated enclave, members can conduct their daily work and leisure activities without extensive interaction with the larger society. In practice, the majority of the immigrants choose the enclave economy over the open secondary economy basically because the enclave offers not only security and shelter against overt ethnic discrimination but also opportunities for upward social mobility. As a result, the cost of employment in the secondary labor market for immigrant workers can be effectively reduced. In this sense, being confined to the enclave does not necessarily mean the "failure" of assimilation, for the enclave economy helps immigrants surmount structural obstacles and raise themselves socioeconomically; it is simply another mode of immigrant incorporation. Thus, immigrants have always undergone adaptation to American society, and they will continue to do so. Yet, the direction, pace, and the manner in which the second or later generations become integrated depends on the modes of adaptation and economic accomplishment of the earlier immigrants.[15]

These theoretical models have, in one way or another, tackled some of the most important research issues of immigrant adaptation. The assimilation model, based on the melting-pot assumption, argues that immigrants have to compete with native workers and other ethnic groups for economic opportunities in the larger society and that ethnic enclaves depend for their economic success or failure upon the opportunities provided by the open market. The opportunity is typically an "ethnic niche," which is supposed to best fit an ethnic group. The assimilation process, thus, is viewed as a series of stages culminating in absorption of the dominant social values and cultures of the mainstream, or at least one of its subsegments.

The ethnic-cultural approach rests on the hypothesis that some cultures predispose their members toward the successful pursuit of certain specific goals. It perceives assimilation without acculturation. In a culturally pluralist situation, immigrants are able to retain their own distinctive heritage while interacting with other groups in the larger society. Under cultural pluralism, differences in values and norms do not result in prejudice and discrimination; each group is allowed to function on relatively equal ground.

Finally, the enclave-economy model rejects the view that the success of immigrant adaptation depends solely upon individual traits, abilities, and motivations. By focusing on the social and structural context in which immigrants become incorporated, it integrates some parts of the ethnic-cultural model and assumes an ethnic-specific economic structure in which an enclave economy can participate.

Chinatown as a Socioeconomic Enclave

New York City's Chinatown emerged as a direct result of the anti-Chinese campaign on the West Coast and the Chinese Exclusion Act. It was not until the 1880s that a significant number of Chinese added the long transcontinental trip to their transpacific voyage. Frustrated that years of hard work had not rewarded them with gold to bring home, frightened by unjust treatment in the West, and intimidated by the dominant white society, the eastbound Chinese never again wanted to take the risk of hunting for quick fortunes in a new place. Instead, they clung to each other in the hope that some day their "gold dream" would come true and they could all go home with lots of gold to honor their ancestors and families.

Old Chinatown began to take form in a ten-block area bounded by Canal Street on the north, Park Row on the south, Baxter Street on the west, and the Bowery on the east on the Lower East Side of Manhattan (Figure 1-1). For half a century, this enclave housed almost all of New York City's Chinese. Even after World War II, when New York City gained more Chinese population as a result of the repeal of the Chinese Exclusion Act and passage of the War Brides Act, Chinatown was still home to the majority of the immigrants (approximately ten thousand of them). Today, the traditionally delineated Old Chinatown has expanded over its ten-block boundary uptown to Houston Street and to Essex Street on the east, with some clusters near Fourteenth Street and in the surrounding neighborhoods.

New York City's Chinatown has shown many faces to the American public since the late nineteenth century. For thousands of tourists and New Yorkers, Chinatown is simply viewed as one of the most interesting

Figure 1-1. Chinatown in Lower East Manhattan, New York City
Source: Department of City Planning, New York City.

tourist attractions, a place where they can wander about to escape from the boredom of their routine work, treat themselves to a special meal, and have some fun bargaining with the aliens. Other than that, it is merely an immigrant ghetto, an undesirable place to live and an alien world to which they do not belong. Even many Chinese immigrants take Chinatown for granted. It is a place where they can speak their own language; share their pleasure, pain, nostalgia; and feel a sense of home. They are all too pre-occupied in their daily struggle to find out what makes Chinatown tick and how far they can go from there.

Yet, in the eyes of many serious scholars and researchers, the view of Chinatown turns gloomy. They generally perceive Chinatown as a de-teriorating slum. Its dank and filthy cubicle dwellings, run-down housing with ever-skyrocketing rents, stifling air, and seemingly demeaning life-style are totally incomprehensible to the larger population. The squalid living conditions are only part of the story. Chinatown is plagued with vice. The long-standing protection rackets, high-stakes basement gam-bling dens, and houses of prostitution increasingly branch out into extor-tion, armed robbery, street-gang fights, large-scale heroin importing, and the smuggling of illegal aliens. Furthermore, Chinatown is geared toward an ethnic elite who build their fortunes on the exploitation of cheap im-migrant labor through extremely low wages, poor working conditions, long hours, and so on. People lament, "There are no norms anymore, no rules, no values, and the code has broken down." [16] Chinatown works only for the ethnic elite that has risen at the expense of other Chinese. [17] Most group members continue to be "trapped" in the ghetto: they will never be able to rise to decent positions in their new country; instead, they will eventually suffer the same fate as the emerging urban underclass as they increase in numbers and get stuck there. [18]

Less attention is paid to the bright face of this dynamic community. There are signs of prosperity, hope, and solidarity everywhere. Busi-nesses are growing and thriving. The community is expanding beyond its traditional boundaries, bringing life to the decaying areas surround-ing Old Chinatown. Every morning streams of Chinese workers pour into Chinatown from nearby subway exits, along with the delivery trucks, to join the local residents in beginning a day's work. In the evenings the commuting workers rush down the subway and quickly melt into the peak-hour traffic on their way home. During weekends and holidays, life is even more vigorous. Families and friends who live elsewhere gather in Chinatown to attend movies or plays, join in various games, or celebrate their recent achievements, family events, or special occasions, such as the purchase of a new home, weddings, birthday parties, and family reunions. Day in and day out, Chinatown carries on with its own rhythm and internal vitality.

Chinatown's residents and many of the new immigrants may live in dilapidated housing, they may work long hours at low-wage jobs, and they may be poor, but they are not impoverished. In Chinatown, a cohesive ethnic culture—a work ethic, persistence, self-esteem, a spirit of self-sacrifice and family commitment—helps them unfold their American dream. After years of hostility, exclusion, and struggle, Chinatown is now changing and learning a new self-confidence with hope and inspiration. So prosperous and full of life is it today that it little resembles what it was in the old days. After more than a hundred years, Chinatown—one of the city's oldest and most dynamic immigrant enclaves—has grown into a consolidated immigrant community. It is from there that hundreds and thousands of newer immigrants are striving to secure their own subsistence and build better lives.

New York City's Chinatown was selected for this study primarily for three reasons. First, New York City's Chinese population has grown at an unprecedented rate, from 33,000 in 1960 to 124,372 in 1980 by census count, the largest Chinese population of any single U.S. city in 1980. During the decade 1970–1980, San Francisco, where the nation's oldest Chinatown is located, had only a quarter (82,244) of the Chinese population in California, but 85 percent of New York State's Chinese were concentrated in New York City. Moreover, from one-fifth to one-fourth of all Chinese immigrating to the United States every year since 1965 have settled in New York City. Second, New York City's Chinatown, once a bachelors' society situated in a ten-block area, has expanded in all directions beyond its traditional boundaries in recent years. The influx of recent Chinese immigrants and their families has changed the social and economic structures of the ethnic enclave, and it also accounts for much of the decentralization of Chinatown. The city's outer boroughs, such as Queens and Brooklyn, have developed visible Chinese populations and satellite Chinatowns, in part from the outward movement of people from Manhattan's Chinatown and in part through the family networks of new immigrants. Third, Chinatown's economy has developed from within and has a strong geographical base, with outlets spreading all over the city. Also, the enclave economy has a relatively long history, and it has seen a succession of first-generation immigrant entrepreneurs. I believe that results generated from this study are representative and have significant meaning for Chinatowns in other metropolitan cities, though variations among different Chinatowns across the nation may exist.

Chinatown is a dynamic immigrant enclave that is constantly changing and developing. Past studies of American Chinatowns were predominantly limited to historical and anthropological frameworks and tended to view Chinatowns simply as a survival strategy—a means of self-reliance and self-defense—or as a first stop along a unilinear assimilation path in which immigrants entered at the bottom of the socioeconomic ladder to begin a process of acculturation and mobility lasting several generations.[19] Other social scientists have challenged this traditional view and linked Chinatown to the political economy of the larger system of capitalism. Peter Kwong sees the self-maintenance and self-reliance in Chinatown as sustained by the dynamics of an informal politico-economic structure within the larger economic system of capitalism. He argues that because of the capitalist need for an exploitable labor force, Chinatown has increasingly divided the ethnic Chinese into a small elite class and a large working class.[20] The external forces from the larger political economy of capitalism have combined with the interests of Chinatown's elite class to preserve and strengthen the existing politico-economic order of the community, further polarizing it. Social mobility for the ethnic working class is largely constrained by the dominance of the ethnic elite. Members of the elite class have managed to shift the minority disadvantages onto their less fortunate co-ethnics and have built their fortunes on extreme exploitation of the ethnic working class within the enclave. The end result of Chinatown, therefore, is neither a declining urban ghetto, like many black and Latino slums in inner cities, nor a diminishing remnant of ethnic symbols, like Little Italy.

I take a different stand from these past studies to approach Chinatown as a socioeconomic institution that provides immigrant Chinese with advantages and opportunities that are not easily accessible in the larger society and helps them to make headway in society without losing ethnic identity and solidarity. Throughout this book, I treat Chinatown as an economic enclave embedded in the very nature of the community's social structure, offering a positive alternative to immigrant incorporation.

According to the enclave-economy model, economic enclaves are created by certain immigrant groups as their distinct mode of incorporation into the receiving country. Portes originally defines the enclave as containing "immigrant groups which concentrate in a distinct spatial location and organize a variety of enterprises serving their own ethnic market and/or the general population. Their basic characteristic is that a significant proportion of the immigrant work force works in enterprises owned by other immigrants." [21] He later modifies this definition to emphasize enclave participation by place of work: "Enclave entrepreneurs are immigrant owners of firms in an area where similar enterprises concentrate. Enclave workers are employees of these firms." [22]

An economic enclave is distinguished from an ethnic neighborhood, which is usually equated with and stereotyped as a homogeneous residential area where poor and more recent immigrants concentrate, with little diversity in their economic activities. Portes and Bach note: "We must also distinguish enclaves from immigrant neighborhoods. Most immigrant groups initially resettle in ethnically concentrated communities and generate a few small businesses to serve immediate, specialized consumption needs. Ethnic neighborhoods fulfill important social support functions, but lack the extensive division of labor of the enclave and, especially, its highly differentiated entrepreneurial class." [23]

The economic enclave is thus a partially autonomous economic system, constituting a distinct labor market. This labor market (and possibly also a consumer market) supports ethnic businesses and helps them compete more successfully in the larger economic system. The highly differentiated ethnic market makes it possible for participating immigrants to achieve social mobility through the enclave economic structure.

New York City's Chinatown, which consists of a wide range of businesses owned by the Chinese and a sufficiently large labor pool, fits the general description of the economic enclave. The enclave, however, is not so much a strict geographical concept as an organizational one. Whereas most of the Chinese-owned businesses are highly concentrated in Chinatown, others have spread throughout the city to other satellite Chinatowns. The 1982 *Survey of Minority-Owned Business Enterprises* indicated that 87 percent of all Chinese-owned firms in New York State were located in the New York metropolitan area (5,413 of 6,216 businesses). And of the 5,978 total entries in the 1988 *Chinese Business Guide and Directory for Metropolitan New York and Boston*, close to 60 percent of Chinese firms were located in Manhattan's Chinatown, and many firms were segregated in Flushing and Brooklyn where they could be supported by a large concentration of the ethnic population. [24] The outlying Chinese-owned businesses, though physically detached from Chinatown, retain strong ties to, or display similar characteristics to, the organizational structures of the enclave economy. Non-Chinese-owned firms based in Chinatown are excluded from the enclave definition. Although they are

located in Chinatown and may have a large body of Chinese employees and a majority of Chinese customers, they are different from ethnic
firms in ownership patterns, resources, market channels, business performance, management norms, labor control, and many other aspects. Yet,
these businesses certainly have a strong effect on Chinatown's enclave
economy.

Another significant characteristic of the economic enclave is its "embeddedness." As Mark Granovetter has argued, economic behavior is
closely embedded in the ongoing structures of social relations.[25] This embeddedness denies that the individual is a self-interested organism who
bases his or her rational calculation purely on maximizing benefits and
minimizing costs. It also endows the individual with resources beyond
his or her control.[26] These resources—namely, a specific social context,
extensive family and kinship networks, interpersonal relationships constrained by sentiment, trust, obligation, and other cultural values and
norms, and so on—constitute a pool of social capital specific to ethnicity.[27] If it is generated from an ethnic enclave, this social capital can
give its group members a competitive edge in their struggle for socioeconomic mobility, despite their limited material and human-capital resources.

Immigrant Chinese participating in Chinatown's economy are largely
affected by the long-standing structures of social relations. They depend
on Chinatown not because they are willing to accept low-wage jobs, poor
working conditions, and exploitation but rather because they view it as
a better option. In Chinatown they are provided with a familiar work
environment in which they are effectively shielded from deficiencies in
language, education, and general knowledge of the larger society. They
can obtain firsthand information on employment and business opportunities through their family members, kin, and co-ethnics and so avoid the
expense in time and effort involved in finding "good jobs" in the larger
market. They are able to work longer hours to accumulate family savings
more quickly. They can gain access to rotating credit, clan associations,
and the family for financial support and resource mobilization. Finally,
they can get job training and cultivate an entrepreneurial spirit at work,
possibly preparing themselves for eventual transition to self-employment.
Thus, social capital reciprocally benefits both the enclave entrepreneurs
and the workers. The "willing self-exploitation" of the enclave workers
apparently brings about profits for ethnic entrepreneurs, but the entrepreneurs are also obliged to help train the workers in occupational skills
and to promote eventual transition to self-employment.[28] Chinatown's

recent development shows that many new business opportunities have been created with ethnic resources. The potential for self-employment—an important indicator of social mobility—has grown within the reach of many ambitious immigrant Chinese. For instance, the 1980 census shows that the rate of self-employment for immigrant Chinese males in the New York, NY–NJ SMSA (Standard Metropolitan Statistical Area) was 13 percent as compared to 7 percent for the general male labor force in the area.

In sum, New York City's Chinatown is an economic enclave backed by a consolidated ethnic social structure. Adding a social dimension to the study of Chinatown's economic enclave provides a better understanding of the modes of immigrant incorporation in the United States.

Scope of the Study

This book focuses on the effects of post-1965 Chinese immigration on Chinatown and how Chinatown affects immigrant incorporation in the United States. I am interested in how quantitative changes, caused by large-scale Chinese immigration after the U.S. immigration policy reform in 1965, stimulated qualitative changes in Chinatown. I used the cut-off point of 1965 analytically. It should be noted that Chinatown's qualitative changes—from a bachelors' society to a family-oriented community—began as early as the 1940s. However, only after 1965 was the change sufficiently radical to alter the face of Chinatown completely. By the same token, Chinatown's economic organization changed from a self-maintained marginal subeconomy to an interdependent and integrated enclave economy after this cut-off point.

The chapters that follow primarily deal with several hypotheses. First, Chinese immigration to the United States has been determined by specific contexts of exit and reception. The contexts of exit can be defined by pull and push factors.[29] The pull factors are subject to not only structural opportunities and the need for cheap immigrant labor but also the need for family reunification in the receiving country, whereas the push factors depend on the sociocultural, political, and economic situation of the sending country. The contexts of reception can be defined by the government policies and labor-market conditions of the receiving country and by the preexisting social and economic structures of the immigrant community.[30] Members of immigrant groups are unavoidably caught in an ethnically stratified system created to protect the status and interests of native workers and to block the upward mobility of immigrants deliberately. They are also inevitably bound by an entangling network of social relationships, which is framed by cultural solidarity and mobilization around the symbols of a common ethnicity. Specific strategies and modes of adaptation vary to accommodate the changing contexts.

Second, Chinatown is no doubt a form of segregation; it represents a particular mode of adaptation of immigrant Chinese to American society. However, it is not completely sealed off from the rest of the world. On the contrary, it has always interacted with the larger society, and the interface between the two worlds has increased over the years depending on specific goal orientations of the immigrant group.

Originally, Chinatown emerged as a direct product of structural, legal, and cultural barriers. It functioned to serve the sojourning needs of its residents, mostly single males who came only to make money and did not intend to stay. The short-term orientation and the prospect of eventual return for early immigrant Chinese constrained the scope of community development and hindered assimilation. As immigrant Chinese began to adopt a more permanent lifestyle in America, once discriminatory immigration legislation was repealed, Chinatown underwent a structural transformation from an isolated urban island to a prosperous economic enclave, facilitating assimilation. Although the new immigrant Chinese are as likely as their predecessors to end up in Chinatown, their experience and the consequences of enclave participation are substantially different. Today's Chinatown has developed a structure of opportunities that works to channel immigrants into the larger American society.

Third, Chinatown's enclave economy, though dominated by small and marginal businesses that are extremely competitive and susceptible to business succession, is not simply an extension of the larger secondary economy. Rather, it has developed beyond the margins of the large economic structure. The enclave is represented by a structural duality—a protected sector and an export sector—that operates partially by its own principles. The protected sector is secured by the enclave's own ethnic capital, labor, and consumer markets, and the export sector serves the needs of the larger economy. On the one hand, this structural organization enables the enclave to circulate capital between the two sectors and to prevent resource drain. It also works to increase the interface between the enclave export sector and the larger economy, hence gradually incorporating itself as a distinctive segment of the larger economy. On the other hand, this structural duality makes it possible for the enclave economy to diversify, generating a wide range of opportunities for immigrant

Chinese to pursue careers commensurate with their past human-capital investment despite initial disadvantages associated with immigration.

Fourth, the boundaries around Chinatown provide tangible benefits to group members—employment security, shelter against overt or covert ethnic discrimination, and for some, opportunities for upward advancement within the enclave. Social capital—unique family and kinship networks, reciprocal obligations, and cultural values and norms—minimizes the economic cost traditionally associated with immigration and segregation and gives immigrants a competitive edge in overcoming initial disadvantages. Thus, participating in Chinatown does not necessarily mean being trapped in a dead end. The seeming "failure" of assimilation represents a positive alternative for first-generation immigrants, who actually pave the way for their children to assimilate more successfully.

Finally, the development of the economic enclave reproduces a dialectic of spatial expansion and decentralization. In the case of New York City's Chinese, residential patterns are linked not simply to higher socioeconomic status but also to factors associated with bonds of kinship and family, the economic enclave, and its related ethnic housing market. Those who are able to leave Chinatown physically have retained social relations embedded in the enclave. Residential dispersion has, in fact, resulted in decentralized ethnic enclaves—satellite Chinatowns, which maintain strong ties to the original enclave. In general, the outward residential mobility of the Chinese within the city has not provided strong evidence of spatial assimilation; rather, it has shown signs of resegregation of the decentralized ethnic population.

Methodologically, I relied principally on three sources of information to conduct this study: fieldwork research, which was done between 1988 and 1989; documentary studies of historical data; and the U.S. census data. Fieldwork and documentary data were as useful and essential as statistical data in exploring the theoretical concepts, identifying interesting new issues, and better understanding the phenomena under study. Their representativeness, however, was limited in that the fieldwork data were collected in a rather unstructured manner through a community network of family and social relations and the documentary data were also selective. Even the U.S. census data exhibit a certain degree of bias because Chinese immigrants were not quite as cooperative as expected. However, the three sources of data, taken together, proved effective.

Chapter 2 discusses the early history of Chinese immigration to the United States and examines involuntary and voluntary factors affecting early Chinese immigration and settlement patterns. The network character of the immigration process and the sojourning character of Old Chinatown are emphasized.

Chapter 3 examines the changing contexts of reception, the changing contexts of exit, and the changing mentality and goal orientation of the recent immigrant Chinese. These changes have greatly affected the patterns of integration of Chinese immigrants and their communities into the larger American society.

Chapter 4 provides a detailed description of post-1965 Chinese immigration. Emphasis is on the heterogeneous demographic and socioeconomic characteristics of the recent immigrant Chinese in New York and how the process of uprooting affects their adjustment in their new country.

Chapter 5 digs into Chinatown's economic system. It goes beyond survival strategies to examine the structural context in which the enclave economy emerged. It describes different phases of economic development and treats recent Chinese immigration and the influx of foreign capital as important factors in the development of the enclave economy. It conceptualizes a dual structure of the economic enclave, looking specifically into the interrelationships between the protected sector and the export sector to account for the diversification of economic activities in Chinatown, which creates ample opportunities for recent arrivals.

Chapter 6 looks into another dimension of the Chinese population in New York—the male ethnic labor force. The Chinese, both foreign-born and native-born, are compared with non-Hispanic whites in education, occupation, and earnings. I also report results from empirical analyses based on a recent controversy over the earnings and occupational returns on human capital for male enclave participants. I attempt to answer several important questions associated with immigrant incorporation, such as: Will improvement in the overall levels of human capital increase chances of economic assimilation? Are there any positive occupational and earnings returns on human capital? Can human capital yield significant positive earnings returns for immigrant Chinese workers participating in the enclave?

Chapter 7 looks into another important component of the enclave labor force—women. By emphasizing the interacting roles of wife, mother, and wage worker, the analysis focuses on the employment position and occupational attainment of immigrant women and the family strategy for social mobility.

Chapter 8 examines the decentralization of Chinatown and the residential mobility of immigrant Chinese. It attempts to show that unique characteristics of the enclave economy, kinship ties of new immigrants to the ethnic community, and ethnic segmentation of the housing market work together to structure the locational pattern for New York City's Chinese.

Chapter 9 concludes the book by summarizing the main results and highlighting how these results fit into the current theoretical debates concerning immigrant incorporation. It also draws practical implications pertaining to urban enclaves and the urban underclass.

2

Memories of Sojourning

Chinese immigration to the United States dates back to the early 1840s after the Chinese defeat in the Opium War (1838–1842). The one-and-a-half-century history is fairly long in a country that is only a little more than two hundred years of age. Studies on early Chinese immigration have focused on various aspects of the life and experience of immigrant Chinese in the United States.[1] These studies have served as invaluable background sources for the study of today's Chinese-Americans. Why did the Chinese emigrate, to start with? Was it because of the "American dream"? Without a doubt. Or was it because of the hope of economic independence and freedom? Yes, in part. But these ideas were too general and remote and were often taken for granted. There were distinctive motivations other than these to spur the Chinese on. Like thousands of early European immigrants who were driven by an American dream, early Chinese immigrants also had a dream of their own—the "gold dream."

In contrast to the American dream of economic prosperity, freedom, and individualism, the gold dream is typically Chinese—a sojourners' dream. It connotes a strong desire to make a great fortune for the family and entails a sense of personal sacrifice and collectivism. In Chinese culture, gold bears symbolic meanings deeper than the prosaic one. Gold not only means money, food, clothing, and land, but also refers to glory, splendor, and the rank of the family. In classical Chinese literature and folk arts the search for gold has been among the most popular themes. The color gold was once reserved exclusively to the imperial family and was applied only to such sacred objects as the legendary dragon and the Buddhas.[2] Gold is also regarded as a symbol of luck, and it appears in many traditional Chinese holiday decorations. Even in the names people give their children, the word "gold" (*jin*) is commonly used. A Chinese laborer who left his wife and children to sojourn in America for over thirty years included the word in the names of all his seven children—Jin-man (golden affluence), Jin-rong (golden glory), Jin-ping (golden peace), Jin-ming (golden light), Jin-hui (golden brilliance), Jin-gen (golden root), and Mei-jin (pretty gold). He had hoped, like many of his fellow laborers, to return to China with lots of gold, but found himself exhausted and penniless instead. He finally rejoined his "gold" children and family in China in the 1940s and died on his own soil with his gold dream kept alive by his children and grandchildren.

In a more general sense, the gold dream reflects the wish of the Chinese for an affluent life and a stable family anchored on their own land. Few Chinese had ever thought of leaving home for a strange world until they became convinced that there was a "shortcut" to make their gold dreams come true. When thousands of Chinese laborers left home to start their gold-seeking journey across the Pacific, they always remembered that they would return to their families and their land of birth someday.

This chapter traces memories of the past. Such a historical description of early Chinese immigrants helps us better understand how changes in the process of immigration have greatly altered the patterns of immigrant incorporation.

The Gold Mountain: An Illusion

The Gold Mountain has been a synonym of America for years among the Cantonese. Many of the American Chinese have roots in Canton (now the southern part of Guangdong Province surrounding the capital city, Guangzhou), for it is from Canton that large numbers of emigrants to the United States were originally drawn. Since the first ship of Chinese contract labor sailed out of the South China Sea in the late 1840s, the Gold Mountain was mythicized and glorified as a source of hope and fortune and was gradually built into the everyday speech of many Cantonese at home. The phrase "Is your grandfather digging *gum shan* (meaning the Gold Mountain in Cantonese)?" was frequently used to mock a person who seemed too obsessed with luxurious goods or a child who complained about food or made excessive demands for toys and candies.

What caused the Chinese to emigrate? It has commonly been taken for granted that poverty at home and California's Gold Rush during the late 1840s brought the first wave of Chinese immigrants to the United States. Although these push and pull factors—escape from poverty and quest for gold—may embody meanings far deeper than generally assumed, they tend to overshadow the real determining factors. Of course, the lure that one day's pay in America is worth a month's hard work at home is strong enough to pull people out of their homeland, but the wage gap itself or poverty alone does not account for actual emigration. Studies on international migration have found evidence that a more significant set of determining variables than poverty at home is needed to induce emigration.[3] Western penetration of China, emigration and immigration policies of the sending and receiving countries, a change in mentality and tradition for the emigrating Cantonese, and kinship connections all contributed to Chinese emigration.

Historically, the Chinese were known to be family-bound and clannish; they were industrious, thrifty, and self-sacrificing. In order to bring home gold and other good fortune, they were always ready to work for any price, in any place, and even to sacrifice their individual lives. However, the Chinese were not an emigrating people. Leaving home, let alone emigrating to another country, was considered shameful. Extremely ethnocentric values and traditional family bonds often held the Chinese to their land of birth. Even though some had to leave home to search for gold, they did so not for themselves but solely for their families; and they were always expected to return with wealth to glorify their families and honor their ancestors.

The Manchurian Qing Dynasty also made and enforced various laws to discourage emigration. Emigrants who left home and "deserted" family graves to seek profit were condemned as rebels, traitors, and "human trash." They could be punished by the death penalty.[4] Not until 1894 did the emperor abolish the death penalty for emigration. Before then, the extremely restrictive emigration policies simply did not permit people to leave the country at will, whether to escape poverty and hunger or for any other purposes.

The idea of emigration as a livelihood and the illusion of the Gold Mountain came from the West. The intrusion of Western colonial powers did not come until after China lost the Opium War with Great Britain in the early 1840s. This defeat resulted in the cession of Hong Kong to the British; the opening of five ports—Guangzhou (Canton), Xiamen (Amoy), Shanghai, Tianjin, and Ningbo—to foreign trade;[5] an increase of Chinese taxes; frequent uprisings of the peasant class; and the penetration of Western ideas into the country (mainly the coastal provinces, through missionaries). China before the Opium War did not recognize any other nation as equal to itself. Foreign countries were treated as "tributary states" by the emperor. Since 1757, maritime trade by foreign ships in China had been limited to the single port of Canton, and foreigners in China suffered various kinds of restrictions in trade and everyday life.[6] After the end of the Opium War, further Western penetration of China proceeded. The freedom with which Western merchants and missionaries could move throughout the empire increased, and foreign goods began to compete successfully with Chinese products.

This Western invasion of China began to undermine the traditional Chinese values and imperial control. Particularly hard hit by the "west wind" were two provinces: Canton (now part of Guangdong) and Amoy (now part of Fujian), where large volumes of Chinese emigration started. The country's door was smashed open. People began to see an alternative means of livelihood abroad, and the imperial power could no longer exert complete control. In the late 1840s, when gold was discovered in California, emigration from China to America began to take place on an unprecedented scale.

Among other reasons, information about the Gold Mountain was probably one of the most important stimuli to vivify the gold dream. Before the Opium War, China was practically free of Western contact and almost completely sealed off from the rest of the world, though a very small number of visitors and students traveled out of the country and some came to America.[7] In the early nineteenth century, with the rise of Western expansionism—the drive for foreign markets and the tremendous demand for labor—Western colonialists acquired vast areas in Southeast Asia, the Caribbean, and South America. With the outlawing of the slave trade and, later, slavery itself, cheap labor began to be contracted out of China in small numbers through the notorious "coolie trade." These Chinese contract laborers were first shipped to plantations in British and French colonies in Southeast Asia—Indochina, Siam, Burma, Malaya, Indonesia, and the Philippines—and then to the Caribbean and Latin America, particularly Cuba, Peru, Chile, and the Sandwich Islands, which were in the hands of the Portuguese and Spaniards, following lines of contract that had originated much earlier.[8] When gold was discovered in California, a larger number of laborers were contracted out to America to work in the gold mines.

Initially Chinese laborers went overseas under contract. Later, as knowledge of opportunities abroad began to filter back home, more and more free emigration took place. As years passed, some went home to get married and went overseas again, and some simply returned permanently to China.[9] After several years' hard work abroad, many of these early laborers returned home to show their village, in one way or another, that they had made fortunes they would not have made at home. The idea of seeking gold abroad gradually spread in areas where labor was first contracted out of the country. Those who had been abroad were honored as "guests of the Gold Mountain" (*gum shan haak* in Cantonese) and their return showed their fellow villagers a possible alternative means of making a living. Mr. Lee, an eighty-year-old immigrant now residing in Long Island recalled:

> I was originally from Punyu [now Panyu County in Guangdong]. I still remember the first time I saw my grandpa—a bony little old man. He had gone to *gum shan* before I was even born. Grandpa had been away from home for almost twenty years, and he came back really like a *gum shan haak*. He bought a big buffalo and a brand-new plow set, and he also brought with him some queer-looking clothing and a lot of candies and crackers that I had never seen. He built a new tomb for the great-grandparents and rebuilt our shabby, run-down home. For a while, everybody in the village respected him, admired him, flattered him and treated him as some sort of god. People started to believe that there was a real *gum shan* across the ocean. I also felt that people suddenly looked favorably upon my family. Only then did I start to dream about going to dig *gum shan* and make a lot of money to bring home after I grew up. Afterward quite a few people in the village started to leave home to dig *gum shan*.[10]

Mr. Lee's grandfather never returned to the United States, but about fifteen years later, Mr. Lee's dream came true. He himself came to America. He worked as a merchant, helping his uncle with the family's trading business between Hong Kong and New York's Chinatown. But he was never able to go back to China with a great fortune as he had originally planned; instead, he drew his whole family into chain migration.

Emigrating Chinese were from places along the south and southeast coast. Those who came to America were principally from the Pearl River delta—the areas south of Canton.[11] The Chinese villagers learned about *gum shan* from *gum shan haak*. They were interested in the possibility of making fortunes abroad. Yet, their minds were full of illusions that anywhere outside China there was a better way of making a living and that in America gold was lying on the ground for anyone to pick up.

Not only had the return of *gum shan haak* in the Canton area spread news about the Gold Mountain, the penetration of Western ideas following the Opium War had also fostered in the minds of the Chinese an increasingly strong desire to emigrate. Meanwhile, Western influence from missionaries and trading contacts also encouraged people to emigrate. The opening of the port of Canton had not only pushed open the country's southern door but had also opened up the minds of the Cantonese. They were among the first in the country to know that "there is a *gum shan* across the Pacific," a "wonderful world outside China." Trading between Canton and the Western countries further broadened the vision of the Cantonese and alerted them to the possibility of another means of enriching one's life. Moreover, social stability and economic order in the Pearl River delta area after the Opium War were constantly disturbed by territorial conflicts among warlords and by peasant uprisings that drove people into deeper misery and suffering. Since their daily routine was being dislocated by unpredictable chaos, the Cantonese were compelled to look overseas for a means of supporting their families. However, poverty alone could not explain emigration, for though the country was certainly poverty-stricken, the Pearl River delta, known for its fertile land and rich farming resources and its versatile commercial activities, had always celebrated a relatively more affluent lifestyle and a more open-minded attitude toward tradition compared to the rest of the country. Thus, this area was certainly not the poorest. The poorest regions, in the west and north, simply did not have access to the information and family networks associated with emigration.

Westward expansionism and American colonialism in California also contributed to Chinese emigration. When gold was found in California in 1848, American colonialists flocked there to open up gold mines and develop the area for their own profit. By then, capitalism in America was on the rise. Edna Bonacich argues that the development of the West Coast followed two lines: one was dependent capitalism, depending upon Eastern and European investments and producing raw materials for those markets. The other was the independent manufacturing capitalism that grew out of a small producer class. Dependent capitalism, represented by mining, railroads, and agriculture, tended to produce raw materials rather than manufactured goods. In order to be competitive in the international and national markets for capital and sales, these industries had to keep labor costs, the only flexible cost, as low as possible. Yet, the cost of available free white labor was too high for capitalists to make a handsome profit; they had to seek cheap labor across the Pacific. The independent small producer class also came to California with the Gold Rush. When gold was exhausted, these producers turned to manufacturing for the local market. Their development was based on the accumulation of capital within the local area and was not confronted with competition from the Eastern or European markets. Even though their labor cost was high, they managed to pass on this cost to their customers. However, they still had an interest in using cheap labor to compete with each other.[12] A large supply of labor had to be found, but without a transcontinental railroad, labor had either to be shipped around Cape Horn from the eastern seaboard or to be moved overland by wagon train.[13]

Either means was very expensive. One solution was the importation of Chinese labor across the Pacific. The coolie system, which later developed into a somewhat more humane "credit-ticket" system, began to import labor to meet the needs of gold mining and America's West Coast development.[14] The coolie trade—later described by the Chinese as the "selling of pigs"—produced the extreme form of the contract system at that time. Large ports such as Canton and Amoy were centers of the trade, and the credit-ticket system was the dominant mode of labor transport from Hong Kong to San Francisco. Under this system, money for the passage was advanced to the laborers in Chinese ports to be repaid out of their earnings in California.[15] The emigrants first made their way to Hong Kong or Macao. Both cities were then under foreign rule, and ships could be found to make the journey. The passage fees were extremely expensive—fifty dollars for the passage and twenty for emigration—an enormous amount of money for the Cantonese, who then lived on about one dollar per week. Only a few managed to collect money from their families, their clans, and others in the village to pay for their passage and emigration fees; the majority were forced into labor contracts, incurring a debt that they later found hard to pay off.

The contract system was not just a way of transporting labor; it was a form of exploitation, too. The contracts bound the coolies to pay so much per month or to work a certain length of time in return for their passage across the Pacific. But as the illiterate coolies could not even read the contracts and usually signed the papers before the blanks were filled out, the system left plenty of room for the Western labor recruiting companies, the Western sailing vessels, and the Chinese coolie brokers and merchants to make a profit. In 1850, forty-four vessels left Hong Kong for California, each carrying about five hundred contract laborers. By the end of 1851, it was estimated that there were about twenty-five thousand Chinese in California working in mines or in domestic and manual labor.[16] As the demand for passages and freight increased, enormous profits were generated. During the year 1852 alone, $1 million in easy profit was made from the voyage fees paid by thirty thousand Chinese who embarked at Hong Kong for San Francisco.[17]

Thus, the Chinese immigrants were shipped under contract to California, basically to meet the increasing economic need of the West Coast for an adequate supply of cheap labor and the demand of the Chinese labor contractors for profit.[18] The emigrating Chinese were mostly laborers with a sojourning goal—to make quick money and return home. Most of them did not know what they were headed for. They went with an illusion that there was plenty of gold in California. They were, in fact, a group of "bitter strength" (or bitter labor in Chinese) and might never be able to fulfill their sojourning goal once they started the long and lonely journey. Even if some anticipated the hardships and risks, the desire for gold and the willingness to sacrifice for the welfare of their families was just overwhelming.

Bitter Strength: The Sojourners

The gold dream of the early Chinese immigrants had a sojourning character. Instead of wanting to make a new life in America as thousands of European immigrants did, the early Chinese immigrants intended to stay only a little while. Thus, they had a tendency toward isolation and little interest in assimilation, in settling down in their new country.[19] The primary objective of the transpacific journey for early Chinese immigrants was to make fortunes for their families at home. Most of the Chinese strongly believed that there was gold in America and hoped that, with hard work and personal sacrifice, they would be able to bring home gold and money. This sojourning character of early Chinese immigration to the United States shaped the mode of adaptation for the early Chinese in America and the structure of Chinatown.

Early Chinese immigrants were predominantly peasants from the Pearl River delta, from counties in Canton such as Taishan (Toishan), Kaiping (Hoiping), Enping, Xinhui, Xunde, Nanhai (Namhoy), Panyu, and Zhongshan (Chungshan), where the news of the Gold Mountain reached shore first. The Pearl River delta area was rich farmland, and the Cantonese were ambitious and adventuresome. For hundreds of years, they not only worked in the fields but also tried every possible occupation that promised a livelihood. They knew that they could not just depend on farming to get rich; many of them either traveled to nearby cities to trade as peddlers, shopkeepers, or merchants, or did odd jobs, such as carpentry, fish farming, wood crafting, and basket weaving. As they traveled, they became familiar with urban life in such big port cities as Hong Kong, Macao, and particularly Canton, which was then the only port where foreigners could trade in southern China. The adventurousness of the Cantonese and the modern ideas of emigration greatly shaped their decision to go abroad.

Another characteristic of the Cantonese was clannishness. The villages in the area were much alike, each mostly inhabited by people who had the same family name or were related in some way to one another. The families and the clans were close-knit. They shared the same traditional values and spoke the same dialects. Wherever they went, they formed family or clan associations to help each other get adjusted in the new place. Thus, when they went abroad to try their luck, they were often assured of meeting and getting the aid of fellow villagers and clansmen who had gone earlier.[20]

Many of those who came across the Pacific were young men, mostly married men who left their wives behind in their native villages to bring up their children and care for the elderly in their extended families. They came merely as laborers, not as settlers. The emotional ties with the family, the veneration of the ancestors, and the desire to save enough money to live an affluent life back in the country village in China sustained them in the strange and hostile world. Even the Chinese merchants who were able to bring their families with them (only a very small number) still thought of China as home. Because Canton was for a long time the center of emigration, early Chinatowns carried a Cantonese version of the Chinese culture in the form of Cantonese foods, handicrafts, and dialects.

Work in America was very hard and living was even more difficult for the Chinese laborers. During the first few years of emigration, the Chinese were tolerated and even welcomed in San Francisco. They either worked in mines or performed basic services such as cooking and laundry, desperately needed by the American men who had left families to seek a quick fortune in the goldfields.[21] But by 1852 the rich surface mines were exhausted, and miners were forced to penetrate deeper into the ground in order to generate a fair return. This deeper mining required capital resources only large companies could command, and a much cheaper labor force—the coolies—were employed in the mines. There, for the first time, they found themselves competing for jobs with white miners. This competition later triggered the anti-Chinese hostility. For the Chinese laborers, America was a place where they could possibly make a fortune but a place where they did not belong. Things in American made little sense to them, and they were extremely lonesome. They had to cling to each other for social and emotional support.

The Chinese worked for very low wages, and a considerable portion of their wages was deducted each month to pay back their labor contractors and brokers. Moreover, they were subject to heavy taxes. In 1852 California imposed a three-dollar-a-month license tax on foreign miners, many of whom were Chinese. After a year, the tax was raised to four dollars per month. Most of the tax was actually collected from the Chinese because they did not have the desire to become permanent citizens. The tax they paid made up one of the largest sources of revenue for the new state of California. It was not until 1870, after the tax had been paid for sixteen years, that the U.S. Supreme Court ruled it unconstitutional. The Chinese had already paid $5 million, 85 percent of the total tax collected; yet not a single cent was refunded.[22]

In the late 1850s, when most of the gold mines were exhausted, the demand for cheap labor shifted to railroad construction. Chinese were then hired by the railroad companies to complete the most difficult part of the transcontinental railroad in the Rockies, and they began toiling on the long iron trail.[23] Almost always, they were employed in the jobs that were the most difficult and dangerous, the jobs in which few white workers were interested. When the railroad was nearly completed, the Chinese began to branch out into other areas of economic activity in the West, particularly into construction, agricultural industries, and manufacturing, such as woolen and knitting mills and small-scale manufacturing of boots, shoes, and cigars.[24]

The early Chinese immigrants made an enormous contribution to the development of the West and the construction of the transcontinental railroad. Yet, as history moved on, few of them made fortunes; and most found only back-breaking toil, poverty, loneliness, and too often, death in the quest for gold.

Exclusion: The Chinese Must Go

Chinese immigrants came to participate in the Gold Rush; yet, ironically, they did not reap even the slightest amount of gold before they found themselves the objects of discrimination and exclusion. Their contributions and hard work were not credited; instead, they were accused of building "a filthy nest of iniquity and rottenness" in the midst of the American society and driving away white labor by their "stealthy" competition.[25] They were called the "yellow peril," the "Chinese menace," and the "indispensable enemy." The anti-Chinese anger eventually flamed into a campaign slogan—The Chinese Must Go!—put forward by the workingmen's party in California in the late 1870s in the campaign for laws to exclude the Chinese.[26]

Strong anti-Chinese movements in California during the last quarter of the nineteenth century were evidence of the exclusion and exploitation of nonwhite groups by the dominant white society.[27] The Gold Rush attracted much cheap immigrant labor from abroad and also brought many economically depressed white workers from the East Coast. During the early 1870s, the United States underwent a serious economic depression. Everything came at the same time: drought, the decline of mineral production, speculation and panic in stocks and real estate, land monopoly, and the rise of a labor movement. The completion of the railroad put twenty-five thousand railroad workers out of work, and unemployment was further intensified by the one million westward migrants from the East Coast.[28] Job opportunities for Californians and incoming white workers were limited; yet Chinese laborers still continued to be shipped into California, keeping labor costs as low as possible so as to generate higher profit for the capitalists. The white working class, whose ideology encompassed the notion of the "dignity of labor," was joined by small farmers and artisans to form an anticapitalist class and fight against slave labor.[29] Conflicts between the white workers and capitalists were taken out on the cheap labor, particularly on the Chinese.

Because they were sojourners, the Chinese laborers remained unassimilated and isolated. Because the coolie trade was a form of slavery, the Chinese were not simply torn between the white working class and capitalists; they were entirely excluded from the American working class. Having no intention to stay, eager just to make quick money to go home, they were ready to accept inhumane working conditions and wages far below standard, directly contradicting the ideology of the white working class. As more and more Chinese were shipped in to take jobs for which white workers were in direct competition, anti-Chinese sentiment fermented, and the Chinese laborers soon became the target of racial prejudice and discrimination. The anti-Chinese movement rapidly gathered strength. A sense of the times can be seen in the propositions offered by the California workmen's delegation to the state constitutional convention in 1877. One of the propositions stated:

> Aliens should not be allowed to trade, peddle or carry on any mercantile business; no person not eligible to be a citizen should be allowed to settle in the State, and any person encouraging such

should be fined; aliens, ineligible to citizenship, should be prohibited from bearing arms, giving testimony in the courts in cases involving white persons, from fishing in the inland waters of the State and from employment on public works; a per capita tax of $250 should be levied on each Chinese immigrant.[30]

Although these propositions were not passed, they were used to justify the anti-Chinese movement. As a result of the political campaign by the white working class, the U.S. Congress passed the first Chinese Exclusion Act in 1882, one of the few federal laws to exclude a whole group of people based merely on national origin. The law stipulated that

the coming of Chinese laborers to the United States be, and the same is hereby, suspended; and during such suspension it shall not be lawful for any Chinese laborer to come, or, having so come after the expiration of said ninety days, to remain within the United States.

. . . the master of any vessel who shall knowingly bring within the United States on such vessel, and land or permit to be landed, any Chinese laborer, from any foreign port or place, shall be deemed guilty of a misdemeanor, and on conviction thereof shall be punished by a fine of not more than five hundred dollars for each and every such Chinese laborer so brought, and may be also imprisoned for a term not exceeding one year.

. . . thereafter no State court or court of the United States shall admit Chinese to citizenship; and all laws in conflict with this act are hereby repealed.[31]

The act, designed to keep Chinese laborers out of the U.S. labor market,[32] suspended immigration of all Chinese laborers, skilled or unskilled, for ten years, with some exceptions for diplomatic officers, scholars, students, and merchants and for travelers who paid short visits. The law also prohibited the naturalization of all Chinese already in the United States, because the coming of Chinese laborers to this country endangered the good order of "certain localities in the United States."

In September 1888 Congress passed another act to prohibit Chinese laborers from entering the United States. The law stipulated:

That from and after the date of exchange of ratifications of the pending treaty between the United States and His Imperial Majesty the Emperor of China, signed on the twelfth day of March, anno Domini eighteen hundred and eighty-eight, it shall be unlawful for any Chinese person, whether a subject of China or of any other power, to enter the United States. . . .

That from and after the passage of this act, no Chinese laborer in the United States shall be permitted, after having left, to return thereto. . . .

That no Chinese laborer within the purview of the preceding section shall be permitted to return to the United States unless he had a lawful wife, child, or parent in the United States, or property therein of the value of one thousand dollars, or debts of like amount due him and pending settlement. . . .

. . . And that no Chinese laborer shall be permitted to re-enter the United States without producing to the proper officer of the customs at the port of such entry the return certificate herein required. A Chinese laborer possessing a certificate under this section shall be admitted to the United States only at the port from which he departed therefrom, and no Chinese person, except Chinese diplomatic or consular officers, and their attendants, shall be permitted to enter the United States except at the ports of San Francisco, Portland, Oregon, Boston, New York, New Orleans, Port Townsend, or such other ports as may be designated by the Secretary of the Treasury.[33]

From 1888, the entry and reentry of Chinese laborers were further restricted. Chinese laborers who had returned to China to visit their families were not permitted to return. Although there were some exceptions, none were made for the majority of the Chinese laborers. Few Chinese laborers could actually match the requirements for return certificates, because not many of them had families in the United States. In the following years, about twenty thousand Chinese who had gone back to China to visit their families were denied reentry to the United States, even though many of them held the required return certificates.[34]

In 1892 the Extension of the Chinese Exclusion Act of 1882 was renewed and extended to further prohibit the entry of all Chinese laborers.[35] In subsequent years legislation extended restrictions on Chinese immigration to the island territories of the United States.[36] The definition of "Chinese laborers" was broadened to as many categories of work as possible. Salesmen, clerks, buyers, bookkeepers, accountants, managers, shopkeepers, apprentices, agents, cashiers, physicians, restaurant owners and cooks, housekeepers, laundrymen, peddlers, and many others—all became "laborers" who were denied entry under these new laws.[37]

The effects of the exclusion legislation were augmented by extralegal

Decades

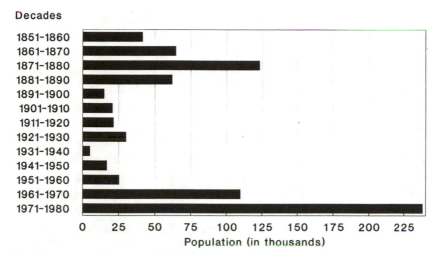

Figure 2-1. Chinese Immigration to the United States by Decades, 1851–1980
Source: INS Statistical Yearbook: 1986.

persecution and vigilantism as rage and frustration grew among white workers. The Chinese were driven out of the mines, farms, woolen mills, and factories and forced to cluster in urban enclaves for self-protection, which later developed into Chinatowns. Even in Chinatowns, however, they were hardly left alone. Armed mobs constantly intimidated the Chinese with shouts, blows, and pistol shots. They threw stones at the Chinese walking on the street, chopped off their pigtails, broke into and set fire to houses and buildings, and looted Chinese stores.[38]

During that period, many Chinese laborers were forced to return permanently to China. Others, who could not afford the return journey (either because they had no money for the trip or because they had no fortunes to bring home), departed for the East Coast to pursue their sojourning goal. Even those who returned to China temporarily to visit their families were not allowed to come back to America. Many merchants who had small shares in business ventures or debts owed them suffered heavy losses because return was impossible.

The number of arrivals from China dropped sharply after the Chinese Exclusion Act and the subsequent legislation. In the 1880s the number of Chinese immigrants admitted to the United States (61,711) decreased by 50 percent from the previous decade (123,201), and Chinese immigration reached its lowest point at 4,928 in the 1930s (See Figure 2-1). The trend did not change significantly until the 1970s.

During the years of exclusion, no laborers were allowed to immigrate, and no Chinese were eligible for naturalized U.S. citizenship. Some, who were merchants or members of a merchant's family, were able to come legally under earlier exclusion laws. Others came through illegal channels, most commonly through falsified birth certificates identifying the newcomers as the sons of merchants who traveled in and out of the country or sons of native-born or naturalized Chinese-Americans. This practice was possible because the 1906 San Francisco earthquake destroyed almost all of the city's official birth records. Chinese merchants, who were able to travel back and forth, assumed "fatherhood" of these "paper sons," usually their own nephews or sons of clansmen, and brought them back to the United States. They did so mainly to fulfill family obligations.[39] Similar stories are often told in New York's Chinatown. A ninety-two-year-old Chinatown merchant, who retired in Westchester County but made frequent trips to Chinatown, recalled:

> In those days, entering the United States was very difficult, because the law forbade Chinese immigration. I came as a merchant to trade between New York's Chinatown and Hong Kong, leaving my wife and children at home back in Taishan. Each time I went back from China, I claimed that I had a son and acquired a birth paper [certificate]. In this way, I managed to bring my younger son and a couple of nephews here to New York, leaving my older son at home to take care of my wife, who had never come with me until only recently. A lot of other merchants did the same thing; otherwise, who could possibly come?[40]

As a direct outcome of the Chinese exclusion laws, San Francisco's Chinatown, which had first been established as a sojourners' settlement, became more consolidated as an immigrant community, insulated from the larger society for self-support and self-protection.[41] Shortly afterward, Chinese began to disperse to other parts of the country, most of them moving eastward to escape the antagonism of the white working class in California. Chinatowns thus became visible in many major cities, including New York, Chicago, Boston, Baltimore, and Philadelphia. Those who came to New York City settled in Chinatown, which was then an insignificant and tiny enclave on the Lower East Side of Manhattan. Gradually, Chinatowners were sealed off from the outside world and were forced to conduct marginal economic activities to sustain their daily survival needs. Different from the sojourners, they became another type of worker, running laundries and restaurants, or working as domestic servants. Unlike European immigration, early Chinese immigration to the United States was subject to exploitation, harsh taxation, racial discrimination, and social injustice.

Chinatown: Involuntary and Voluntary Segregation

The emergence of Chinatowns in the United States involves both an involuntary and a voluntary process. Chinatowns were a product of legal and institutional exclusion, systematic racism, and prejudice. Anti-Chinese and discriminatory remarks were often reflected in the press. Stuart Miller quotes an example from the *New York Times* that is typical:

> Although they are patient and reliable laborers, they have characteristics deeply imbedded which make them undesirable as a part of our permanent population. Their religion is wholly unlike ours, and they poison and stab. The circumstances would need to be very favorable which would allow of their introduction into our families as servants, and as to mixing with them on terms of equality, that would be out of the question. No improvement of race could possibly result from such a mixture.[42]

If the isolation of the work camps in which early Chinese miners labored under the strict control of their employment companies strengthened their adherence to their customary way of life, then Chinatown was certainly a mode of accommodation to a hostile American society. Excluded from all aspects of American life—social, political, legal, and economic—Chinatown developed its own reactive mechanism in response to the hostile environment.[43]

In a classic study of Chinatowns, D. Y. Yuan notes that segregation in Chinatown is both voluntary and involuntary.[44] Denied structural assimilation because of discrimination, the Chinese had no choice but to develop insulated enclaves for self-protection. In a society where most of the options of life were unavailable to them, immigrant Chinese tended to depend on each other. Involuntary segregation developed and strengthened a sense of ethnic identity and solidarity, which in turn reinforced ethnic segregation.

However, the Chinese were also inclined to cluster (or to segregate themselves) in Chinatown for practical reasons. First, they came to work for money and did not intend to stay for long. Their adaptation to the American society was oriented only toward a short-term goal. Thus, they did not see the need to learn English, the need to become educated, the need to get involved in politics for workmen's rights, the need to be Americanized. All they needed was to find work that enabled them to accumulate some money. When they were rejected by the larger society, they adapted to the rejection by creating their own niches in Chinatown. Moreover, many of them led a bachelor's life and had no families with them. They needed a form of social life that resembled home. Thus, they came to Chinatown, where they could speak their own language, eat their own food, play their own games, exchange news from home, and share common experiences with fellow countrymen day in and day out. They could rely on each other to share hardships and comforts in a community on which their common identity was based. Furthermore, culturally the Chinese were clannish. Many of them had come to the United States through a family or kinship network. Upon arrival in a foreign country, they naturally turned to their kinship groups for help and were thus guided into Chinatown. Within Chinatown, people were grouped according to their clans or under the same family names and were bound by cultural obligations specific to these subgroups.

Early Chinatowns primarily served three functions. First, they were originally residential shelters isolated from the hostile society. New York City's Chinatown was home for hundreds of laborers who were driven out of the mines and farms on the West Coast and forced to move eastward to look for other means of livelihood. Although it is believed to have existed before the 1880s as a four-block enclave, Chinatown grew during the time of exclusion.[45] It was demographically abnormal, a bachelors' society with a highly skewed sex ratio. At the turn of the century, about four thousand men and thirty-six women lived in Chinatown—a ratio of 110 males for every female. By 1940 Chinatown, still a bachelors' shelter (603 males per 100 females), had grown into a nine-block area bounded by Canal Street on the north, Park Row on the south, Baxter Street on the west and the Bowery on the east, making a home for about ten thousand Chinese immigrants.

Second, Chinatowns served as an economic base where workers could earn just enough to keep alive their hopes and guarantee their acquiescence to the system. In order to avoid confrontation with the white working class, the Chinese had to find economic niches that were left vacant by the larger economy and not in direct competition with the white working class. With the increasing need for hand laundry, most of the laborers were transformed into laundrymen and took up laundry work for a living.[46] The laundry business became the backbone economy in China-town: in the 1920s, some 37.5 percent of all Chinese workers in New York City were engaged in laundry work.[47] This remained a Chinese-dominated business until steam and machinery came into widespread use and, later, laundromats developed.

Besides the laundry business, the Chinese were also able to penetrate into marginal economic activities that were not interesting to the white workers or even to European immigrants. Many found employment as servants and cooks in substantial households; others were able to set up gift shops or other small businesses.[48]

Another base of the Chinatown economy during the bachelors' era was the restaurant business. Unlike the laundry industry, which catered to non-Chinese customers, restaurants emerged primarily to meet the needs of the sojourners. The bachelors who had left their families behind had to spend so much time working that they hardly had the time or inclination to cook. As the number of bachelors became larger, tea-houses, coffee shops (the old Chinatowners were heavy coffee drinkers), and restaurants sprang up. These drinking and eating places, usually very small, were originally set up to satisfy the immediate needs of the Chinese laborers. Later, when Chinese cooking became accepted by the general population, they were extended to cater to a much broader clientele.

Third, early Chinatowns functioned as social centers of support that gave the workers in an alien environment the illusion of home. The majority of the early Chinatowners were married men who had left their wives at home and come to seek fortunes, hardworking men obsessed with the desire to accumulate money to return to China, but they were lonesome. Without any knowledge of English or of American culture and constantly confronted with racial prejudice, they could not possibly go beyond Chinatown to share "joys" in the melting pot. Thus, the restaurant business was important in Chinatown not simply for economic reasons. For the Chinese sojourners, the eating places were also where they could spend their limited free time together. Instead of going back to their crowded slum housing to rest after a day of work, they would gather in restaurants to have their meals, chat over things happening at home and around them, play cards or gamble a bit, or share a few minutes of dirty jokes with each other to overcome the daily boredom of hard work and homesickness.

Although the Chinese seemed to hold stubbornly to their chopsticks, old-fashioned lifestyles, and clannishness, they were not innately unassimilable. There were reasons for them to be self-segregated. The sojourning orientation, interacting with external factors, defined their life in early Chinatown.

From Sojourners to Settlers

Few statistics exist that accurately depict the social and economic characteristics of the early Chinese immigrants. However, it is generally believed, and somewhat self-evident, that early Chinese immigrants were predominantly male sojourners, poor and without much education and English skills but with dreams of gold. Unfortunately for most of the sojourners, their gold dream remained illusory.

The dreams and lives of the early Chinese immigrants revolved about three primary objectives: to earn and save money, to pay off their debts, and to rejoin their families in China for a life of peace and comfort. However, long misfortune and ill treatment in the United States, coupled with the desperate situation in China, particularly during the civil war in the late 1940s that resulted in the Communist take-over of the country, finally shattered the last hope of making the gold dream come true. Terrified by the radical destruction of the traditional social order and the confiscation of private property by the new Chinese Communist government, which took control of the country in 1949, and further influenced by the extreme anti-Chinese propaganda of the McCarthy era in the United States, the sojourners started to rethink their future for the first time. Since returning was too uncertain, they might just as well stay.

Meanwhile, the sixty-year-old Chinese Exclusion Act was repealed in 1943, and the War Brides Act of 1945 was passed, making it possible for the Chinese to become naturalized U.S. citizens and for their families to reunite with them here in America.[49] Moreover, the growing awareness that there was a whole world outside Chinatown, a world that could offer possibilities of a promising future, opened the long-closed eyes of the Chinese, as racist encounters became less frequent and prejudice more covert. A permanent life in the United States began to be accepted as a substitute for the traditional goal of returning to China. Chinatown's sojourners were, like it or not, slowly transformed into settlers, making a home in the United States. Many Chinese who came after the war intended to find a home rather than to sojourn in America.

An immigrant worker in his fifties recalled coming to New York in the early 1950s:

I came from Hong Kong as a teenager to join my uncle here in New York after my family had just fled from China. My parents kept telling me that I should work very hard to get settled down so that I could help my younger brother to immigrate to America in the future. Unlike many Chinatown workers, I did not have any roots in China. The only thing I had in mind was my parents' words about building a life here so as to get my brother out. I came with the help of my uncle and I wanted to settle down here. I had no intention to return to Hong Kong.[50]

During that period, women began to come and join their husbands in America. By 1947, approximately nine thousand had come; 80 percent of all Chinese immigrants who entered between 1945 and 1947 were women. Since then, the percentage of women admitted to the United States has been slightly higher than that of men, because male immigrants usually returned to China to get married and brought their wives out soon afterward. As a result, the sex ratio in the Chinese community gradually became more balanced (see Figure 2-2).

Still another group of Chinese was forced to make a home here. When the Communists gained control of mainland China in 1949, some five thousand people who had been admitted to the United States since World War II to pursue specific objectives were stranded. These people were students, tourists, businessmen, government officials, journalists, and other temporary visitors who had not originally planned to stay when they entered.[51] Moreover, after the Communist government gained control of China, a large number of Chinese refugees were granted visas to enter the United States to escape communism. Most of these refugees were from the elite class in China. The new immigrants and those who had changed their sojourning goal started to orient toward a permanent life and transformed the old image of the unassimilable sojourners—with an imputed "filthy" and "immoral" second nature—into a new, more sympathetic image of a model minority. The Chinese, after a century of sojourning, finally abandoned their traditional goal for the promise of a life defined no longer in terms of mere survival but in terms of social mobility in the American society.

Conclusion

Chinese immigration to the United States has a relatively longer history than the immigration of most other non-European groups. An examina-

U.S.

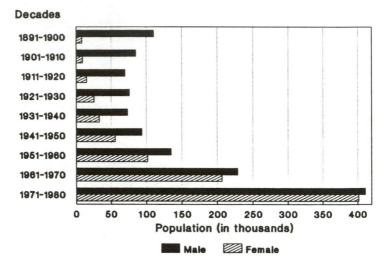

New York State

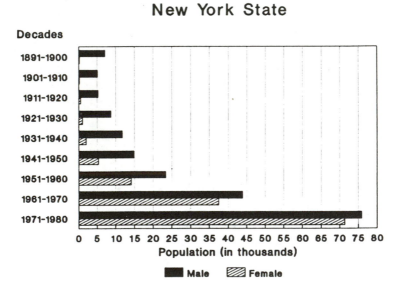

Figure 2-2. Chinese Population by Sex, 1900–1980
Source: U.S. Census of Population: 1980.

38

tion of the old-timers in Chinatown serves as a point of departure for more detailed analyses of the effects of recent Chinese immigration and patterns of immigrant assimilation in later chapters. During almost two-thirds of their history in America, Chinese immigrants were confronted with hostility and legal discrimination. For many old-timers, the journey to the Gold Mountain was long, painful, and unrewarding, and the gold dream many had held was shattered. Questions of why they came, why they clustered in Chinatowns, and why they couldn't return are not unanswerable. They came with a gold dream, they built Chinatowns for survival, and they stayed because of their unfulfilled goals and the fear of communism. Their experience was paradoxical: many Chinese sojourners were obsessed with the idea of making enough to go back to China, and yet they remained and endured; few actually went back. The struggle between a sojourning goal and a reality of endurance became a way of life unique to Chinatown, which affected the settlement patterns of those old-timers.

In sum, this part of the history indicates that Chinese immigration from the beginning had a network character. Information about a livelihood abroad from Western traders, travelers, and ministers and from immigrants themselves was filtered through family and kinship networks to feed back to those who remained behind, and kinship networks helped pool resources to facilitate the journey. Without extensive kinship networks that functioned as information providers as well as sources of support, the transpacific journey would not have been possible. Furthermore, settlement patterns depended on the motivations and perceptions of the immigrants themselves. Motivated merely by a sojourning goal and hence perceiving their stay in the new country as temporary, the Chinese simply tried to work as much as possible at anything they could lay their hand to and for whatever wages were offered them. Their life was simple: to work and to save; their social contact with the larger society was marked by both indifference and alienation. It was not that the Chinese were unassimilable by nature, but just that they never tried or wanted to be. Finally, isolation in Chinatown was both involuntary and voluntary. The involuntary factors were straightforward; they derived from the competition for economic opportunities. While immigrants were oriented toward a sojourning goal that made their stay a direct threat to the white working class and their way of life incompatible with that of the larger society, they were excluded. Racial resentment and discrimination forced them to stay together, to develop their own community as a self-contained enclave, and to take up leftover work in the narrow margins of the larger economy. While sojourners prevailed, Chinatown could not simply be treated as a springboard from which immigrants could jump into the mainstream, through socioeconomic achievement, for its members did not intend to jump. Because of the need for social and cultural support from fellow sojourners and the need to maintain ethnic identity and kinship ties with China, immigrants chose a way of life in Chinatown that reminded them of home. This voluntary self-isolation created a stereotype of unassimilability that in turn reinforced the community's irrelevance to the larger society.

3

Changes in Recent Chinese Immigration

The year 1965 was a significant milestone in the history of immigration to the United States. In that year the U.S. government revised the discriminatory immigration law to abolish the national-origin quotas that favored immigrants from northwestern Europe, predominantly white, Anglo-Saxon Protestants.[1] The United States has achieved most of its population growth in the past two hundred years, primarily through immigration. Significant waves of immigrants poured into the United States in the 1850s when the country was badly in need of labor for development and industrialization. During the first decade of this century, immigration reached a record high of 8.7 million, about 85 percent of which was from Europe. The 1980 census reported a total of 14 million foreign-born members of the American population, about 6 percent of the total. Although this percentage was far less than it was in the 1920s when immigrants made up 13 percent of the total, recent immigration has greatly affected people and society. The Center for Immigration Studies reported that the number of legal immigrants between 1981 and 1990 will equal or surpass the 8.7 million total between 1901 and 1910, making a second peak in the history of immigration since 1820.[2]

The trend has reversed since 1965. As opposed to the earlier peak, about 85 percent of the new arrivals are now from Asia or the Caribbean and South America. Europeans account for only about 11 percent of the total. This is a sharp contrast to the predominantly European and Protestant people making up the American majority. In the early 1960s only about 7 percent of all immigrants, approximately twenty thousand per year, came from Asia. Since then, Asian immigration to the United States has increased more than tenfold. The biggest influx across the Pacific has been mainly from Hong Kong, Taiwan, China, Korea, and other Southeast Asian countries such as the Philippines, Vietnam, Laos, and Cambodia. The U.S. withdrawal from Indochina in the 1970s led to a more diverse wave of refugees, a portion of whom were of Chinese origin. Recently, approximately 264,000 immigrants each year, 44 percent of the nation's total annual arrivals, are from Asian countries. In the 1900s, Asian-Americans made up only 0.3 percent of the total population. In 1990 this percentage grew to 3.0. It is estimated that by the year 2080, Asian-Americans will make up 10 percent of the total U.S. population.

The Chinese, being the first to immigrate to the United States, have formed the largest ethnic group of Asian immigrants. It is expected that the recent Chinese immigration stream from China and Hong Kong will continue at a rate of thirty thousand to thirty-five thousand each year. In addition a separate quota of twenty thousand per year has been given to Taiwan and a sizable number of ethnic Chinese immigrants come in from other Southeast Asian countries.[3] Moreover, the Immigration Act of 1990 treats Hong Kong as a foreign state effective with fiscal year 1995, allocating a separate quota of ten thousand per year.[4] The rapid growth in Chinese immigration has been a direct result of the changes in the contexts of reception, the contexts of exit, and the mentality of the new arrivals. This chapter examines the conditions under which massive Chinese immigration has occurred and how these changes have affected the mode of Chinese immigrant incorporation.

The Changing Contexts of Reception

In *Immigrant America*, Alejandro Portes and Rubén Rumbaut point out that the most relevant contexts of reception are defined by the policies of the receiving government, the conditions of the host labor market, and the characteristics of preexisting immigrant communities.[5] Changes in these contexts can have significant impact on the trend of immigration and the mode of immigrant incorporation.

Immigration Policies

Prior to 1965, the U.S. immigration laws favored European immigrants. Before then, most Asian-Americans were descendants either of the Chinese who dug in gold mines and built railroads in the nineteenth century or of Japanese farmers. The discriminatory quota systems effectively cut off the inflow from non-European countries. The Chinese, one of the largest and oldest non-European immigrant groups, were subject to a series of harsh discriminatory laws. Beginning with the Chinese Exclusion Act of 1882, the Chinese and the family members of the Chinese already in the United States were denied of entry for more than sixty years. Under the restrictive immigration policies, there was virtually no new immigration from Asia after the 1920s. Very few Chinese were able to complete the transpacific journey to America, and the Chinese population in the United States was growing very slowly. Even after the repeal of the Chinese Exclusion Act in 1943 and the passage of the War Brides Act in 1945, the number of Chinese (other than wives under the nonquota preference category) who could enter was limited to an annual quota of only 105. Table 3-1 shows that the Chinese population experienced a continuous decline in the first two decades of this century and only a slight increase in the 1930s and 1940s. Both New York and California, the two largest receiving states of Chinese immigrants, showed similar trends.

On October 3, 1965, President Lyndon B. Johnson signed the law that ended the national-origin quota system that had regulated the inflow of non-European immigrants into the United States. Reflecting the spirit of the times, the new immigration law was intended to serve two fundamental interests—the humanitarian interest in reunifying families and the economic interests in obtaining skilled and needed workers from foreign countries. This law put each of the sending countries on a relatively equal footing with an annual limit of twenty thousand.

Under the relaxed immigration legislation, immigrant visas are granted according to six preference categories with numerical limitations: (1) unmarried sons and daughters of U.S. citizens (20 percent); (2) spouses and unmarried sons and daughters of permanent residents (26 percent); (3) the talented with exceptional ability (10 percent); (4) married sons and daughters of U.S. citizens (10 percent); (5) brothers and sisters of U.S. citizens (24 percent); and (6) skilled and unskilled labor (10 percent). Parents, spouses, and minor children of U.S. citizens are exempt from the quota allocations. Immediate relatives of adult U.S. citizens who come for short-term visits are not limited by the proportional allocation.

After 1965 basically three types of immigrants have been granted visas to enter the United States: more than three-quarters are family immigrants, some 20 percent are employment-based immigrants, and the rest are diverse immigrants. Under the new law, twenty thousand immigrants were allowed to enter the United States annually from China, including Hong Kong and Taiwan. This quota doubled in 1981 when Taiwan was permitted a separate quota of twenty thousand.[6] A fairly large number of the immigrants (parents, spouses, and minor children of U.S. citizens) entered without having to qualify for any of the numerically limited

Table 3-1. Chinese Population in the United States and the States of New York and California, by Sex, 1900–1980

Year	U.S.	New York	California
1980	812,178	147,250	325,882
Male	410,936	75,885	163,060
Female	401,242	71,365	162,822
1970	435,062	81,378	170,131
Male	228,565	43,919	87,835
Female	206,497	37,459	82,296
1960	237,292	37,573	95,600
Male	135,549	23,406	53,627
Female	101,743	14,167	41,973
1950	150,005	20,171	58,324
Male	94,052	14,875	36,051
Female	55,953	5,296	22,273
1940	106,334	13,731	39,556
Male	73,561	11,777	27,331
Female	32,773	1,954	12,225
1930	102,159	9,665	37,361
Male	76,388	8,649	27,988
Female	25,771	1,016	9,373
1920	85,202	5,793	28,812
Male	70,141	5,240	24,230
Female	15,061	553	4,582
1910	94,414	5,266	36,248
Male	85,210	5,065	33,003
Female	9,204	201	3,245
1900	118,746	7,170	45,753
Male	110,750	7,028	42,297
Female	7,996	142	3,456

Source: U.S. Census of Population: 1970 and 1980.

categories. The increase in sheer numbers, from an annual quota of 105 permitted by the repeal of the Chinese Exclusion Act in 1943 to twenty thousand in 1965, is monumental. As a direct effect of this single piece of legislation, the number of Chinese immigrants admitted to the U.S. between 1961 and 1970 reached 109,771—four times greater than the number for the previous decade (a total of 25,201 between 1951 and 1960). In the 1970s, the number reached 154,957—41 percent higher than the 1961–1970 figure—and after that, the number of immigrants from China and Hong Kong consistently exceeded the annual limit of twenty thousand, suggesting that a large number of new arrivals were admitted through nonquota categories. The total population of Chinese descent in the United States, more than 60 percent of which was foreign-born, increased substantially, from 237,292 in 1960 to 435,062 in 1970 and to 812,178 in 1980 (see Table 3-1). In New York City, the Chinese population grew from 33,000 in 1960 to 124,372 in 1980, by census count.

Conditions of the U.S. Labor Market

Why do people immigrate? The "push-and-pull" thesis emphasizes the structure of job opportunities in the United States and the specific motivation of migrant workers relative to the motivation of workers born and raised in the country in which they work.[7] This argument focuses on the structural conditions that give rise to the observed differences in circumstances and behavior of various immigrant groups.[8] It perceives the larger economy of the receiving country as consisting of a dual structure: the core and the periphery, corresponding to the primary and secondary labor markets. The labor force is segmented into two or more labor markets.[9] The core, or primary, economy is dominated by large firms that handle staple products and is characterized by high wages, knowledge-intensive jobs, good working conditions, promotion chances, and career stability. In contrast, the peripheral, or secondary, economy is filled by small-scale firms that cater to the unpredictable or fluctuating portion of demand and is characterized by low wages, labor-intensive work, long working hours, little upward mobility, and job instability. The two sectors tend to be noncompeting; hence, each offers a sheltered position to firms that may be established by different segments of the population.[10]

This line of argument depicts a process of queuing. Jobs in the secondary labor market are viewed as unattractive to, and often avoided by, native workers, who are more interested in long-term career prospects.

As more and more native workers head for the core sector, the problem of filling secondary jobs becomes serious.[11] Immigrants are one solution to this problem. That is, immigrants come because there is a demand from the secondary labor market. As they enter the new country, immigrant groups are structurally denied equal access to the larger economy, presumably because they are newer entrants in the labor force and have less experience, fewer skills, and perhaps less education. For this reason, they have little opportunity to participate in the primary labor market but most of the time take jobs that are left over even in the peripheral economy. By queuing up in the labor market, they gradually move on to better jobs as time passes.

While international immigration may be initiated by the structure of job opportunities in the receiving country, its consequences vary depending upon both the motivations and the experiences of immigrants, which are distinctive from one ethnic group to another. The dual-labor-market thesis does not intend to deal with group characteristics that affect immigrants' labor-market participation in their new country and the consequences of labor migration. On the one hand, the migration process links the sociological characteristics of the workers at their place of origin to the roles they are supposed to play at the destination, and such linkages are often different for each ethnic group. On the other hand, international migration often causes a clash of interests between native workers and immigrants, for unlike slaves, immigrants are theoretically free to sell their labor and move between jobs in the labor market.[12] Moreover, since the postindustrial economy has a limited and perhaps declining need for labor in the core economy, large portions of the population must be relegated to the low-wage competitive sector, the welfare economy, or even the underground economy.[13] As a result, the secondary labor market has disproportionately drawn from racial minorities, women, and immigrant workers, since the system as a whole requires that some sector of the population fill the undesirable jobs.[14] Because of the political and economic vulnerability of immigrants, they often encounter various social and labor-market barriers that are systematically created to block their upward movement.

Recent studies have argued that immigration to the United States has been highly selective.[15] The U.S. immigration laws have been responsive to the internal labor-market conditions. After the first wave of European settlers, immigration into the United States became a system to furnish labor. In response to the growing demand of industrial development, European immigrants entered the country by the thousands in the second quarter of the nineteenth century. The coming of large numbers of Chinese laborers in the third quarter of the previous century primarily served the need for cheap labor in developing the West and building the transcontinental railroad. Internal politico-legal, social, and economic systems were not designed to incorporate the Chinese laborers into the U.S. society. As the U.S. economy experienced recession, the Chinese were among the first victims of exclusion, under the rationale that the Chinese laborers affected the wages and job opportunities of the American white working class.

On the other hand, the United States has been competing with other countries in an immigration market for immigrants' human and physical capital in the same manner as countries compete in the worldwide market to exchange goods and services.[16] There have been concerns about the economic effects of immigration on the U.S. labor market, that is, whether the family reunification emphasis of the current immigration law would cause an explosive family-chain migration, which would negatively affect the U.S. labor market by depressing skills and wages and displacing native workers. However, studies have shown optimistic results that family ties that influence immigration decisions actually increase the skill level of the immigrant flow because they attenuate the unfavorable selection in the immigration process.[17] Moreover, many immigrant groups are able to depend on the availability of material resources in their preexisting communities. Within the structural constraints, segments of immigrant communities can mobilize resources through a variety of means.[18] Therefore, opportunities offered by the U.S. labor market may not necessarily be limited to the vacant niches in the secondary economy.

Access to opportunites in the labor market for today's immigrants, particularly for those with education and occupational skills comparable to those of native workers has become much more open than before. Although some immigrants may have begun to displace native workers in the middle and upper end of the larger American labor market,[19] overall, immigrants may not necessarily overwhelmingly pour into the larger labor market and take away jobs from native workers. Many immigrant groups are able to mobilize ethnic resources to develop ethnic economies that resemble many positive features of the core economy.[20] Again, different immigrant groups may have different experiences in intergroup competition and may adopt ethnic strategies depending on the interaction of opportunities and group characteristics.

Recent immigrant Chinese, the majority of whom are family immigrants, have been injecting two major types of capital—human and physical—into the United States and are helping to diversify the economy in Chinatown. Unlike early immigrants, who were predominantly poor and uneducated sojourners, recent immigrants are demographically and socioeconomically heterogeneous and oriented toward permanent settlement. The 1980 census showed that immigrant Chinese from China, Hong Kong, and Taiwan had a greater percentage of high school graduates than the general U.S. population, and almost three times as many college graduates (76 percent versus 67 percent high school graduates and 44 percent versus 16 percent college graduates, respectively). The immigrants from China, who were more disadvantaged than their counterparts from Hong Kong and Taiwan, also had levels of educational attainment higher than the national average and higher than those for other minorities. The median household income for Chinese immigrants exceeded that for the general U.S. population.

Chinese immigrants with strong human capital usually had achieved middle-class status and well-established lives before immigration. According to reports from the Immigration and Naturalization Service, about 42 percent of the Chinese immigrants admitted to the United States between 1982 and 1986 left behind executive, administrative, or managerial positions or professional specialty occupations. This segment of the immigrant population comprised persons who tended to have better resources than other immigrants and so were able to refuse a passive acceptance of their low immigrant status. They were able to avoid starting from the lowest rung of the socioeconomic ladder. These immigrants were highly motivated and were willing to take risks in pursuing self-employment in order to sustain and improve the standard of living that they had established before immigration. However, the options of Chinese immigrants, despite strong human capital, were limited by initial disadvantages associated with immigration. Most of them did not speak English, lacked access to information about the larger society, and had limited access to networks of employment in the larger labor market. Many first-generation immigrants were simply not aware of the possible employment opportunities, if any, in the larger labor market upon arrival. They also tended to assume that whatever was available outside their community had to be at the lower end of the occupational scale (i.e., jobs that gave them little chance to upgrade or reinvest in their human capital). For this reason, they depended on Chinatown, where they could take advantage of ethnic networks and the community. Even for those who had to work low-wage jobs, their priority was not individual achievement but the welfare of their family and their children.

The influx of immigrants into New York City's Chinatown in recent years has boosted the enclave economy in Chinatown through extensive investment. Old immigrants shifted their patterns of sojourning to permanent settlement and became increasingly interested in making long-term investments and reinvestments after their family members rejoined them. New immigrants and their families were uprooted from their country of origin and brought with them all the family wealth and savings to start a new life in their new country. Furthermore, political uncertainty in Hong Kong, Taiwan, and Southeast Asia (e.g., the scheduled return of Hong Kong to China in 1997), caused investors to look for secure capital outlets in the United States. As a result, New York City's Chinatown experienced a boom in property investment and expansion in a wide range of local businesses. The most significant change can be seen in the rise of the garment industry, which replaced the laundry business as one of the basic industries in Chinatown. Services that apparently had an ethnic clientele—accounting, banking, insurance and real estate, restaurants and food stores, medical doctors and herbalists, barber and beauty shops, jewelry stores, etc.—all experienced tremendous growth. The case of New York City's Chinatown provides convincing evidence that family immigrants are not displacing native workers in the larger labor market. Rather, they contribute significantly to the U.S. economy as a whole by creating economic opportunities in the enclave labor market.

Preexisting Kinship and Family Networks

The humanitarian and compassionate ideals of the new immigration laws have accounted for the majority of the total influx of immigrants to the United States in recent years. The centerpiece for U.S. immigration policy is family reunification. The policy recognizes that families ease the sociocultural and psychological dislocations associated with immigration by serving as buffers and mediators between the individual immigrant and the host environment.[21] Because of this policy, 80 percent of all immigrants entering the United States are either immediate family members or close relatives of U.S. citizens or permanent residents. The migration chains that have developed along the family lines have facilitated immigrant incorporation into the American society.

Immigration from one's home country to a totally new one is not an exclusively individual decision. Politico-legal constraints can effectively suppress an individual's desire to think about, to start, and to carry on the journey of immigration. People who have extensive kinship and family networks are more likely to immigrate than those who do not.[22] Immigration opportunities for prospective immigrants would be close to zero without family or kinship connections. Most current studies have taken the 1965 reform of U.S. immigration law as a primary factor contributing to the recent peak of U.S. immigration, and chain migration or networking have become an apparent pattern.[23]

To take advantage of family preference in the U.S. immigration law, Chinese-Americans and their relatives in China and other parts of the world remain in close contact with each other, either to consolidate the existing extended family or kinship ties or to establish new links to the networks. The recent trend of Chinese immigration to the United States is partly an unintended result of earlier decisions: most of the new immigrants have not come simply from isolated nuclear families. They do not finish dealing with the U.S. Immigration and Naturalization Service once they obtain a Green Card (permanent residence) and, eventually, U.S. citizenship. Instead, they try every possible means to qualify their relatives for the immigrant categories and to help them to obtain a Green Card in this country.

Usually, the process starts from one of two points: Either an immigrant has become a naturalized U.S. citizen or has secured permanent residency status. It takes approximately five to six years for a permanent resident to obtain a U.S. citizenship. Immediately after an immigrant acquires citizenship, he or she petitions to send for spouse, minor children, and parents (nonquota) and adult unmarried children (first preference). It takes about two to three years to get married children out (fourth preference) and about five to six years to get siblings out (fifth preference). The spouse of a citizen must wait about three years to become a naturalized U.S. citizen. Once the relatives arrive, they are automatically issued Green Cards and are thus eligible to petition for immigrant visas for their own spouses or parents (and parents-in-law) or minor children. Later (after five to six years) when they become naturalized citizens, they can duplicate the process of the initial petitioner to bring over other members of their extended families.[24] Also, the unmarried children can create another network through marriage, and the parents-in-law can bring a whole new family line into the migration chain. The networking is circular in action and continuously expands over time. Previous research has found that naturalized petitioners from mainland China have most frequently petitioned for their parents (84.5 percent for parents as compared to 14.3 percent for spouses and 1.2 percent for children); more women (52 percent) than men (48 percent) petitioned for their parents; and native-born petitioners were more likely to petition for a spouse.[25]

Another equally effective way for Chinese to immigrate is to find some means to tie into the family-chain network. The most common shortcut, perhaps, is marriage. For example, a woman (or a man) in China without any connection to the family migration chain could marry a U.S. citizen or a Green Card holder and come to the United States. This spouse can then send for her or his parents, who could then send for their minor children, and when these immigrants become U.S. citizens, they can send for their siblings or married children and so on. Thus, a transpacific marriage can bring a new chain into the migration process, as many in Chinatown testified. Mr. Peng's immigrant experience was typical:

> My brother-in-law is a naturalized citizen. But he was not the one who helped us out, for it would have taken at least eight years. We came because of our daughter. She married a Chinatown worker in 1982, and had her citizenship in 1986 and got us out the next year. Then we were able to petition for our two adult sons and get them out shortly. If my daughter had sent for her brothers, there would have been a five-to-six-year wait. But we got them out more quickly.
>
> My elder son is twenty-six now and he will go back to China to marry his girlfriend and then she can come and her family will too in the future. People are very smart, they know how to get here quickly through the family connection.[26]

Because marriage appears to be one of the most effective ways to get through the process, some Chinese women have tried this means in order to come. They are able to do so because many male Chinese immigrants have an inclination to marry within the group, and there are simply not enough unmarried Chinese women available in the in-group marriage market. Thus, these Chinese immigrant men will turn to their family or kinship networks to look for wives in China.

Back in China, it is not unusual for a twenty-year-old woman to marry a *gum shan haak* her father's age, and such a marital relationship can sometimes be established within a single month, after the first meeting. Once married, she is able to come to the United States within six months, and then she is obliged to get her extended family members out. Generally, a *gum shan haak* is introduced to his future wife by one of his relatives. The woman knows her husband-to-be solely through the descriptions of the go-betweens, and from references obtained through the kinship network. At that point, emigration to the United States is perhaps more important to her than how her future life will turn out. Such women are concerned less about their personal happiness than about finding a means to get themselves and their families out of China. Their own future lives, they worry about only later. Mrs. Cheng, a Chinatown garment worker, told her story when asked how she first met her husband:

I was from a village in Nanhai. One day, my neighbor came to my door and told Father that a son of her cousin in New York wanted to look for a wife at his home village, and that he was an honest and diligent worker. My father trusted our longtime neighbor, who herself actually hardly knew anything about her relative in person, and talked to me about that. I agreed to have a meeting with the stranger. I had often dreamt of going to the U.S., and this might be a chance. So when I first met the man (now my husband), all I had in mind was how to impress this man to marry me so that I could get out of here. Later on, I could possibly get my brothers out, too. He stayed only for three weeks and we agreed to get married during his next trip. A few months later, he came back to the village and married me. That was how I got here. But I was not the only one in the village who did this.

To think back, this was really scary. It was like you bet your life and you couldn't afford to lose. I think I am really lucky. We get along well and I am quite satisfied with what I have now—a child, some money to send back to my parents, and possible help at a later time to get my brothers out.

There are many young women in New York who are like myself, but not all are as lucky. Some are beaten and abused by their husbands, and they have to tolerate that because they do not have others to help. There are also some women, especially some of these vain city girls, who take advantage of their honest husbands. I knew a woman from Hangzhou who came here by way of marriage and dumped her husband for someone else after little more than a year. Many women back in China are still trying to find someone here to marry. In newspapers here in Chinatown and back in China, you can see a lot of such advertising. Those answering the ads are taking many more risks than those introduced by their relatives. With references from your relatives, you feel safer. If you don't want to try this, you will end up in China forever.[27]

The nonquota and first-preference advantages for spouses of U.S. citizens and legal alien residents have unintentionally built some side roads to the United States. Some people attempt to come through fake marriages, and these, especially those arranged within the kinship networks, are hard for immigration officers to detect. Though a gamble with big risks, they appeal to some Chinese who want desperately to emigrate. A thirty-four-year-old Chinatown electrician, who agreed to have his interview quoted, provided an example:

> I am still legally married to my cousin though we are not husband and wife in real life. She is a nineteen-year-old college student and her mother is my aunt. I now live with her parents and her two younger brothers in Brooklyn. Her family came here in 1981 because my aunt's father-in-law helped them, and they became naturalized citizens in 1987. My father had hoped that my aunt could get me out, because I am the only son of the family, and yet the only way that seemed feasible was to find me a U.S. wife. Then my aunt worked this out by arranging for her daughter to marry me on paper and bring me out. And so it worked and I came.
>
> In a year or so, we will have a divorce. I plan to go back to China to find a wife, because there aren't many women available here. My cousin will still go on to her higher degree at college and may marry someone she loves when the time comes. I am not concerned too much about legality here. This is solely a family matter. Without family help I would not have been here talking to you.[28]

The extended families who help their members immigrate through fake marriages do so principally to fulfill traditional family obligations, though some do ask for money in return—usually from four to ten thousand dollars. But compared to the prices charged by underground agencies that specialize in this illegal enterprise in big entry cities such as San Francisco, Los Angeles, and New York, the amount of money involved is insignificant. These marriages are much less risky, for both the persons involved are likely to be members of the extended family or kinship network. While transpacific marriages work for many immigrant families, there are negative consequences, too. For example, family violence and wife abuse are more frequent in Chinatown today than before, partly because marriages are built not on mutual understanding and long-term commitment but on a short-term goal of immigration.

Fake marriages are severely penalized by immigration law. According to the Immigration Marriage Fraud Amendment of 1986, a spouse can come only under a conditional immigrant visa.[29] The immigrant who comes under a conditional visa has, by law, to stay married for two years before he/she can apply for permanent residence. Marriage fraud can be penalized by heavy fines and deportation. This law is meant to prevent

Table 3-2. Chinese Immigrants Admitted to the United States, by Region, Sex, and Age, 1982–1985

	China	%	Hong Kong	%	Taiwan	%
Total	101,027	100.0	21,555	100.0	53,955	100.0
Male	46,459	46.0	10,496	48.7	25,185	46.7
Female	51,320	50.8	10,599	49.2	28,535	52.9
Unknown	3,248	3.2	460	2.1	235	.4
Under 20	19,151	19.0	10,796	50.1	16,205	30.1
Total	19,151	100.0	10,796	100.0	16,205	100.0
Male	9,740	50.9	5,612	52.0	8,155	50.3
Female	8,774	45.8	5,041	46.7	8,005	49.4
Unknown	637	3.3	143	1.3	45	.3
20 to 59	65,868	65.2	10,342	48.0	35,745	66.2
Total	65,868	100.0	10,342	100.0	35,745	100.0
Male	29,385	44.6	4,712	45.6	16,122	45.1
Female	34,172	51.9	5,322	51.5	19,445	54.4
Unknown	2,311	3.5	308	2.9	178	.5
Over 60	16,008	15.8	417	1.9	2,005	3.7
Total	16,008	100.0	417	100.0	2,005	100.0
Male	7,334	45.8	172	41.2	908	45.3
Female	8,374	52.3	236	56.6	1,085	54.1
Unknown	300	1.9	9	2.2	12	.6

Source: INS Statistical Yearbook: 1982 to 1986.

marriage fraud, but it unintentionally makes women more vulnerable to family violence or wife abuse; they are reluctant to report such crimes or to leave the abuser for fear that they might face possible deportation. However, it would not be easy for immigration officials to block this illegal channel built by the family.

In recent years, the number of immigrant women has been considerably higher than that of men, particularly in the twenty-to-fifty-nine age group (Table 3-2). This statistic indicates that women have come to join their husbands here, but it also implies that many Chinese-Americans may have gone back to China to get married and then brought their wives out of the country at a later date.

Legally or illegally, the Chinese could not just come on their individual initiative to achieve economic goals. They are, in one way or another, backed by their families and kin within a consolidated social network.

Family-chain migration has positive effects on immigration assimilation in U.S. society, because it indicates uprooting rather than sojourning. Families facilitate immigrants' social, economic, and political integration and enhance their ability to assimilate successfully into American society.[30] Also, families provide important social support and information to help immigrants overcome initial disadvantages associated with immigration.[31] In the near future, family migration under the present immigration law will continue to affect the rate of Chinese immigration and the growth of the Chinese community in the United States.

The Changing Contexts of Exit

Emigration Policies

More liberal emigration policies in China have also played a crucial role in recent Chinese immigration to the United States. In the past, emigration from China was not free. There were harsh laws to prevent the Chinese from leaving the country under the imperial regime. Even under the control of the Nationalist government, when China was open to the outside world (1911 to 1949), emigration was legally discouraged. After the Chinese Communist party gained power in 1949, China's door to the West was once again closed tight. The country was totally isolated from the West and maintained restrictive emigration policies for three decades (1949–1979). During that period, even if the door might open a little, it was for a different purpose and with a very different hand upon the knob. Few people were allowed to leave the country, even to travel or visit relatives abroad. During the restrictive period, Chinese passports were issued almost exclusively to those who were on business, particularly handling the government's diplomatic affairs. There were only a limited number of exit permits issued for those who petitioned to emigrate to Macao and Hong Kong to rejoin their families. Very few were able to obtain exit permits to come to the United States or other Western countries.

The cold war between China and the Western countries cut information and communication channels. The Chinese received very little information on immigration and their contacts with family members abroad were disconnected. Although the U.S. immigration policies began to favor family reunification as early as 1945, with the War Brides Act, and the immigration law was liberalized in 1965 to give an annual quota of twenty thousand for Chinese nationals, very few in China were able to take advantage of the reform. China was then about to be engulfed in the extremely destructive political turbulence of the Great Proletarian Cultural Revolution, which lasted from 1966 to 1976.[32] During this period, people in China were prosecuted and sent to prisons or labor camps merely because they had *hai-wai-guan-xi* (relatives abroad).

After the Cultural Revolution, particularly in the 1980s, China gradually lifted the barriers to emigration. However, the process is selective: only those with close family connections and adequate emigration papers are qualified to apply for passports and exit permits. Persons with exceptional professional skills and higher educational degrees (higher-ranking doctors, professors, Ph.D.s, and the like) or sensitive positions in government or scientific research institutions (intelligence agents, researchers of military defense and the space sciences, for example) are not allowed to emigrate, not even to rejoin their families. Moreover, various administrative barriers at different levels of government deliberately function to slow down the application and screening process. It usually takes three months or longer for an application to go from the applicant's work unit to a superior agency that supervises that work unit and then to the public security bureau of the local government and finally to the public security bureau of the provincial government, which issues ordinary citizens' passports.

Self-supporting and exchange students who wish to pursue a higher degree at universities outside China with their own funding are subject to further restrictions. Those with undergraduate degrees are allowed to leave only after five years' service, and those with master's degrees, seven years' service; otherwise, they must pay up to thirty thousand yuan back to the government to compensate for their college education costs, which have been paid by the government (equivalent to fifteen years' salary for an average college graduate). All government-sponsored students on exchange programs are required to sign a contract with the government before they can leave the country, promising that they will return in a certain number of years or that their parents must be responsible to pay a fine of up to fifty thousand yuan. Those who are still at college and wish to leave before graduation must pay approximately twenty-five hundred yuan per year of college completed in order to get exit permits, and they must provide numerous appropriate notarized funding documents and notices from universities that accepted them. And so on.[33]

Despite all these strict requirements and administrative barriers, however, emigration has been rather flexible in family unification cases. According to statistics from government sources, the number of Chinese citizens applying for emigration is increasing. Table 3-3 provides infor-

Table 3-3. Number of Exit Permit Applications and Approvals, China, 1986–1990

Year	Applications	Approvals	% Approved
1986	80,828	77,064	95.3
1987	118,074	107,297	90.9
1988	244,243	212,182	86.9
1989	248,689	238,301	95.8
1990	290,235	278,988	96.1
Mean	196,413	182,766	93.0

Sources: Southern Overseas Chinese Journal, June 1990; *People's Daily* (overseas edition), May 21, 1991.

mation on passport applications between 1986 and 1990. Over the five-year period, an average of 196,413 applications per year went through the provincial public safety bureaus for exit permits, and about 93 percent of them were approved. Between 1979 and 1990, China issued 1,346,909 exit permits nationwide from 1,554,916 applications, an 87 percent approval rate. Although the approval rate appears fairly high, these statistics may be misleading in that the number of applications that made it to the end of the administrative ladder—the provincial public security bureau—were only those that had survived the screening from the previous two or more levels of government bureaucracy. Relaxation of the Chinese emigration policies has granted only partial rights of emigration; the policies remain restrictive and selective.

Nevertheless, more and more people are granted exit permits, raising the obvious questions of where they go and how they get there. With an annual immigrant quota for Chinese nationals of twenty thousand, plus a sizable number of nonquota visas, the United States has become the largest receiving country of Chinese emigration. Other Chinese successfully emigrated to Canada or other Western countries. But many did not manage to leave China despite their exit permits. Between 1979 and 1990 of those who held exit permits (a total of 1,346,909), only a little over half (700,000) were able to obtain entry visas from another country and actually emigrate. From 1986 to 1990, only about 54 percent were able to obtain visas to enter another country. Most of the U.S. immigrant visas were issued at the American embassy or at consulates in China under the six preference categories of the current immigration law. Immigrant visas for professionals or those with exceptional ability in science and arts under the third preference category were mostly issued to those who were already in the United States, either as students or as temporary workers. Since the number of people eligible for family-chain immigration far exceeded the annual quota of twenty thousand, the waiting time has increased to as long as eight to ten years for the fifth preference category. As for nonimmigrant entry visas, such as tourist or student visas, the approval rate is fairly low, said to be less than 1 percent in 1988 in the U.S. Consulate General in Guangzhou, for example. Many tourist and student visa applications were rejected because the applicants are suspected of intending to immigrate illegally. Some people have held their Chinese passports for four years or more (Chinese passports are generally valid for five years) but have never been able to leave.

Disparities between Life Expectations and Reality

The Chinese are not an emigrating people. Strong tradition and ethnocentrism emphasize attachment to the land of one's birth. Even in the past when people tried to leave the country to look for a living, they tended to sojourn rather than settle down and tried to return to the land of their birth as soon as they could. Today, the situation is different. Many Chinese desperately want to leave their country. Why have so many Chinese attempted to emigrate, particularly to the United States?

It is generally assumed that poverty, unemployment, and low wages at home are the primary pushing factors, and economic prosperity and higher-paying jobs are the pulling factors. Immigrants are said to be economically depressed and desperate. On the one hand, they have lost hope for their own country ever to become developed. On the other hand, they have perceived America as a paradise with lots of opportunities. They believe that, with determination and hard work, they can make it there, not so much for themselves as for their children. Coming to America and becoming a part of it is their long-term dream.

However, many studies point to the opposite. Several independent studies on Caribbean immigration to the United States find that many immigrants from developing countries are not among the poorest and unemployed. Other studies show that very few Mexican immigrants were unemployed in Mexico, and those who immigrated tended to have above-average levels of education compared to their homeland population. Among immigrants from the Dominican Republic, the majority were from cities. They had much higher levels of literacy and were more skilled than the general Dominican population as a whole.[34] The recent wave of Asian immigration reveals a similar pattern. As is shown in the following chapters, the majority of Chinese immigrants come from the more open and economically prosperous regions relative to the rest of China. Those from Hong Kong and Taiwan were among the middle-class, better-educated, and professional groups. The first wave of "boat people"—refugees from Vietnam and Cambodia—was largely business-men, traders, and capitalists and their families escaping Communist control.[35] The Korean immigrants almost uniformly come from urban Korea with a strong middle-class background.[36] Therefore, it is not simply poverty or lack of jobs, but well-paid jobs, economic and political free-dom, the effects of immigration/emigration policies, and a network of family and kinship relations that fuel immigration to the United States.

People emigrate for various reasons. Many Chinese hope for politi-cal stability, economic prosperity, and the well-being of their families. Disappointed and frustrated at what they could do under the repressive regime, they began to perceive a wider and wider gap between their aspi-rations and expectations and the means for fulfilling them in China. The huge economic gap, or income differential, between the sending and re-ceiving countries is not the sole cause of emigration. Many of the Chinese immigrants came from the more well-to-do segment of the population in the most economically prosperous regions of the country.

After the Cultural Revolution in 1976, a group of liberal and open-minded senior government officials adopted open-door policies and led a national economic reform. In 1979 China and the United States nor-malized diplomatic relations, and in subsequent years, China's door to the outside world was opened wide, and economic reform brought about substantial growth nationwide. During that period, the general standard of living improved significantly. According to the State Statistical Bureau of China, the gross national income increased from 1,166 million yuan in 1964 to 3,940 million in 1981 and 6,822 million in 1985.[37] The coastal areas in the east and southeast and the three independent municipali-ties of Beijing, Shanghai, and Tianjin especially benefited. For example, Guangdong Province, which sent a majority of the Chinese emigrants to the United States, ranked fourth in national income of the twenty-nine provinces and fifth both in gross output values of agriculture and indus-try and in net income per capita for rural households in 1985 (Table 3-4). Annual income per capita in urban areas increased from 243 yuan in 1964 (before the Cultural Revolution) to 500 in 1981 (after the Cultural Revolution), and further to 821 in 1985.[38]

Meanwhile, the normalized relations between China and the United States permitted frequent contacts to resume between relatives in the two

Table 3-4. National Income and GOV, by Province, China, 1984 and 1985

Province	National Income 1984 (100 million yuan[1])	GOV[2] 1985 (100 million yuan)	Income Per Capita[3] 1985 (yuan)
Beijing	157.30	356.08	775.08
Tianjin	121.68	326.50	564.55
Shanghai	341.20	892.67	805.92
Guangdong	397.38	895.47	495.31
Anhui	221.17	405.24	369.41
Fujian	128.70	236.22	396.45
Gansu	83.07	160.59	255.22
Guangxi	128.17	213.77	302.96
Guizhou	94.51	144.76	287.83
Hebei	282.01	560.61	385.23
Heilongjiang	264.84	468.08	397.84
Henan	306.16	567.41	329.37
Hubei	293.39	620.01	421.21
Hunan	247.88	448.19	395.26
Inner Mogolia	96.18	159.07	360.41
Jiangsu	466.31	1,268.70	492.60
Jiangxi	141.65	264.51	377.31
Jilin	147.28	301.95	413.74
Liaoning	354.15	805.97	467.84
Ningxia	18.27	32.95	321.17
Qinghai	19.51	30.58	342.95
Shanxi	152.10	285.07	358.32
Shaanxi	121.71	255.87	295.26
Shandong	477.86	895.47	408.12
Sichuan	403.34	759.49	315.07
Tibet	9.10	8.66	352.97
Xinjiang	74.26	123.95	394.30
Yunnan	122.64	204.57	338.34
Zhejiang	276.70	677.97	548.60

Source: SSBC 1986, pp. 37, 44, 586.

[1] Yuan is the unit of Chinese currency. One yuan equaled about one-third of a dollar in 1985.

[2] GOV—Gross Output Value of agriculture and industry.

[3] Net income per capita for rural households.

countries. Those people who were once victims of the Cultural Revolution because of *hai-wai-guan-xi* were suddenly looked up to and became envied and prestigious. With various amounts of money sent them by relatives abroad, they could afford many more luxurious consumer goods, and their living standards were much higher than those without *hai-wai-guan-xi*, who depended solely on wages. For instance, in the early 1980s, a color television was a luxury rarely found in ordinary homes in China. Only those with overseas remittances could possibly afford one, because a basic set cost about three years' salary of an ordinary state worker at that time. The other group of recent emigrants was the students, most of whom were from better-off families with at least some overseas connections. For example, of the nearly forty thousand Chinese students studying in the United States in 1988, more than 40 percent depended for funding largely on family or kinship sources abroad. During the period of economic reform, many emigrant families were able to reap the benefits and enjoy a relatively comfortable life with high status and prestige before they left China.

Then why should they leave everything they have behind and be uprooted to a strange new world? The reason is apparently not poverty but the gap between what they expect of life and what they can do to fulfill that expectation. In China where individual freedom and advancement are strictly limited, people often find that they are unappreciated and unable to realize their full potential. Although they may not know a lot about what they may be able to achieve in their new country before emigration, one thing they are certain of is freedom to choose a way of life and the opportunity to live up to one's expectations. An interview with Mr. Liao, a newly arrived twenty-six-year-old immigrant who works in Chinatown as an electrician, reflects this view.

> Before I came, I lived with my parents in a spacious three-bedroom apartment with all possible sorts of goods—a color TV, a piano, a stereo sound system, a luxurious sofa set, a refrigerator, a microwave oven, a washing machine, and many other things. Most of these came from money sent by my grandpa from Taiwan. And I had a pretty stable job in a factory as an electrician, making a decent salary compared to my fellow workers. Right now, I do not yet have all the things I left behind, I have to work at least sixty hours a week, and I am a nobody. But that is okay; I believe this is only temporary. I will surely make it in a few more years. Even if I can't, I would accept it, bad luck or lack of ability, because I have already been given all the possible chances.[39]

Mrs. Zhao, a garment worker who married a Chinatown dishwasher and came from Taishan a few years ago, recalled:

> I still consider myself a country girl without much education, but I believe hard work should be rewarding. In the village back in Taishan, I worked very hard in the rice fields for a whole year and could not earn enough money even for food, let alone for some nice clothing. Back there, working hard just did not make a difference. But here, there is a difference: I can make more simply by working hard. I am now paid by the piece in the garment shop. I work very hard and can make an average of fifty to sixty dollars a day, while some of my fellow workers can only make about forty a day.[40]

The Hong Kong exodus also illustrates this point. Recent emigrants did not just try to escape poverty and come for money. A large number of them were well established at home. They were wealthy entrepreneurs, well-educated professionals, who had achieved upper- or upper-middle-class status at the place of origin. They came to the United States primarily for political stability, personal security, and the freedom to protect their already established status, which they believed would be threatened by an unpredictable political situation and possible abuse of human rights after the Chinese take-over in 1997.

China's rigid Communist system and unpredictable, unstable policies have widened the gap between life expectations and the means to fulfill them, creating a strong push toward emigration.

The Changing Mentality

Compared to the earlier period, Chinese immigration to the United States after 1965 has been different in many ways. The most significant difference is found in the changing mentality, which was caused by changing conditions in the contexts of reception and exit.

On the U.S. side, the repeal of the Chinese Exclusion Act opened the door for a limited number of Chinese immigrants to rejoin their families after World War II. China, however, did not open the door for emigration at the end of the war. Instead, after 1949 the two countries entered into a cold war, and the anti-U.S. Communist government banned emigration. Thereafter, the country was stricken by a prolonged period of uninterrupted revolution. During the following three decades, few people were allowed to leave, and equally few to enter. The Chinese barriers have been almost impenetrable except for a small number of people who risked

their lives to cross the borders to Hong Kong to take advantage of the tiny
American immigration quota.[41] Other immigrants were those who earlier
escaped China to Taiwan. Political repression under the rigid Communist system and the subsequent economic crisis caused a nationality crisis,
which has in turn resulted in a change of attitude toward emigration.

For the Chinese-Americans, the 1949 Communist take-over in China
and the repressive control of the Communist party over all aspects of
people's lives, plus vehement propaganda from both China and the United
States during the cold war, have completely shattered the gold dream that
they had long held. The effect felt by American Chinatowns was direct
and immediate. While many old-timers tended to support the Nationalist government that had fled to Taiwan, they became more realistic,
abandoned the sojourning idea, and rebuilt their lives in their adopted
country. To them, going back to a country where all forms of private
ownership were abolished and all aspects of the social and private lives
of individuals were controlled seemed absolutely senseless, if not crazy.
Mr. Chan, a sixty-eight-year-old Chinatown resident and senior leader
of a Chinatown kinship association, recalled what was generally felt by
many of the old-timers at the time:

> Many of us had always hoped to *fan tong shan* [return to China] to buy
> land and settle down. But all of a sudden, we were cut off from all
> the contacts with China and learned that returning was impossible.
> We just could not take it. You know, most of us had aging parents
> and wives and children at home, and routinely we used to send home
> remittances and promises to return to fulfill family obligations. This
> had been the only reward of our hard work and bachelors' lives here.
> With all these gone, what else was left? Many of us were desperately
> depressed, frightened, and intimidated for a period of time. Some
> drank and gambled heavily and went around with prostitutes to let
> themselves down. But after a while, we started to hope that some
> day, we could bring our families out here instead. Still, even now, I
> feel sad for not being able to return; but it is not important any more
> that I should return to my land of origin to die, which I had always
> kept in mind.[42]

The impact on those who were left behind in China—the relatives of
the Chinese-Americans—was even more intense. What made it worse
was that they were not even allowed to think of their loved ones abroad,
nor could they maintain any hope of rejoining their families. During the
repeated class struggles and political campaigns that culminated in the

Cultural Revolution, those who had even the slightest *hai-wai-guan-xi*—the slightest kinship connections with the outside world—were considered rebels and enemies of the proletarian class. They were suspected of helping with subversion attempts by the Nationalist government in Taiwan and the U.S. imperialists or, at the very least, were considered untrustworthy. They were always targets of public criticism and were discriminated against badly in education, jobs, housing assignments, promotions, and many other opportunities. Some were sent to prison for years for *li-tong-wai-guo* (having illicit relations with a foreign country) on the evidence of a single letter from a relative abroad. Others were sent indefinitely to remote, undeveloped areas and labor camps for "re-education" under unbearable hardships. Even young children were affected by having a distant relative abroad, whom perhaps even their parents might not have met.

Having *hai-wai-guan-xi* was a liability as well as a shame during those days.[43] Severe political repression made prospective emigrants of this group of people, most of whom lived in constant fear of an unpredictable future and had lost hope for even a moderate standard of living and peace of mind in their own country. Whenever possible, they would leave and might never come back. Mr. Peng recalled,

I followed the People's Liberation Army down south in the early 1950s and was a cadre with administrative responsibilities in a planning unit of the city government. That was when I was only twenty-two and a pure Chinese revolutionary, meaning without any *hai-wai-guan-xi*.

Then I got married, and my wife happened to have a brother who fled to Hong Kong and later immigrated to the U.S. This *hai-wai-guan-xi* that I had married into caused a series of problems for me and my family. I was never promoted since then and remained on and off my job from those never-ending political campaigns. Whenever there was a political campaign, I was the target of criticism and investigation, and then I got rehabilitated after. This was repeated over and over again many times during the past thirty years, and I spent almost eight years in a labor camp.

My wife was a nurse and not in any leadership position, but still she was never trusted. My three kids did very well in school, but they were often deprived of the prizes and honors they deserved and of the right to participate in many of the after-school activity programs, such as science group, singing and dancing groups.

The absurd thing was that I had never met this brother-in-law and my wife had never contacted him directly, and he was actually a Chinatown worker, 100 percent proletariat. I was so frustrated and depressed and yet could not utter a single word of complaint. For some time, I hated this brother-in-law wholeheartedly.

But later, I changed, hoping that he could simply get us out. With this kind of repressive and rigid political system, nothing is going to happen to your good. The situation after the Cultural Revolution seemed much improved, but I was still haunted by Mao's prediction that a revolution would happen every seven or eight years. I don't have much hope any more. I simply could not take it another time. This world is large—why should I be in China to make a living?[44]

Mr. Peng's brother-in-law did not help his family get to the United States. It was his own daughter, who married a Chinatown worker and later became a naturalized U.S. citizen, who finally got the whole family out. Only then did he meet this brother-in-law for the first time. There are many Chinese immigrants like Mr. Peng who simply want to leave the country and move on to find a better life somewhere in the world.

During the closed-door period, those who had no *hai-wai-guan-xi,* often regarded as politically pure, were forced into alignment with the Communist party to fight a constant struggle against U.S. imperialism, subversion from the West, and the "corrupted" lifestyles of the bourgeoisie and all sorts of "foreign trash." As time went by, the negative effects of the repression were felt. People became doubtful of the legitimacy of the system and started to lose confidence. Even so-called revolutionaries began to get tired and tried to find ways that could enable them or their children to leave the country for another place. It has been continuously reported in the official party newspaper—the *People's Daily*—and other sources, both in China and abroad, that many senior Chinese government officials abuse power to their own benefit, by exchanging public goods with, or by kowtowing to, Westerners to help their children out of the country.[45]

The corruption of government officials has further shaken the confidence of people and has led to a nationality crisis. The logic seems straightforward: when work is unrewarding, there will be no alternative but increasing inertia and frustration. Also, when a person with a college education makes much less than a street vendor, how can children be encouraged to go to school? Furthermore, when a man earns $2.00 per day and knows that he can earn at least $3.25 per hour in another country, he surely will be tempted. But most important of all is the unpredictable and politically unstable future. Uninterrupted political campaigns, educational discouragement, the low work ethic and incentives, accompanied by growing frustration, discontent, and anger, have created a vicious cycle that feeds back to affect the general well-being of the country and further erode national pride and national identity.

China's recent brain-drain problem and Hong Kong's 1997 syndrome[46] serve as the best evidence of this erosion. According to a recent survey by the Chinese Students' Association of Political Science in the United States, only 2.6 percent of the 360 Chinese students sampled in ten major universities across the United States intended to go back to China after graduation. Two-thirds of the students listed political stability and democracy as the major reasons for staying.[47] In Hong Kong there are no plugs for the brain drain. There, the middle class, many of them made-good refugees from China, fear that China will expropriate Hong Kong's wealth when it takes over in 1997 just as it did Shanghai's forty years ago. As the deadline draws nearer, wealthy businessmen, with their big companies and assets, have managed to move offshore to invest in the United States, Canada, Australia, and other areas in Southeast Asia. Well-educated professionals have also managed to acquire foreign passports and have left. Many middle-class people have spent tens of thousands of dollars, legally or illegally, in order to obtain passports to leave the island. According to statistics, Canada issued 22,130 immigrant visas for persons from Hong Kong, and Australia issued 14,000 in the year 1989 alone. The Hong Kong government estimated a record high of 62,000 persons emigrating from the island in the year 1990, more than 1,000 a week.[48] Most leave behind successful jobs and stable homes to head for at least two or three years of possibly lower salaries and lower status in their newly chosen countries. The majority of this exodus is due to the 1997 take-over and a national identity crisis. For many people in Hong Kong, a foreign passport is a form of "political insurance."

Conclusion

Fallen leaves no longer return to their roots.[49] This proverb reflects the changing mentality of recent Chinese immigrants to the United States. However, the changing mentality alone did not cause massive Chinese immigration; it simply defines a motivation distinct from that of the earlier immigrants, which affects later adaptation to a new country for immigrant Chinese. Several general conclusions can be reached concerning the effects of changing conditions of recent Chinese immigration.

First, liberalized U.S. immigration policies are among the most important factors responsible for the recent wave of Chinese immigrants. The U.S. immigration law determines whether immigration can occur at all, to what extent, and of what type. Also, as an effect of the family-reunification preference in recent U.S. immigration legislation, a family network has developed to facilitate immigration. Whether as blood or marriage kin, for every immigrant to enter the United States, there is a potential set of future immigrants. This family-chain migration has already produced a number of social consequences. Overall, the 1965 immigration reforms not only eliminated the explicitly racist national-origin quotas but also shifted visa preference toward family reunification. The unlimited number of immediate family members (parents, spouses, and minor children) of U.S. citizens has tended to multiply and become very large. The immediate effect is an increasing volume of Chinese immigrants (both immediate and extended family) at an accelerated speed, swamping other categories of legal immigration. Furthermore, the family-chain migration affects incorporation patterns of recent immigrants upon arrival in their new country. On the one hand, the new arrivals are a more heterogeneous group with regard to age, human capital, and economic resources. Thus, their path to socioeconomic achievement is more likely to be wide, with more choices, not just limited to certain marginal options. On the other hand, immigrants are tied from the very beginning to the family network and kinship relations. They are therefore more likely to adopt a collective strategy to climb up the socioeconomic ladder, in contrast to the individualistic ideology of assimilation. Also, since the family network is, in fact, a branch of the larger ethnic social network, immigrants are more likely to attach themselves to and continue to seek support from this network. The Chinese community has, thus, to expand to meet the needs of the newcomers, and in turn, it helps retain an ethnic identity and provide an institutional base for a cohesive Chinese-American society.

Second, the shift from sojourning to uprooting partially results from the changing contexts of exit. The 1949 Communist take-over and the subsequent uninterrupted revolutions and political repression in China, along with the heated propaganda of the cold war from both sides, have created a national identity crisis for the Chinese at home and abroad. The Chinese are increasingly aware that there exists a wide gap between aspirations and the means to achieve them in China, and they have started to perceive immigration as the most effective means of fulfilling their goals for a better future. These perceptions suggest that the ambition and drive for success and integration in a new country for most of the Chinese immigrants are much stronger than they were for those who came here merely to sojourn.

Finally, the transpacific journey for recent Chinese immigrants is characteristic of an uprooting process distinct from the sojourning of the old-timers. No longer is it true that "fallen leaves always return to their roots," a traditional Chinese belief that had kept the gold dream alive for so many years. Newcomers no longer follow their predecessors' footsteps to sojourn and search for gold to bring home from the United States. Rather, they, like many European immigrants, come with or to join their families to rebuild their lives and fulfill an American dream. The new belief to justify this change is to "let fallen leaves establish roots wherever they land." The change in mentality implies that recent immigrants will be more ready to assimilate into and identify with their adopted country. Nevertheless, they may not have to follow the traditional road to parity. Instead, they are likely to adapt or recreate some important aspects of their former culture, which, in turn, will affect their mode of incorporation.

4

Uprooted: The New Arrivals

"We finally made it to the Gold Mountain, and we are here to stay." These words express the new attitude of many Chinese immigrants, who now seek a home and a better life in the United States rather than "gold" and a return "home" to their land of origin. Since 1965, the Chinese have ceased to be an unimportant residuum in the larger U.S. population. Their number more than tripled over the period between 1960 and 1980, reaching a record high of 812,178. Unlike the early sojourners, who were obsessed with the desire to make enough money to return home, the new arrivals are settlers. Working hard to fulfill their dreams of economic prosperity, opportunity, and freedom, they stand out as a group in their adopted homeland and continue to make contributions but in a much more visible way.

The increasing influx of Chinese immigrants has brought diversity to a previously more homogeneous Chinese population. The new arrivals have already displayed remarkable differences from their predecessors not only in mentality and aspirations, but also in socioeconomic characteristics and modes of adaptation. This chapter examines the heterogeneity of recent Chinese immigrants and how the process of uprooting affects their adaptation in United States.

Diverse Origins

Early Chinese immigrants were predominantly laborers from the Pearl River delta in rural Canton, south China. Although they spoke various local dialects, most commonly Taishanese, the old-timers were basically from the same geographical region and shared a common language, Cantonese. Many of the Chinese words that were incorporated into English are Cantonese, especially those words that are related to food, for example, dim sum, bok choy, wonton, chow mein, and so on. Cantonese was the sole language in America's Chinatowns for many years.

Before World War II, Chinese immigrants were predominantly Cantonese, mostly from rural Canton, the original sending area, and a few from Hong Kong. Before then, very few native Taiwanese emigrated from the island. Recent Chinese immigrants, however, have come from diverse geographical regions. Today's Chinatowns are still dominated by the Cantonese culture, but the non-Cantonese population is growing rapidly. Cantonese is no longer the sole language spoken in Chinese communities in the United States. Now Mandarin, the official and most widely used language of both China and Taiwan, is being accepted. In such newly established Chinatowns as the one in Flushing, New York, Mandarin is now the most commonly used language. Recent Chinese immigrants can be roughly categorized into three groups by place of emigration: those from mainland China, those from Hong Kong, and those from Taiwan.

Immigrants from Mainland China

The majority of immigrants from Mainland China have been admitted under the relative-preference categories. According to the Immigration and Naturalization Service annual reports, about one-fifth of the Chinese entering between 1982 and 1985 came to join their spouses; they were exempt from the numerical limitation. Ninety-four percent of those subject to the numerical limitation entered under the first, second, fourth, and fifth categories (unmarried children of U.S. citizens, spouses and unmarried children of permanent residents, married children of U.S. citizens, and brothers and sisters of U.S. citizens). The number of persons who came under the third category (the skilled and professionals), the sixth (the skilled labor), and the refugees, was small, because of strict emigration controls in China. Talented and higher-ranking persons in China were discouraged from emigration for fear of "brain drain," and political dissidents were also forbidden to leave the country. Most recently, however, this number has increased as many students and visiting intellectuals have decided to stay in the United States instead of returning home upon completion of their exchange programs.

As discussed in the previous chapter, the Chinese have emigrated for various reasons, partly because of the legacy of underdevelopment, poverty, and overpopulation and partly because of China's extreme leftist policies and the constant power struggles between the ruling political elites. Thus, the major pushing force does not simply derive from material shortages—inadequate housing, limited supplies of food, clothing, and consumer goods—but also from political repression, limited individual freedom, unrewarding work, and lack of opportunities and economic independence. As the United States has relaxed its unequal immigration quota system based on national origin, and as China itself has become more open to the outside world, people have started to emigrate. But only those with close relatives abroad are likely to be able to do so.

Family-chain migration, which characterizes recent Chinese immigration, has facilitated emigration both from rural Canton and from urban China. The majority of the earlier emigrants and potential emigrants lived in rural Canton, where emigration started and where most Chinese-Americans have retained family or kinship connections. However, in the past forty years, a sizable number of the rural Cantonese and their children moved to cities in different parts of the country. Thus, potential emigrants—relatives of Chinese-Americans—have been spreading out to areas other than Canton.

Because of the big development gap between rural and urban China, many of the rural emigrants, like their relatives who emigrated earlier, are relatively poor, with little education, no English-language ability, and few transferable skills. Upon arrival in the United States, their initial disadvantages often render them less competitive even in the ethnic labor market, and completely ineligible for the larger labor market.

The urban emigrants are much more heterogeneous. They are from different parts of China, not just Canton. Although they have moved with their families to cities in the Canton area and in other parts of the country, they are related to people in America and are thus eligible for emigration. A good portion of the non-Cantonese emigrants either enter family-chain migration networks through marriage or are students and intellectuals who came to the United States on exchange programs but were stranded or later decided to stay. Urban emigrants have much better education and job skills than their rural counterparts, though they lack English-language ability.

Despite differences in geographical and socioeconomic backgrounds, both rural and urban emigrants from China have shown similar motivations, cultural inclinations, and orientations toward the future. They have emigrated to escape a repressive political regime; they perceive emigration as a step up the path to economic betterment; and they are prepared to work hard and make it in America.

Immigrants from Hong Kong

Statistics from the Immigration and Naturalization Service show that the number of immigrants from Hong Kong admitted to the United States between 1951 and 1960 was about 15,544. The following decade, the number increased five times to 75,007; and a much larger number (113,467) came during the 1971–1980 decade. Emigration is nothing new in Hong Kong. However, it became an issue when the Communists seized control over mainland China in 1949, and now, as the 1997 deadline draws nearer, the wealthiest, most talented, and best-educated people are leaving the island in large numbers.

Many recent immigrants from Hong Kong or their families were originally mainlanders. Some left in the early 1950s to escape the Communist take-over, and some had illegally crossed the border in later years. They had not trusted the Communist government on the mainland to begin with and, thus, did not have any faith in the prospect of Hong Kong's transfer to Chinese sovereignty in 1997. People left the island in large numbers for fear that history would repeat itself, and the Communist government would turn Hong Kong into another Shanghai. They left because they did not believe that their freedom would remain intact after 1997.

The extremely large recent exodus is directly attributable to the 1997 syndrome, characterized by brain drain and capital flight. According to a study by Survey Research of Hong Kong in 1988, 38 percent of the financial center's managers and professionals said that they were prepared to leave in the coming nine years. Banks and other industries have found it difficult to plan programs because of the high turnover rate among emigrating staff members. It was estimated that by the year 1997, 10 percent of the population of 5.5 million will have departed Hong Kong, leaving at a rate of fifty thousand a year.[1] Also, a loss of business confidence in Hong Kong has contributed to an estimated tenfold increase in capital outflow, totaling HK$22.34 billion (US$2.86 billion) in 1989, according to the monthly reports of the Hong Kong and Shanghai Bank. Economists predicted that there would be another outflow of HK$32 to 33 billion in 1990.[2]

Many emigrants left for Canada and Australia, where immigration of skilled workers and entrepreneurs was encouraged. The United States had an immigration quota of five thousand per year, determined mainly by family and kinship relations. Recently, the United States increased the quota and opened a new category for entrepreneurs willing to invest a million dollars or more in a business with at least ten employees.[3] Therefore, while a large number of immigrants came under the relative-preference category, many came, and will come, from the wealthy elite. In the fall of 1990, the U.S. Congress passed a new Immigration and Naturalization Act, and President George Bush signed it into law. This act treats Hong Kong as a special district, increasing its annual quota over three years from five thousand to ten thousand. After 1994 it will be treated as an independent region, allowed an annual quota of twenty-five thousand, plus a separate quota for professionals working for U.S. companies in Hong Kong.

Compared to their co-ethnics from the mainland, immigrants from Hong Kong differ primarily in four respects: First, almost all of them are urban. They are from one of the most industrialized and fastest growing regions in Asia and are used to the lifestyles of the laissez-faire capitalist. Their way of life, work ethic, and mentality were fostered and developed in a physical environment close to the one they have immigrated into. Thus, they tend to have fewer adjustment problems than their mainland counterparts, who are mostly rural or semirural and come from a different economic system. Second, they are educated within a system heavily influenced by the British in particular and by the West in general. They usually have a better command of English, one of the official languages in Hong Kong. In this respect, they are less likely to be blocked by the language barrier and nontransferable education than their mainland co-ethnics. Third, the work experience, training, and professional skills they acquired in Hong Kong are more likely to be applicable or transferable to the United States, since the colony of Hong Kong is mostly Westernized. In this way, their options in the larger labor market are generally wider than those of the mainlanders when they immigrate to the United States. Fourth, they are much better off economically, and many of them immigrate with sufficient capital to start their new life.

Immigrants from Taiwan

Taiwan, ruled by the Guomindang Nationalist government that fled the Chinese mainland in 1949, is one of the western Pacific's more remarkable success stories. It has changed from an underdeveloped backwater to a flourishing industrialized economy with an overall trade surplus of US$19 billion.[4] The island's foreign reserves reached a peak of US$ 76.7 billion in 1987 and were still at US$ 69.4 billion in 1990, among the largest in the world and enough to cover nearly two years' worth of imports.[5]

In Taiwan, the population of nearly 20 million enjoys good education, health facilities, and a steadily rising standard of living. But Taiwan's political development has failed to match its economic accomplishments. Martial law was lifted only in 1987 after being in force for thirty-eight years. Not until late 1986 was permission granted for an opposition party to organize. Power still remained concentrated in the hands of the transplanted mainlanders. The legislature itself was controlled by members who were last elected nearly forty years ago. Taiwan's growing middle class became increasingly restive and resentful because of lack of political freedom. Some political activits among the native Taiwanese (84 percent of the population) formed opposition groups to call for the island's independence—an idea that was simply not tolerated either by the Communists in Beijing or the Nationalists in Taipei. Meanwhile, China persisted in its effort to resume control of the island and did not rule out possible military action against the Nationalists. The unstable political situation and the potential threat from both the independence movement and the Communist mainland haunted many Taiwanese, both former mainlanders and natives. Thus, the pushing force for emigration in Taiwan derived mainly from lack of political stability on the island and fear of the prospect of Communist take-over. After the defeat of the Nationalist government in 1949, former mainlanders who had originally fled from the Communists began to emigrate to other parts of the world. In recent years, the exodus from Taiwan occurred on a much larger scale.

Emigration from Taiwan to the United States is a relatively recent phenomenon. Significant emigration did not occur until 1949, when refugees who had escaped the mainland to Taiwan began to immigrate to the United States. Some of them were students who came on nonimmigrant visas. After they finished their education here, the students managed to change their student visas to work visas and then to apply for immigrant visas under the preference category of needed professional expertise and skills. Today, students from Taiwan constitute one of the largest international student groups at U.S. colleges and universities. Many of them are expected to stay permanently. Once their immigrant status was secured, the former students could bring in family members through family-chain migration, which remains common for immigrants from China and Hong Kong. As in Hong Kong, nervous talk of capital flight was common in Taiwan. Outward direct investment from Taiwan grew so rapidly that the cash-rich island suffered a net capital outflow and a loss of confidence in its currency.

Generally, immigrants from Taiwan, like many of those from Hong

Kong, are affluent, well educated, and skilled. Many have received education and training in the United States. Most of the Taiwanese are not from Canton. They speak Mandarin and a Fujian (Fukien) dialect and carry a cultural tradition somewhat different from the Cantonese. Because of these differences in socioeconomic background and culture, they have tended to stay away from the Cantonese-dominated old Chinatowns, and establishing their own enclaves. Flushing, New York, and Monterey Park, California, are two of these new Chinatowns.

Work Experience

Another noticeable feature of recent Chinese immigration is the diversity of the work experience of immigrants, which is related to the geographical diversity. Table 4-1 shows that between 1982 and 1986 about 47 percent of the mainland Chinese immigrants admitted to the United States declared a previous occupation of some sort. Most of those who were without occupation were peasants from rural areas of China, were under twenty years old, or were retirees (see Table 3-2).[6] Mainland Chinese immigrants showed a relatively higher percentage of laborers and agricultural workers (not counting the peasants) and a lower percentage of persons with managerial and professional positions than their counterparts from Hong Kong and Taiwan. However, compared to the old-timers, who were predominantly peasants, this group displayed a drastic change in occupational distribution. Close to one-third held managerial and professional positions before emigration. Thus they possessed much more valuable human capital than their predecessors. An even larger percentage of immigrants from Hong Kong had held executive-managerial and professional occupations, and nearly 68 percent of the recent Taiwanese immigrants were from executive, managerial, and professional positions (Table 4-1).

Despite diverse geographic origins, the majority of recent Chinese immigrants, particularly those from Hong Kong and Taiwan, have immigrated for the purpose of securing their already well-established life and to preserve their middle-class standard of living, which they perceived as threatened by the Communist system. They immigrate not only with human capital—work experience, professional expertise, and education—but also with monetary capital, with "fortunes" small or large. They uproot themselves from their home country for a single goal: They or their children must succeed in America. They are determined not to fail. With this ambition and a well-defined future-oriented goal, new immigrants are more inclined to take risks rather than just accept the

Table 4-1. Chinese Immigrants Admitted to the United States, by Region of Emigration and Major Occupational Group, 1982–1986

Occupation	Total	China	Hong Kong	Taiwan
Total	220,087	126,132	26,576	67,379
With occupations	91,752	58,613	8,349	24,790
% With occupations	41.7	46.5	31.4	36.8
% Executive-managerial	15.8	11.1	16.4	26.6
% Professional specialty	26.1	19.4	28.4	41.2
% Sales	6.3	4.7	7.0	10.0
% Administrative support	7.9	6.3	17.0	8.7
% Precision production, crafts, and repair	4.6	5.3	6.7	2.1
% Operators, fabricators, and laborers	16.1	22.8	9.8	2.4
% Farming, forestry, and fishing	12.8	19.3	0.8	1.4
% Service	10.4	11.1	13.9	7.5

Source: INS Statistical Yearbook: 1983 to 1986.

low immigrant status borne by their predecessors. Although some may find the education and expertise attained in China, Hong Kong, or Taiwan nontransferable to the new country and thus may experience a brief period of downward mobility in the first few years, they are usually able to adjust quickly and move back up to match their previous status. Even those from rural China, who are poor and less educated, share the same goal, the same motivation and determination to work hard to make their dreams come true.

Table 4-2 illustrates some socioeconomic characteristics of immigrants from China, Taiwan, and Hong Kong with data from the 1980 census. The table shows that significant emigration from Taiwan to the United States has occurred more recently than that from Hong Kong and mainland China. College graduates were almost twice as common among immigrants from mainland China and nearly four times as common among those coming from Taiwan as in the U.S. population. Those declaring professional specialty occupations represented a proportion of the Chinese immigrants similar to that in the total American working population. Median household income was higher than that of the larger population.

Table 4-2. Socioeconomic Characteristics of Immigrants from China, Hong Kong, and Taiwan, 1980

	China	Hong Kong	Taiwan	U.S. Average [1]
Total Persons	286,120	80,380	75,353	226,545,805
Males per 100 females	102	102	86	95
% Immigrated 1975–1980	27.2	34.9	54.6	—
% Naturalized U.S. citizens	50.3	38.3	28.9	—
% High school graduates [2]	60.0	80.3	89.1	66.5
% Completed four years of college or more [2]	29.5	42.7	59.8	16.2
% In professional specialty occupations [3]	16.8	19.1	30.4	22.7
% In service occupations [3]	24.4	18.6	13.7	12.9
Median household income	$18,544	$18,094	$18,271	$16,841

Sources: U.S. Census of Population: 1980. See also U.S. Bureau of the Census, 1984. Socioeconomic Characteristics of the U.S. Foreign-Born Population Detailed in Census Bureau Tabulations.

[1] The total U.S. population.
[2] Persons 25 years and over.
[3] Persons 16 years and over.

Demographic Features of the Chinese in New York

Age

The age pyramids in Figure 4-1 show that compared to the non-Hispanic white population in New York City in 1980, the Chinese were much younger, and therefore, their prospect for continuing rapid population growth was certain. About 53 percent of New York City's Chinese were between the ages of twenty-five and sixty-four, supposedly the age for participation in the labor force, similar to the percentage for the city's non-Hispanic white population. But 38 percent of the Chinese were twenty-four and under and only 9 percent were sixty-four and over, as compared to 28 percent and 20 percent, respectively, for non-Hispanic whites.

The foreign-born Chinese population had a disproportionately high number of adult persons aged twenty to fifty-nine. Recent immigration

Non-Hispanic Whites

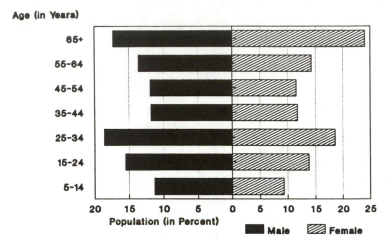

Chinese

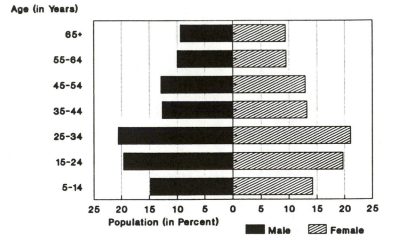

Figure 4-1. Age and Sex Distributions, New York City, 1980
Source: U.S. Census of Population: 1980.

statistics from 1982 to 1985 show that 65 percent of immigrants from China, 48 percent from Hong Kong, and 66 percent from Taiwan during this period were between twenty and fifty-nine years of age; 19 percent from China, 50 percent from Hong Kong, and 30 percent from Taiwan were under twenty years of age. About 16 percent of those from China were over sixty, and of those from Hong Kong and Taiwan, only 2 percent and 4 percent, respectively (see Table 3-2). The foreign-born Chinese population in New York showed a similar age structure.

The particular age composition of recent arrivals implies some significant effects on the Chinese community in New York. First, they tended to bring with them cultural traditions, varied ways of life, and a network of social relations that had been built up over the years in their place of origin. This previous experience affected their mode of adaptation in two ways. Negatively, their cultural heritage, which was considered irrelevant to the society they were transplanted into, would hinder integration. Positively, however, they were more likely to organize and develop alternative modes of adaptation through their ethnic enclaves, that is, through an enclave economy, which in turn would speed up integration of immigrants and their children. Moreover, the influx of adult immigrants provided a large labor pool for the ethnic economy, in which cultural heritage and ethnicity could be turned into social capital. They were ready to work as soon as they reached shore in America. Thus, they were more likely to rely on their past work experience and human capital credentials to participate in the enclave labor market, overcoming their initial disadvantage as new arrivals. In turn, the enclave is assured of a continuous influx of immigrant labor.

Sex

Another demographic feature in the Chinese population in New York also demonstrates changes in recent Chinese immigration into the United States. Before 1943, Chinese immigrants were ineligible for U.S. citizenship and, so, unable to bring in their family members. They were denied political rights, a normal family life, even the right to intermarry with whites in many states.[7] As a result, they had to isolate themselves in Chinatowns, concentrated only in a few large cities such as San Francisco and New York. In these bachelors' societies, dominated by male sojourners, there were few women. At the turn of the century, the census showed that there were seven Chinese females per hundred Chinese males in the United States, eight per hundred in California, and only two per hundred

Table 4-3. Chinese Population, by Sex, New York State, 1900–1980

Year	Total	Male	Female	Females per 100 males
1980	147,250	75,885	71,365	94
1970	81,378	43,919	37,459	85
1960	37,573	23,406	14,167	60
1950	20,171	14,875	5,296	36
1940	13,731	11,777	1,954	17
1930	9,665	8,649	1,016	12
1920	5,793	5,240	553	11
1910	5,266	5,065	201	4
1900	7,170	7,028	142	2

Source: U.S. Census of Population, 1910–1980.

in New York State. In New York City's Chinatown, the sex ratio was only one female per hundred males in the late 1800s.

Most of the early immigrants led a bachelor's life in the United States. With the strict Chinese Exclusion Act, they could hardly bring their families here. Although the "paper sons" kept entering in small numbers, they too were confined in Chinatown and they too became bachelors because there were few Chinese women in the community. In order to fulfill family obligations, most of the young bachelors, like their fathers or uncles, had to return to China to get married, and this practice led to the immigration of more "paper sons." Most always wanted to have a real family but were unable to do so until restrictive immigration laws were relaxed.

In 1945 the United States began to allow entry to a limited number of wives of Chinese-Americans who had served in the U.S. military. Between 1944 and 1953, on average, more than eight times as many women as men immigrated. In 1948, for example, 3,317 female Chinese immigrants entered the United States, compared to only 257 Chinese men. In the years that followed, the nation continued to admit more women than men, and the imbalance began to equalize (Table 4-3). By 1980, the census showed about 96 Chinese females to 100 males in New York City (as opposed to 114 females to 100 males for non-Hispanic whites). New York State's female Chinese population in 1980 was more than five times larger than it had been two decades before. The number of females per hundred males jumped from thirty-six in 1950 to sixty in 1960, climbed to eighty-five in 1970 as a direct result of the 1965 immigration law, and reached ninety-four in 1980.

As more and more women and children immigrate, Chinatown is no longer a bachelor's temporary shelter, marginally attached to the larger society. It has become a full-fledged, family-based, ethnic community, woven, though very slowly, into the city's social mosaic. Meanwhile, many special problems caused by the strains of settlement and assimilation have begun to affect the community. There are greater demands for various social and cultural institutions to cope with increasing problems and for goods and services, especially those culture-specific ones that cannot be satisfied by the institutionalized delivery mechanisms of the larger society. Also, as immigrant population growth continues to put pressure on Chinatown, a wide range of economic activities and businesses geared toward the problems of immigrant adjustment have arisen, opening opportunities for ethnic economic development. Furthermore, many small-scale, labor-intensive enterprises that require only minimum start-up capital have emerged to absorb the surplus cheap labor. In sum, the changing structure of Chinatown from an all-male, temporary settlement to a family community provides a social basis for the development of an enclave economy.

Preferred Destination

Recent Chinese immigration to the United States is urban-bound. Almost all Chinese immigrants settle in big metropolitan areas; less than 3 percent of the Chinese immigrants admitted to the United States between 1965 and 1980 have settled in rural areas. Moreover, only a few large cities host most of the immigrants. Over the years, the pattern of preferred permanent residence has been consistent: More than half of the immigrants tend to choose California and New York as their final destination (Table 4-4), and many concentrate in San Francisco and New York City, where the nation's two biggest and oldest Chinatowns are located.

New York City concentrates a large number of first-generation and recent Chinese immigrants. As recorded in the 1980 census, more than one-fifth of the Chinese reported that they had moved from abroad since 1975. Once they arrive, the Chinese tend to stay in the same metropolitan area, close to their ethnic communities. About 57 percent of the Chinese reported to the 1980 census that they had lived in the same house for at least five years, and another 20 percent had lived in the same county for that long, though they had changed residences.

Among the primary reasons why Chinese immigrants continue to cluster in traditional entry ports are the job opportunities, the social sup-

Table 4-4. Chinese Immigrants Admitted to the United States, by Intended Permanent Residence, 1960–1977

Year	Total[1]	California	%	New York	%	Other	%
1960	3,681	1,430	38.8	1,040	28.3	1,211	32.9
1961	3,213	1,168	36.4	818	25.4	1,227	38.2
1962	4,017	1,562	38.9	1,058	26.3	1,397	34.8
1963	4,658	1,695	36.4	1,132	24.3	1,831	39.3
1964	5,009	717	14.3	954	19.0	3,338	66.7
1965	4,057	1,597	39.4	926	22.8	1,534	37.8
1966	13,736	6,316	46.0	3,526	25.7	3,894	28.3
1967	19,714	6,700	34.0	5,150	26.1	7,864	39.9
1968	12,738	4,193	32.9	3,323	26.1	5,222	41.0
1969	15,440	5,584	36.2	3,845	24.9	6,011	38.9
1970	14,093	4,460	31.7	3,290	23.3	6,343	45.0
1971	12,908	3,079	23.9	3,607	27.9	6,222	48.2
1972	17,339	4,340	25.0	4,919	28.4	8,080	46.6
1973	17,297	4,648	26.9	4,782	27.6	7,867	45.5
1974	18,056	5,449	30.2	4,548	25.2	8,059	44.6
1975	18,536	5,654	30.5	4,536	24.5	8,346	45.0
1976	18,823	6,085	32.3	4,215	22.4	8,523	45.3
1977	19,764	7,027	35.6	3,546	17.9	9,191	46.5

Source: INS Annual Report: 1960–1977.
[1] Including those from Taiwan.

port system in Chinatown, and the nature of family-based migration. First, jobs, particularly entry-level jobs, are more accessible in big cities and those cities experiencing rapid economic growth. The urban-bound movement became self-perpetuating once immigrants found out about the existence of such opportunities.[8] Urban concentration, in this respect, has been a way of economic adaptation for new arrivals who must struggle to overcome such initial disadvantages as lack of information about the larger society, lack of transferable education and skills, lack of language proficiency, and so forth. However, the tremendous immigrant flow into particular cities cannot always be accounted for by job accessibility in the larger economy. In recent years, the locational patterns of immigrants have often been found to be unaffected by changing economic circumstances in the larger society. For example, in the 1970s New York City suffered a severe financial and economic crisis; a sharp drop in population, largely due to net out-migration; a phenomenal decline in manufacturing jobs, which decreased by almost one-third; and the massive destruction of low-cost housing. Nevertheless, despite declines in both population and jobs, New York City is still a large urban agglomeration, full of opportunity for immigrants.

Another reason immigrants cluster in cities is to take advantage of the social and economic support of their ethnic community. Preestablished immigrant communities in big cities continue to attract co-ethnic members, and the continuous influx in turn stimulates enclave economic development to accommodate growth. For instance, between 1969 and 1980, the number of jobs in the large midtown garment center in Manhattan fell sharply, from forty thousand to twenty-five thousand. During the same period, the number of jobs in women's apparel in the Chinatown area doubled, from eight thousand to sixteen thousand, and reached almost twenty thousand in 1982.[9] Moreover, as a result of the booming enclave economy, jobs that are made available in the ethnic community are a major magnetic force to pull recent arrivals into or close to the community.

A third reason, perhaps most important, is linked to the family-chain-network character of Chinese immigration. Recent immigrants simply follow their predecessors' footsteps and settle where their relatives or social networks are, and thus the trend of residential segregation persists. Post-1965 Chinese immigrants have kept to the residential pattern established before 1965, though recent Chinese immigrants are generally more ready to integrate into the American mainstream and better accepted by the general public. It does not naturally follow, however, that today's Chinese immigrants are more assimilable than their predecessors simply because they have the motivation to make a permanent home here and because they encounter fewer structural barriers on the path of incorporation.

When they arrive in the United States, many immigrants find a gap between what they want to do and what they are allowed to do. Most of the recent immigrants realize that in order to be fully "Americanized" and to assimilate quickly into the larger society, they have to stay away from and avoid identifying themselves too much with Chinatown. Nevertheless, they often find themselves ending up in Chinatown because many options in the larger society are closed to them, primarily because of their linguistic handicap.

In New York City, the majority of the Chinese immigrants have concentrated in Chinatowns in lower Manhattan, Flushing in Queens, and Sunset Park in Brooklyn, or in other enclaves recently established to accommodate the rapid population growth. For example, in such areas

Table 4-5. Chinese Population of the United States and New York City, by Sex, 1970 and 1980

	1970	1980	% Growth
U.S. Total	435,062	812,178	86.7
Male	228,565	410,936	
Female	206,497	401,242	
N.Y.C. Total	69,324	124,372	79.4
Male	37,504	64,018	
Female	31,820	60,354	
New York County	39,366	52,165	32.5
Male	21,970	27,225	
Female	17,396	24,940	
Queens County	12,855	39,526	207.5
Male	6,449	19,997	
Female	6,406	19,529	
Kings County	11,779	26,067	121.3
Male	6,236	13,348	
Female	5,543	12,719	
Bronx and Richmond Counties	5,324	6,614	24.2
Male	2,849	3,448	
Female	2,475	3,166	

Source: U.S. Census of Population: 1980.

as Woodside, Jackson Heights, Corona, and Elmhurst in Queens, and Ridgewood and Bay Ridge in Brooklyn, Chinese residential enclaves have become visible in the past fifteen years. Between 1970 and 1980, Queens County's Chinese population more than tripled and Kings County's more than doubled (Table 4-5).

The growth of population in the outlying areas suggests that recent Chinese immigrants no longer collect in Chinatown first and then disperse as time goes by. Moreover, dispersion is more likely to lead to further segregation, that is, to neighborhood take-over, rather than spatial integration. Part of the reason is population pressure on the old Chinatown area: Despite tremendous expansion and neighborhood take-over, Chinatown simply could not accommodate the population growth. Part of the reason derives from family-chain migration. Family members who are already here usually provide basic support, such as housing, for those who come later.

Why do the Chinese immigrants continue to cluster in Chinatown? Is it because of ethnic exclusiveness and independence or because of intimidation and rejection by the mainstream society? Historically, Chinatown was a response to the overt or covert prejudice and discrimination of the larger society. Early immigrants were forced into Chinatowns under American working-class pressure and exclusion legislation. They had no other options but to return to China or to build a "Little China" here for themselves. Those who had not saved (and, in fact, would never be able to save) a "fortune" with which to return home chose the latter option.

Today, obstacles of linguistic and cultural differences continue to affect ethnic segregation in Chinatown, albeit less than in the past, but the structural arrangements of the open economy strengthen this segregation. On the one hand, recent Chinese immigrants no longer face overt resistance and antagonism from the American working class, partly because of the accomplishments of the Civil Rights movement and partly because of the declining political power of the working class. On the other hand, postindustrialization and suburbanization have exerted great influence on the opportunity structures of the American economy. Since World War II, employment in traditional production and goods-processing industries has declined markedly, with correspondingly rapid employment gains in information-processing industries. New York City alone gained more than 650,000 jobs in its information-processing industries between 1953 and 1980, while losing more than 525,000 jobs in manufacturing and construction.[10] This transformation has split the economy into a core sector and a peripheral sector. While the rising middle class has been protected from changes in the core sector and has enjoyed all the positive benefits of the transformation, the working class and the vulnerable immigrant groups have been left in the peripheral sector, competing with each other for jobs, housing, and education. Moreover, an interlocking web of barriers to immigrant upward mobility has maintained an ethnic stratification, forcing immigrants to remain on the lowest rung of the social ladder. Although manufacturing jobs in New York City have been radically reduced overall, immigrants have continued to flow into this declining sector and today make up a disproportionate share of the workers within it.

Theoretically, recent Chinese immigrants need not confine themselves to Chinatown, but they may suffer substantial downward mobility in occupation and social status in the larger labor market. Thus, regardless of their socioeconomic background, they have tended to cluster in China-town with their earlier counterparts. The legal, structural, and cultural barriers that used to confine old-timers to Chinatown still effectively limit the options of recent Chinese immigrants, though to a significantly lesser degree. Lack of English-language ability and marketable skills certainly have prevented Chinese immigrants from participating in the larger labor market, and social networks important in immigration have worked to bind people together in Chinatown. These networks, founded in and per-petuated through the emphasis of the U.S. immigration law on family re-unification, have provided sufficient social resources to help immigrants get settled in their new country. The difference, however, is that the re-cent group has given up sojourning and is motivated to get ahead in the U.S. society by way of Chinatown. Instead of being a temporary shelter for immigrants, Chinatown has begun to develop its own ethnic structure of economic opportunities for the immigrants. That is, with the continua-tion and development of Chinatown, Chinese immigrants can possibly use the resources of their own economic enclave to make their dreams come true.

Economic Resources

Population growth in Chinatown has been combined, since the early 1970s, with another trend: extensive foreign investment. As mentioned earlier, many recent Chinese immigrants have come here with their life savings to realize the American dream. Also, political uncertainty and instability in Hong Kong, Taiwan, and Southeast Asia have caused capi-tal investors to look for secure outlets in the United States. The rapid population growth and large influx of foreign capital created a constant demand for development. Even after the financial market crash in 1987, Chinatown's real estate remains a battlefield for Chinese investors and immigrant entrepreneurs. Although Chinatown is perhaps too small to appear in the statistics of those economists who measure foreign invest-ment by billions rather than millions, there seems to be a lot of small investment helping to revitalize the decaying area.

In New York City, it is difficult to estimate accurately the amount of foreign capital flowing in from ethnic Chinese in Southeast Asia. Gigantic corporate acquisitions tend to get the headlines: In 1980 the Hong Kong and Shanghai Banking Corporation, which dominates Hong Kong's financial and commercial affairs, took over the Marine Midland

Bank.[11] In 1985 the same banking corporation acquired $117 million of insured deposits of Chinatown's Golden Pacific Bank, which had been declared insolvent.[12] In 1988 the Peninsula Group of Hong Kong paid an outrageously high price—$127 million—to buy Manhattan's Maxim's de Paris Hotel.[13] Small investors, however, are behind the land rush in Chinatown, pouring in a tremendous amount of cash to exploit real estate and business opportunities. Outside investors are buying up properties in neighborhoods surrounding Chinatown. Areas in the once solidly Italian enclave of Little Italy are now being acquired by the Chinese.

The foreign money, however, is not only large fortunes counted in millions of dollars, but "nest eggs" measured in thousands, just enough money to stake a newcomer in business. Property investment and the expansion of local business have produced a scarcity of space and spiraling rents. Thus, some capital has gone to finance housing development in Flushing, Queens, another growing Chinese enclave in the city. This type of investment does not occur so easily in Old Chinatown because of rent control and restrictive zoning regulations. The influx of foreign capital has helped Chinatown to boom and has decentralized Chinatown's business activities and residents.

Foreign capital investment plays a paradoxical role in Chinatown's economic development. While it directly contributes to the diversification and physical dispersion of Chinatown's economy, it also intensifies internal land-oriented conflicts within the community. Unlike immigrant human capital, which has a visible ethnic label subject to immigrant disadvantages, capital is a neutral resource. Theoretically, it is highly mobile and can move almost anywhere in a market-oriented society. Nevertheless, overseas Chinese capital is invested primarily in Chinatown or an ethnic Chinese market and not elsewhere, and the reason goes beyond simple economic rationality. First, rich Chinese in the Far East have the need to shift capital and part of their business operations to the United States, for they fear that their wealth will be endangered by the unstable political future. Second, overseas investors have a limited information and marketing network concerning where they should invest. Third, overseas and immigrant Chinese generally tend to assume the existence of racism and ethnic prejudice and, thus, are intimidated. They feel that they will lose in competition with the majority group unless their capital volume is far larger. Fourth, the business climate of the larger society favors the native white majority, who have powerful political machines and business coalitions to protect their economic interests. In Chinatown, Chinese investors find a business environment similar to that at home;

and, hence, they feel more confident in the potential return on their investment. Fifth, Chinatown has a high-quality, low-wage, docile labor force. The language barrier may not allow immigrants (even the better educated) to compete successfully in the larger economy. Moreover, immigrants possess skills and creativity specifically relevant to the immigrant population. Further, immigrant labor, under pressure from unemployed immigrants, is more likely to accept low wages and the working conditions offered. Finally, Chinatown's labor force is strongly identified with the community; ethnic commitment reinforces the quality of labor.

Because of the political motivation of the capital flow, Chinese foreign capital moves mainly one way: Profits are not likely to return to Hong Kong, Taiwan, or other Far East countries. This investment does not drain local money out of the community; instead, the profits are reinvested in the United States. In this way, the financial basis of the enclave economy is effectively strengthened. On the other hand, internal competition among ethnic businesses intensifies.

The continuous influx of human and physical capital is a crucial factor in the development of the enclave economy. Without it the economic enclave can easily lose its relatively strong independence.

Conclusion

The impact of post-1965 Chinese immigration on Chinatown is to create a steady influx of human capital and economic resources. The influx of human capital supplies Chinatown with a heterogeneous group of immigrants who settle down in their new country, make their life investment here, and become part of a large group of consumers supporting the ethnic market. Though many are disadvantaged in terms of their human capital, they are by no means sojourners as their predecessors were. They have the strong desire to work hard to move up to self-employment. Recent Chinese immigration brings not only cheap labor but also skilled, well-educated professionals and entrepreneurs into the economy. Thus, the enclave economy is supplied with a qualified labor force that is suitable for a wide range of economic activities in today's sophisticated economic environment. Within an ethnic-specific environment, these two groups can possibly work together to develop the economic enclave and to exploit the economic opportunities available to them.

Recent arrivals differ from the old-timers in many respects. First, the goals of the sojourners and the settlers differ. Sojourners entered the United States in pursuit of a Chinese dream, a dream in which they could find golden marvels to bring home and make a better life for their families. They left home and entered into a life of bondage in defense of the tenets of their culture. They ignored the overtures of assimilation, which had little significance for men seeking to make and save money quickly, to pay off their debts, and to rejoin their families. Most of them accepted only such products of American culture as hats and shoes; a very few adopted whatever promised to bring them closer to their aims. The sojourner mentality kept them separated from the inflow of European immigrants, who always bore an American dream. It is not that the sojourners were unassimilable; it is just that they never tried to assimilate. Recent immigrants, in contrast, have attempted to assimilate into the American mainstream and to make the American dream come true almost from the very beginning of their immigration.

Second, the Chinese population has become socially and economically heterogeneous. Early Chinatown was a homogeneous enclave of bachelors, largely undifferentiated socially, economically, and geographically. The majority came with few economic and human-capital resources other than their willingness to work. Economic activities were often conducted within the family (referring actually more to a family of clansmen than to a nuclear or extended family) for basic sustenance. Recent arrivals come from different social classes, and class distinctions have begun to influence Chinatown's development and to determine the mode of incorporation adopted by the immigrants. New immigrants possess varied levels of educational, occupational, and professional credentials and skills. They no longer passively react to structural changes in the larger U.S. society; rather, they have learned how to take advantage of their human capital and network of social relations to organize and develop economic opportunities within the ethnic community.

Third, the structural conditions under which Chinese immigration has occurred have changed. The historical process of colonial and capitalist development demanded a large supply of cheap labor. Early immigrants came under labor contracts basically to meet this particular demand. They were exploited and treated inhumanely by the capitalists and were often used as strikebreakers against the working class. As a result, they were caught between the greed of capitalism and the antagonism of the rising white working class. Victims of capitalist exploitation and, at the same time, the object of working-class exclusion, they were forced into Chinatown for self-protection and survival. But recent immigrants entered in an era of postindustrial transformation. On the one hand, they entered on relatively equal footing with white Americans. Overt discrimination was somewhat suppressed as a result of the Civil Rights movement and the reform of immigration laws. Moreover, through long interethnic contact, the native Americans gradually accepted the Chinese and came to regard them as a "model minority" rather than strange, incomprehensible aliens. Although prejudice and ethnic discrimination persist, new immigrants have found themselves confronted with fewer legal and structural obstacles than their predecessors.

Fourth, there has been a consistent pattern of ethnic segregation among new immigrants. One of the primary causes is the family-unification emphasis of recent immigration laws. No longer do immigrants have to be confined to Chinatown as did the old-timers. They tend to follow their predecessors' footsteps in the sense that they are still closely linked with Chinatown, and yet, they are not necessarily confined in Chinatown, not even as a first step of settlement. Many of the recent arrivals have actually bypassed Chinatown to make their first residence in outer boroughs of the city. However, patterns of residential dispersion for the Chinese have not been automatically followed by spatial integration. Rather, resegregation is enforced by the network of family relations. (This pattern will be further discussed in a later chapter.)

Finally, the influx of economic resources, in the form of foreign capital, is a distinctive trend in recent Chinese immigration. A good proportion of the recent immigrants not only possess the human capital necessary to secure a better future, but they also possess the physical capital to smooth the transitional path of immigration. These two kinds of resources have been the crucial sources of the booming enclave economy. The nearly one-way influx of monetary capital has helped to generate an exclusive ethnic capital market to finance business activities in the Chinese community. Without such a capital market, the level of independence of the economic enclave would be greatly limited.

The human and physical capital involved in recent Chinese immigration represents a new trend that strongly reverses the traditional vision of immigration, which assumes that immigrants start from nothing upon arrival in the new country and then gradually assimilate when they achieve economic status. Now, this asymmetrical pattern has been somewhat reversed. Immigrants are not necessarily always poor to begin with. The economic resources they bring from abroad make possible economic development within the enclave that, in turn, enables immigrants to achieve economic advantages without leaving the enclave. Hence, the enclave creates an alternative path of immigrant incorporation.

5

The Rise of the Economic Enclave

Like many immigrant enclaves in American cities, New York's Chinatown has always been stereotyped as nothing more than an immigrant ghetto—a rundown residential neighborhood or, at best, a culturally distinctive enclave. It has been thought to serve either as a springboard from which immigrants, crippled by disadvantages related to immigration, can jump into the mainstream or as a cultural center where ethnic-specific needs can be satisfied. Until mass immigration began in the mid-1960s, New York City's Chinatown had primarily been a residential enclave for first-generation Chinese-Americans with a self-sustaining, small-scale ethnic subeconomy.

Since 1965, however, the stereotyped Chinatown has been withering away, and an economic enclave has gradually and steadily taken its place. No longer does Chinatown serve only as a home for immigrant Chinese in the New York metropolitan area. Rather, it has become a consolidated community based on an increasingly strong ethnic economy. Chinatown's enclave economy has been able to mobilize ethnic resources to provide ample job opportunities for immigrant Chinese and a wide range of ethnic businesses that cater to a dispersing Chinese population as well as to the larger population. Chinatown—an immigrant enclave in the full sense—has begun to adopt new functions, creating "golden" opportunities for immigrants. Many immigrant Chinese have been able to support the enclave economy and achieve socioeconomic gains from within it.

This drastic change indicates that Chinese immigrants have been adapting, or trying to adapt, to their new country, yet taking an alternative path. In this chapter I want to go beyond the stereotype of Chinatown to describe the impact of recent Chinese immigration on economic growth there. My analysis goes beyond the notion of Chinatown merely as a residential neighborhood and also beyond the simple survival strategies typical of areas where immigrants from poor, non-Western countries concentrate. To describe how the enclave opens up various economic opportunities for immigrant Chinese and how it serves as a positive alternative for economic integration, this chapter treats the structure of the economic enclave as a segmented sector of the U.S. economy.

Chinatown's Traditional Economies

Historically, the original Chinatown, a ten-block area on the Lower East Side of Manhattan, developed as a place of refuge for displaced immigrant laborers left jobless by the completion of the transcontinental railroad and barred from entering the larger labor market by ethnic prejudice and legal exclusion. Confronted with harsh anti-Chinese sentiment and the enforcement of the Chinese Exclusion Act during most of the first half of this century, the Chinese were forced into isolation and developed small niches that enabled them to survive and save enough money to return home. The gold dream had turned into a harsh reality in New York, where life depended on performing jobs that no one else wanted. The Chinese laborers, mostly males, found themselves holding only iron or silver, working at jobs that were traditionally regarded as women's work— laundry work and serving meals.

New York City's Chinatown in the 1930s and 1940s was a dreary place, a bachelors' society where former laborers eked out a living by doing hand laundry for whites and serving cheap ethnic meals. The two major types of businesses share common characteristics: They are labor-intensive; they depend on low wages, poor working conditions, and long working hours; and they provide few opportunities for mobility. Both were considered ethnic niches located in the narrow margins of the larger economy. While the laundry industry served a mostly non-Chinese clientele, the restaurant business, in the form of chop suey houses or teahouses, catered principally to the immediate needs of the bachelors' society in the early years.

Why did the Chinese go into these traditional businesses? The old-timers were certainly not born laundrymen or waiters. Many of them were peasants who came to America to work in mines on the West Coast and then switched to railroad building when the time came. When the completion of the transcontinental railroad and labor agitation from the white working class put them out of work, the Chinese were allowed to pick up these two occupations merely because no one else was interested in such low-paying, backbreaking, and unrewarding jobs. Old-timers, forced into these marginal economic activities simply as a temporary means of survival, never intended to intrude in the larger labor market; it had been drilled into them that "no matter what you do, make money and save money, so that you can go back to China as soon as possible."[1] Consequently, they became isolated in their own enclave, developing an exclusive ethnic market for the restaurant business, which was later extended to supply exotic food to the larger population.

The laundry business was not as "fortunate" because it depended almost entirely on the nonethnic market. It suffered gradual decline as a direct outcome of modern technology. Such inventions as home washers and dryers, the development by the textile industry of wash-and-wear fabrics, and alternative opportunities for the labor force, especially the younger generation, almost drove the industry out of business. Although it is still run by first-generation immigrants, the Chinese laundry is now "a dying business."[2]

The conditions for business success in marginal economic activities are largely subject to social, structural, and technological changes of the larger society. The fading laundry business in Chinatown is an example. Ethnic businesses with a protected ethnic consumer market, however, are relatively more independent. Unlike the laundry business, which is vulnerable to changes in the larger consumer market, the restaurant business is built primarily on an ethnic consumer market and only later extended to a non-Chinese clientele. This industry is able to exist and flourish not only because of the changing tastes of the non-Chinese customers, who often regard foreign food as a special treat, but also because of the growing demands of the Chinese themselves. During the sojourning period, chop suey restaurants, as well as other eating and drinking places in Chinatown, mainly served quick and inexpensive meals for the Chinese laborers who had no wives to cook for them. Some common items on the menu were not typical of Canton or any other region in China. Whereas dishes such as chow mein (fried noodles) and lo mein (noodles with spicy sauce) were typical everyday Cantonese dishes carried over from China, chop suey (miscellaneous pieces), moo goo gai pan (chicken with mushrooms), and egg foo yung (scrambled eggs mixed with seafood, pork, or beef) were "Americanized" Chinese food. The food in the teahouses was intended not so much to fit the tastes of the general population, for they could not tell the difference anyway, as to meet the needs of the bachelor Chinatowners, who were willing to pay a small price for a dish with a little bit of everything.

The Chinese did not gravitate to laundries and restaurants "by nature," as was often believed at the time. These businesses represented their only means of adaptation to a very difficult reality. If other jobs had been available to them, without doubt they would have taken them. The concentration of marginal business activities in Chinatown was a result of the generally discriminatory labor market. The limitation of even marginal businesses to but two main alternatives reflected the reality of an ethnic population that was too small and too homogeneous to sustain a diversified economy.

Post-1965 Development

Since the 1965 immigration reform, the Chinese have poured into New York, bringing rapid growth to Chinatown. The original boundaries expanded into decaying adjacent neighborhoods and "satellite" Chinatowns arose in Queens and Brooklyn.

The growing demands of the ethnic population, the availability of a cheap and highly flexible ethnic labor force, and the combined efforts of immigrants with different amounts of human and physical capital produced a boom in property investment and business expansion. Chinatown's enclave economy was diversified and gradually moved beyond the narrow margins of the larger economy. Table 5-1 presents some numbers indicating the range of this growth. The most significant change took place in the garment industry, which replaced laundries as the second most important business in the enclave. Besides the booming restaurant and garment industries, services that rely on an ethnic clientele also experienced tremendous growth.

Listed business activities that could be found anywhere in the larger society were booming in Chinatown. For example, Chinese insurance and real estate agencies increased 8,000 percent between 1958 and 1988; import/export businesses 1,822 percent; and doctors 1,428 percent. The number of Chinese accounting firms increased tenfold in the fifteen-year period. Other enterprises, such as beauty salons, grocery stores, herbalists and herbal medicine shops, jewelry stores, travel agencies, Chinese-language news and communication facilities, and others, also grew by nearly ten times or more. Today, the restaurant and garment businesses are the two basic components of Chinatown's enclave economy. The growth in these two industries, combined with a wide range of other economic activities, has shaped the nature of today's enclave economy.

The 1988 *Chinese Business Guide and Directory for Metropolitan New York and Boston*[3] listed a total of 5,978 entries for the New York metropoli-

Table 5-1. Numbers of Selected Chinese Businesses in New York City, 1958, 1973, and 1988

Type of Business	1958	1973	1988
Garment factories	0	200	437
Laundries	NA[1]	NA	20
Restaurants	304	NA	781
Accountants	3	10	107
Bakeries	4	7	46
Banks (including branches)	2	1	39
Barber shops and beauty salons	7	21	111
Chinese book stores	8	15	32
Dentists	3	8	98
Drugstores	1	5	22
Fish markets	2	2	53
Florists	4	6	17
Gift shops	66	60	65
Grocery stores	41	70	187
Herbalists	11	12	101
Herbal stores	2	NA	53
Importers and exporters	9	25	164
Insurance, real estate, and stockbrokers	4	30	320
Jewelers	6	5	97
Language-training centers	0	NA	8
Lawyers	12	25	186
Meat and poultry stores	16	15	45
Medical doctors	21	30	300
Newspapers and periodicals	5	NA	24
Noodle manufacturers	6	8	18
Photo labs and studios	4	5	19
Restaurant equipment	0	NA	92
Theaters and movie houses	5	7	4
Travel agencies	2	7	115
TV and radio broadcast stations	0	2	12
Video rentals and related firms	0	NA	41

Sources: SAPB 1958; 1973 data adapted from B. Wong 1979, p. 79; Key Publications, 1988.

[1] Not available.

tan area—ranging from financial and legal services, retail and whole-sale trade, manufacturing, food and grocery stores, and gift shops to entertainment and health services—as compared to only 424 entries in a similar directory for the Boston metropolitan area. About one-third of the firms are located in Manhattan's Chinatown area and other satellite Chinatowns, such as Flushing and Sunset Park. Firms in Chinatown, big or small, were mostly Chinese-owned, had a predominantly ethnic labor force, and served the special needs of the community.

The 1987 *Survey of Minority-Owned Business Enterprises* enumerated 89,717 Chinese-owned firms in the United States, indicating a 286-percent increase between 1982 and 1987 as compared with a 14-percent increase for all firms nationwide. In the New York, NY–NJ SMSA the number of Chinese-owned firms increased from 2,667 in 1977 to 11,579 in 1987 (10,864 firms were based in New York City); their gross receipts grew from $98 million to $843 million, and the average receipt per firm grew from $37,000 to $73,000 during the same period. The majority (84 percent) of the Chinese-owned firms in this metropolitan area were self-employment or family-run businesses without paid employees.[4]

The economic boom in New York City's Chinatown opened ample opportunities for immigrant workers, so that an ethnic labor market emerged as an alternative to outside employment. In the early 1980s, Chinatown's restaurants employed approximately 15,000 workers, mostly men. Some 500 garment factories employed 20,000 immigrant women in the extended Chinatown area in Lower East Manhattan. Service and tourist-oriented businesses employed about 15 percent of the immigrant work force.[5] Many of these jobs are characterized by low wages and long hours, making them seem highly exploitative to outsiders. However, the availability of a reliable low-wage labor force represents an important condition for the survival and success of many ethnic small enterprises. From the viewpoint of the workers, Chinese-owned businesses offer material and symbolic compensations that escape a gross accounting of benefits based exclusively on wages.

Today, Chinatown's economic structure no longer fits the stereotype of an immigrant residential enclave. Without the growing demand of recent immigration, Chinatown might still have been caught in the margins of the mainstream economy. With it, however, Chinatown has gone far beyond its traditional boundaries and has produced a strong economic enclave in the city, contributing both to the Chinese community and to the larger society.

While continuing to satisfy newcomers' residential needs, Chinatown has been transformed from an ethnic neighborhood into a strong economic base, serving the needs of the growing Chinese population in metropolitan New York. A second Chinatown, which has already gained a strong foothold in Flushing, Queens, and a third Chinatown, which has begun to take shape in Sunset Park, Brooklyn, both retain strong economic ties to this base. The majority of Chinese-owned firms are located in the extended Chinatown area on the Lower East Side of Manhattan, but more and more have begun to spread out into other Chinese enclaves and other parts of the city.

Major Economic Activities

Restaurants

The restaurant business has been regarded as one of the backbones of the economy in Chinatown. The 1988 *Chinese Business Guide and Directory for Metropolitan New York and Boston* lists a total of 781 restaurants in the area, with about two-thirds concentrated in the extended Chinatown area and Flushing's Chinatown. Many other Chinese restaurants were not listed in the directory. According to a recent report, there were 1,150 Chinese restaurants in New York City in 1988.[6]

Of all their cultural attributes, the Chinese seem to cling most tightly to their food. Wherever they go, especially with the family, they tend to look for their own food. Furthermore, over the years, Chinese food has been accepted as one of the best ethnic foods in America. Thus, the clientele of Chinatown's restaurant business grew in two parts: the ethnic Chinese population, which is one of the fastest growing immigrant groups in New York City; and the general population, which has taken Chinese cuisine seriously. However, Chinatown's restaurants are more dependent on the ethnic clientele than on the wider population.

To accommodate the growing demand of the incoming Chinese immigrants, the restaurant industry has developed into roughly three types: tea and coffee houses; fast-food takeouts; and fancy, expensive restaurants.

The tea and coffee houses are usually run by earlier immigrants and are staffed by their immigrant relatives. In the old days, these tea and coffee houses were called "chop suey houses" or "rice shop kitchens."[7] They served daily meals for the sojourners, laundrymen, and other Chinatown bachelors. Today, the rice shop kitchens have been replaced by the tea and coffee houses, which still retain an old style found fifty years ago, catering to the older Chinatowners and the working immigrants. The interior and other facilities are simple and basic. The food is cheap and is served quickly for breakfast, lunch, afternoon snacks, and dinner. For three dollars or so, one can get a couple of dishes of dim sum or a plate of chop suey with a cup of hot tea or coffee. Such teahouses are concentrated in Manhattan's Chinatown, where their customers live and work. They never move beyond the ethnic enclave, because neither the owners nor the workers have the slightest knowledge of English; nor do they encourage non-Chinese customers—for example, all the menus are written in Chinese only. Such restaurants require low initial capital and have low operating costs; they are able to make a marginal profit only through high customer volume.

A second type of restaurant, the fast-food takeout, has been developed only since the immigration surge. Because almost everybody works long hours in Chinatown, people are often too busy to cook. Even though more and more women, traditionally charged with cooking for the household, pour into Chinatown, most enter the labor force and work long hours—an average of forty-two hours a week. Thus most have little time for housework, particularly cooking, and they prefer to buy already-cooked food to bring home after work. Thus, they created a demand for fast food, and many Chinese, sensing profit, started up their own shops. Now fast-food takeouts specializing in barbecued pork, duck, chicken, ribs, and other ready-made dishes can be seen on every single street in Chinatown. Moreover, fast-food takeout is rapidly expanding beyond Chinatown and penetrating into non-Chinese neighborhoods to compete for customers with mainstream fast-food businesses such as McDonald's and Burger King. The fast-food business also fits the desire of recent Chinese immigrants to make quick money and to be bosses. It requires low initial capital—only about twenty thousand dollars to become an owner—and this amount can often be gathered from individual and family savings.

The fast-food business serves the everyday and immediate needs of the local Chinese, but the Chinese living in or close to a full-fledged ethnic community have needs other than basic ones. They also want places to socialize and to entertain family and friends. A third type of restaurant business responds to this need. Such restaurants are characterized by extravagance, luxuriousness, spaciousness, stylishness, and elegance with culturally conspicuous interior decoration and, of course, expensive menus. These restaurants have completely changed the image of Chinese food from something that is good but cheap. They serve a wide variety of cuisines—southern Cantonese, Hunan, western Szechuan, and eastern Shanghai—and can give banquets for the Chinese on all occasions. Although the food is more expensive, many Chinese can afford to go once a week for a family get-together and to indulge a nostalgia for their culture and ethnicity. On weekends and holidays, these restaurants serve tea and dim sum as brunch, and they are literally packed by families and groups of friends. The restaurants can be reserved ahead of time for extravagant birthday and wedding parties, and reservations around Chinese New Year and other traditional Chinese holidays must be made far in advance, sometimes as much as two years before. Well-known restaurants—the Silver Palace on Bowery Street, the Grand Palace on Mott Street—all have lists of reservations for wedding and birthday parties lined up for two or three years. Those restaurants cater mainly to the ethnic Chinese (about 90 percent) and are usually located in Manhattan's or Flushing's Chinatowns. The Chinese go to these restaurants not simply for the food but to feel the cultural atmosphere associated with their home country. A lot of other Chinese restaurants have expanded beyond the Chinatown borders throughout the city, but they are often modified and Americanized to fit the eating habits and tastes of the larger population. Much larger and more sophisticated than the teahouses and fast-food takeouts, these restaurants require a large initial capital investment and modern restaurant management. The start-up expenses are beyond the means of the average immigrant family. Investors are usually those wealthy immigrants who have been successful in business, recent wealthy arrivals from Hong Kong and Taiwan, or entrepreneurs located abroad.

The development of the restaurant business in Chinatown is relatively independent of the constraints of the larger economy, for it has its own ethnically protected capital, labor, and consumer markets. However, internal competition is extremely stiff, and the turnover rate is high. Ethnic entrepreneurs have to take advantage of ethnic solidarity to maintain their businesses. They organize restaurant associations to reduce cutthroat competition in the business. More significantly, they recruit an exclusively ethnic labor force not only to cut labor costs but also to avoid being charged with violations of labor or tax law. Because more recent immigrants are usually ignorant of the law, bosses feel safer from accusations. A good waiter in Chinatown makes an average of $1,500 to $2,000 a month, a cook about $2,000, and a busboy or a dishwasher about $800, provided that they all work at least forty-eight hours per week. For immigrant workers, who have little education and no English, this rate seems satisfactory compared to the pay they received in China.

Garment Industry

Chinese immigrants took up the garment industry when the segmentation of the larger market halted the long decline of New York City's garment industry.[8] Although the city has lost large numbers of manufacturing jobs because of transformation and relocation, small garment firms emerged to fill a substantial niche in the growing blouse and sportswear segments of the market, producing low-priced, mostly unstandardized goods for a significant spot market. Coincidentally with the stabilization of the city's garment trade and in response to market segmentation, the aging work force was withdrawing from the industry and not being replaced by newcomers.[9] As a result, immigrant Chinese and other recent immigrant groups, such as the Hispanics, were able to fill in and take over.

The development of Chinatown's garment industry has been directly associated with the immigration reform of 1965 which allowed wives and family members of the earlier immigrants into the United States. The influx, especially of women, created a potentially large pool of immigrant labor that was suitable for the garment industry, as well as a group of entrepreneurs who were willing to invest in and manage the garment shops. In addition, the relocation of the city's manufacturing firms left a lot of loft buildings vacant around the Chinatown area, providing relatively inexpensive space for garment factories.

The majority of the garment contractors are recent immigrants. The reasons for their interest in this business are similar to those of the earlier restaurant and laundry owners. The starting capital needed is low. In the early 1980s, twenty-five thousand dollars were enough to open up a twenty-machine shop, complete with a boiler for steam-pressure machines and the necessary electric and gas hookups from equipment suppliers; Equipment suppliers also provided contractors with easy terms to get started—a low down payment of about six thousand dollars, with the remainder to be paid in installments over a two-year period.[10] Many of the immigrant entrepreneurs draw on personal savings or borrow money from family members and friends.

After the start-up, contractors have to compete with each other for orders from manufacturers. If they can maintain a stable average of ten thousand orders per month, they are considered successful (the average net profit was around fifty cents per piece in the mid-1980s). Despite the fact that garment manufacturing is monopolized by non-Chinese manufacturers (mostly Jewish), subject to union control, and vulnerable to international competition, many contractors enter the business to make a quick profit and accumulate capital for transferring into the restaurant business or other ethnic businesses. Because the industry itself is fairly unstable, the Chinese do not consider it a long-term endeavor.

According to a Chinatown garment industry study conducted by the International Ladies' Garment Workers' Union, the number of Chinese-owned garment factories in the Chinatown area increased from 34 in 1965 to 209 in 1974 and 430 in 1980, employing some twenty thousand Chinese workers, most of whom are women.[11] Many of the Chinatown sweatshops are under union control. The Garment workers, who do not speak English and have little education, are paid by the piece; the ILGWU's minimum wage was $3.65 an hour or $128 a week before April 1990, and now is $4.25 an hour. Contractors, however, often have ways to get around the union rules by taking advantage of ethnic familiarity and commitment. A skilled worker usually gets an hourly rate of $5, while an unskilled new hand gets only about $2. Although contractors try to keep a stable staff by offering higher wages, the majority of other garment workers are "rotating" labor, hired and laid off regularly to avoid the accumulation of seniority rights and to keep the overall wage level as low as possible, that is, at a starting rate. This practice is possible only when there is a continuous influx of new unskilled immigrants. When asked whether they ever claimed their right to the minimum wage, the workers usually echoed Mrs. Liang, who said: "You cannot demand higher wages if you are a new hand. Getting a job is only lucky for you; if you complain, you will simply be dismissed and the boss can easily get a replacement. However, if you are really good and quick-handed, the boss tends to keep you; and only then can you make your complaint heard. If you are ignored, you can 'fire' the boss [quit your job and move to another shop]. Thus, skill is a very important bargaining tool for high wages in the garment shops."[12]

The recruitment of workers depends primarily on kinship and ethnic ties. Businesses are typically family enterprises in which spouse, siblings, or relatives share ownership and managerial responsibilities.[13] Workers are mostly immigrants from the same original village as the owners. This familiarity promotes less formal and antagonistic employee relations and fosters a stable work force. Ethnicity, friendship, and kinship tie workers to the factory and encourage them to identify their interests with those of the firm.

The garment industry, by nature, is a marginal activity closely linked to the larger economy. In general, garment workers have been out-competed by cheap labor in the Far East, even back in China, where the hourly wage is below a dollar. The only possible piece of the "pie" left is in the fashion segment, where unpredictable demand for fashionable and seasonal garments have to be met on the short notice of the market. Because the requirements of the industry particularly match the capital-raising capacity and minimal skills of immigrants, many immigrant groups are competing for a share of this small pie. Thus, the industry, which is squeezed into the narrow margins of the larger economy, is fraught with cutthroat competition both within Chinatown and among different ethnic groups. Its survival depends mainly on the marginal demand of the larger society, the efficient mobilization of ethnicity, and the effective use of cheap immigrant labor. Because of the uncertainty of market demand and the instability of the industry, most of the Chinese entrepreneurs enter the garment industry only to accumulate capital for other long-term investments.

In 1988 Mr. Zhao, an ambitious garment contractor who had immigrated only three years before, ran a sweat shop on Canal Street with his wife, who used to be a garment worker. The couple worked very hard on all aspects of the factory operation: hiring, working out the wage scale, competing for orders, fighting for contract prices with manufacturers, dealing with workers and the unions, and many other things. They literally worked all the time. When asked what was good about entering the garment industry, Mr. Zhao replied,

> I think I can make quick, but not easy, money from the garment industry. I believe that if I work hard enough, I can make it. But going into the garment industry is not my goal, because this business is too dependent on the larger market and too unstable for a lifelong investment. I am doing it because it is the only available and feasible way for me to accumulate capital. If I have enough money, I will open a restaurant and develop a McDonald's type of global chain Chinese food industry. I probably can make the first move in another two years.[14]

In fact, many owners of Chinatown's restaurants and import-export companies originally made their money from the garment factories.[15] In this way, the development of the garment industry can greatly contribute to the overall economic well-being of Chinatown, in that the industry is able to draw money from the outside economy and then circulate it back into the community. The contribution of Chinatown's garment industry is extraordinary, both to the enclave economy and to the city's economy. According to the ILGWU, a garment worker earned an average of $5,500 in reported wages in 1981 after accounting for seasonal and part-time work. The twenty-thousand-member Chinatown garment work force made a total of $105 million in wages in 1981, and the owners made $9 million in salaries (an estimated $20,000 per shop). Thus, Chinatown's garment industry directly contributed at least $125 million to Chinatown and the city's economy in 1981. This income was spent on food, housing, clothing, and other goods and services, and a large share was saved. It is estimated that, of the money spent on consumer needs, at least two-thirds was circulated in Chinatown: 94 percent of the Chinese, particularly immigrant households in the city, bought food in Chinatown; 40 percent bought nonfood items; and almost 75 percent found entertainment and recreation in Chinatown.[16] Thus, many Chinatown small businesses gained support from the garment income. A fast-food takeout restaurant owner commented on the effect of the garment industry on his business.

> If the garment industry is off season, my restaurant loses at least one-fourth of its sales. When the women workers are laid off, they do not have as much money, and they will stay home and cook. The garment off-season—September till January—is a tough time for the restaurant business. When the garment workers come back to work, usually in February, they will shop around and buy food and other stuff for the home in Chinatown after work, because, then, they don't have time to cook.[17]

Retail and Wholesale Trade

Wholesale and retail trade is another key sector of Chinatown's economy, boosted, like the others, by the increasing demand of the Chinese population. When Chinatown was small, wholesaling was almost absent. Merchants traveled back and forth themselves between the United States and Hong Kong or China, buying Chinese foodstuffs and other goods and shipping them back to New York. They distributed the goods either to the retail stores or directly to restaurants and made a slim profit out of the business. Retail trade, too, was a basic and small-scale business for Chinatown. It supplied the ethnic community with ethnic-specific goods and a limited stock of daily necessities that were unavailable or inaccessible (because of the language problem) for the Chinatown residents, most of whom were bachelors without a real home.

Wholesale and retail trade has grown in connection with a well-organized import and export business. For instance, the growing restaurant business alone has created a tremendous demand for Chinese foodstuffs and supplies, such as necessary spices, cooking utensils, china-ware, furniture, ornaments, and other decorating materials. Other major imported goods include textile products, herbs and herbal medicines, toys, handicrafts, and other ethnic products.

Wholesaling has established a distribution network centered in New York City's Chinatown. Wholesalers distribute goods not only to other Chinatowns in big cities along the East Coast—Boston, Philadelphia, Washington, D.C., Baltimore, and so on—but also to smaller towns and suburban areas close to those cities where sizable Chinese populations reside. Import and export companies have increased from 25 in 1973 to 164 in 1988. Many retailers, on the other hand, still hold on to their tra-ditional ways of organizing goods; they are merchants themselves. Yet, stores are no longer uniformly small; large department stores and grocery stores, mostly investments by Hong Kong and Taiwan businessmen, have sprung up in Chinatown and have branches elsewhere in the other East Coast cities. Many gift shops and department stores provide a variety of products, mainly imported from China, ranging from padded and quilted silk jackets and rubber-soled fabric shoes to antiques and elaborately carved furniture, from woks and bamboo steamers, chopsticks, bowls, and platters to oiled-paper umbrellas and joss sticks. While the clientele is predominantly Chinese, the retail trade also plays an important role in Chinatown's tourist industry, making money from the numerous tourists and drawing outside funds into the community.

Real Estate

The Chinese traditionally value real estate and regard it as an impor-tant indicator of success, which may be used to honor their ancestors and may be boasted about in front of their children. In the old times, the sojourners did not invest in American real estate; instead, they tried to save money so that they could buy land back in China. Now that the Chinese have decided to stay, the desire to own property in the United States has grown. The demand, combined with the pressure of high rents and inflation, and a large influx of foreign capital, makes Chinatown a profitable real estate market.

Chinatown's real estate lift-off came during the late 1970s and early 1980s. About 62 percent of the properties for sale in the area were pur-chased by Chinese between 1975 and 1987.[18] In the core Chinatown area, foreign capital was at work in housing development projects. For example, Yip Hon, a wealthy Hong Kong businessman, spent $6 mil-lion to construct the Wing Ming Building, an eleven-story full-service office tower, in the early 1970s.[19] The East-West Tower, a $21 million, 143-unit project, was entirely financed by capital from Hong Kong and the Middle East.[20] Chinatown was probably not big enough to absorb much of the foreign Chinese capital. In 1986 the largest real estate deal in the works in the neighborhood was about $18 million, tiny by Manhattan standards and modest even by those of other cities.[21] Moreover, because of the neighborhood's strict zoning regulations, which limit all new development to six stories, only a few new buildings have gone up since 1970. Yet, some developers found they could make a handsome profit on building conversions. Many old, shabby buildings were converted into fancy shops, restaurants, and expensive housing units. According to Mr. Wang, former director of the Chinatown Neighborhood Local Development Corporation, at least a couple of dozen buildings are being renovated within the core area of Chinatown on any working day.

There were also frequent and quick real estate transactions in Chinatown. Some of the Chinatown sales recorded before March 1987 included:

— 198–240 Canal Street, a series of six-story buildings that sold for a total of $11 million, ten times the price they fetched when they last changed hands twenty-five years ago.
— 45 Catherine Street, a five-story walk-up, whose sale price was $420,000 in November 1986, up from $110,000 six years earlier.
— 23 Chatham Square, a four-story building that sold for $795,000 in August 1985; the price increased to $1.6 million one year later.
— 13–17 Elizabeth Street, three six-story loft buildings, sold at a price of $4.7 million, up from $750,344 in 1973.[22]

Many former owners of these properties were not Chinese, but almost all the buyers were. The buying behavior of these Chinese was referred to by the Americans as a "no-brainer"—they bought with their eyes closed.

The unusual boom in Chinatown brought its own kind of inflation. Land and building values and rents were pushed to outrageous heights; many residents and businesses were forced out of Chinatown to relocate elsewhere in the city. While the negative effect was certainly enormous, a positive outcome was that the economic enclave was thus developed beyond the traditional territory, bringing about the development of satellite Chinatowns. The real estate business did not just aim at the turf in Chinatown; it had, indeed, penetrated into other areas where land prices used to be relatively low, for example, Flushing, Elmhurst, Corona, and Jackson Heights in Queens and Sunset Park and Bay Ridge in Brooklyn. This real estate boom, then, gave rise to a second and third Chinese enclave and also inflated the land values there. Now, Flushing has turned into an expensive neighborhood for the middle-class Chinese. Along Eighth Avenue between Fifty-first and Sixty-first streets in Brooklyn, almost half of the houses are owned by the Chinese. The real estate business has even started to expand out of New York into other states as far away as Florida, spreading and decentralizing new investments and immigrants.

Chinatown is practically out of property to sell, but investors are still looking and speculating. With a booming local economy and a continuous influx of immigrants and investment capital from overseas, the buying sprees and conversions have generated so much momentum that Chinese investors continue to scramble for a piece of the ethnic market.

Jewelry Trade

Another remarkable sign of economic vitality in Chinatown is the jewelry shops that line Canal and Bowery streets in Chinatown in far greater numbers than one would expect. These stores all seem to have sprung up at the same time. Before 1973, there were only about five jewelry stores in Chinatown; twelve years later, the number had increased to ninety-seven (see Table 5-1). On what used to be the Italian side of Canal Street (the six blocks between Lafayette Street and Bowery Street), there are about forty-eight jewelry stores. Outsiders, as well as the Chinese themselves, often wonder why there are so many jewelry stores and how they can possibly make a profit on expensive gold jewelry, diamonds, and precious stones and still survive the competition with the world's largest and best-known jewelry and diamond center on nearby Forty-seventh Street. Even on Forty-seventh Street there were some Chinese-owned jewelry shops. It is still unknown why this business has recently become one of the fastest growing in the enclave economy. One thing that is quite certain is that most of the owners are millionaire entrepreneurs back in Hong Kong and Taiwan, who felt that investing in gold and diamond speculation was one way to redirect their surplus capital to a safe place.

Tourism and Entertainment

Chinatown has always been a tourist center for people from all over the country and the world. The community's exotic culture, famous food, fine handicrafts, and other oddities attract thousands of non-Chinese visitors. However, the entertainment business has developed not simply to pull tourists from outside into the community, as has always been the case, but also to serve immigrant Chinese. Early immigrants were far less interested in entertainment. They worked hard and played little, saving every penny they could. These people were reluctant to spend any money on travel or entertainment, for which they had little time anyway. Ironically, as their desire to save money overwhelmed them, some got into the habit of gambling, hoping they would spend a dollar to win a million someday. In Chinatown, gambling seemed to be the only means of entertainment for the sojourners (and new immigrants have also picked up the habit).

Today, immigrant Chinese are willing to travel to fulfill their family commitments, to indulge their nostalgia, or just for enjoyment. Many immigrants still have parents and relatives back in China, Hong Kong, and Taiwan, and they are often expected to go back to weed the graveyard (pay respects to their ancestors at the tomb) once a year. A lot of the old Chinatowners had never been back to China because they worked hard in the early years and had no money for expensive air transportation. Later they could not return because the United States and China broke off diplomatic relations. Since the two countries have normalized relations, traveling back and forth has become more frequent. Return visits to China, Hong Kong, and Taiwan are more routine for new immigrants than for older immigrants, because of their immediate or close relatives who are still left behind. Newer immigrants depend almost entirely on Chinese-speaking agents to help them with the travel itinerary, whereas older immigrants may not necessarily be as dependent on Chinatown's travel agencies or they may travel less frequently for family fulfillment.

As settlement patterns have changed, so have lifestyles. Today, immigrants talk about leisure travel and want to enjoy some fun. They want to see the United States, Canada, and some Southeast Asian countries. Even when they pay return visits to their place of origin, they tend to travel as much as possible in their homeland. As the demand has grown, a large number of travel agencies have emerged. In the 1950s, there were only 2 travel agencies in Chinatown. In 1973, the year when Sino-American relations were normalized, the number increased to 7; by unofficial count in 1988 there were 115 Chinese agencies, mainly located in Manhattan's and Flushing's Chinatowns or wherever they are accessible and convenient for the ethnic clientele. They often help to find good deals from various airlines for non-English-speaking immigrants. From Hong Kong, it is easy to connect with other flights or with train or boat service to Canton and other parts of China. More often, travel agencies provide different packages for group and guided travel, particularly for domestic travel. Travel inside the United States, including short trips to nearby entertainment facilities, has also become more and more frequent. For instance, travel agencies have set up daily bus trips to Atlantic City, where some of the casinos even hire popular singers from Hong Kong and Taiwan for their shows in order to attract Chinese customers.

In Chinatown, many entertainment businesses have also emerged to meet the popular demand. There are now four theaters in Chinatown showing Chinese movies both in Cantonese and Mandarin. Videotape rentals have also become popular for the extended families and families living in Queens and Brooklyn. There are twelve different television and radio stations that provide a wide variety of programs in Mandarin and Cantonese for the Chinese population in the New York metropolitan area. In 1988 video rental stores and video movie production centers increased to forty-one. Nightclubs and bars have also been set up to provide places where immigrants can socialize and have a good time in a somewhat Western style but with ethnic services.

Professional Firms

Chinatown's enclave economy has also seen the development of a wide range of white-collar professional services. This segment of the ethnic economy developed to meet the needs of both the growing population and the booming economy. For example, banks and financial institutions arose to help mobilize ethnic capital and financial resources for businesses and residents. While many Chinese still cling to the traditional way of fund raising for business start-ups or for real estate purchases through family associations or kinship-related credit unions,[23] others obtain loans from banks, particularly Chinese-owned banks. Of the business establishments listed in Table 5-1, there were seventeen Chinese-owned banks with twenty-two branches in New York City in 1989; all of them had their main offices in Manhattan's or Flushing's Chinatown. A more recent report from a Chinatown journal notes that Manhattan's Chinatown alone concentrates about thirty-three banks and branches. Quite a few branches of mainstream banks have also entered Chinatown to compete for a share of the ethnic market. CitiBank has three branches in Manhattan's Old Chinatown, Manhattan Savings Bank has two branches there; others, such as Westminster Bank and Lincoln Savings Bank, have opened branches recently. These non-Chinese branches not only have rich human and capital resources but also have full staffs of Chinese employees, giving them a decidedly Chinese look. These banks, though located in Chinatown, are not considered part of the enclave economy.

Chinese banks are supported by capital from Chinese-Americans, by investment from the mainland, Hong Kong, Taiwan, and some Southeast Asian countries. They remain especially competitive on their own ethnic turf. Schuman S. Tu, the chairman of the board of directors of Great Eastern Bank, voiced his confidence in the competitive advantage of the ethnic network in Chinatown:

> Many Chinese banks do not simply look for profits alone; they have ethnic and community commitments to help circulate money within Chinatown and to prevent money from being drained out. This, in turn, helps them stay competitive in face of the big mainstream banks.
>
> One advantage for us is that Chinese businessmen tend to turn to their ethnic banks for business loans, because ethnic banks usually do not have such strict credit requirements or as much paper work, which often scares away recent arrivals who do not speak English. Chinese immigrants are less likely to be frustrated by turndowns simply based on insufficient proof of credit, because we have easy access to their past credit history through family associations and the preimmigration records, an advantage which the big banks do not possess.
>
> Business loan applications of entrepreneurs who are new immigrants often get turned down by the big banks, because they do not have any credit history here in the U.S. With ethnic solidarity, we are able to make a profit and, at the same time, help the community's economic development.[24]

Chinese-owned banks popped up and spread throughout Manhattan's and Flushing's Chinatowns. Although in 1988 Chinatown had more banks than any of the residential areas in the city, more were still to come. Hang Sheng Bank and East Asian Bank from Hong Kong are expected to set up their branches in Chinatown in the near future.[25] Even some overseas Chinese banks have intruded or plan to intrude into midtown Manhattan—the international financial center.

Other professional establishments—law firms and accountants' offices; doctors' and dentists' clinics; bilingual training centers—also came on the scene to serve the demand of the growing local economy. Before 1965, few such businesses were seen in Chinatown. There were not many Chinese professionals in New York City serving the Chinese community (about twenty-five lawyers, ten accountants, thirty medical doctors, twelve herbalists, and eight dentists in 1973), as the Chinese who entered those professions (except herbalists) tended to stay away from Chinatown.

Today, the number has increased tremendously—186 lawyers, 107 accountants, 300 medical doctors, 101 herbalists, 98 dentists, 8 language-training centers, 12 Chinese broadcasting stations, 24 newspapers and periodicals (see Table 5-1). One main reason why the Chinese professionals have turned back to the enclave is the possibility of moving up to full-fledged partnership. In some cases, economic return is greater than in a mainstream environment, where racial discrimination may intervene. The growth of white-collar and professional firms has largely changed the stereotype of Chinatown's economy as low-wage, labor-intensive, and marginal.

Chinatown continues to grow, so prosperous and full of vitality and promise. It has proved itself a successful enclave in which the Chinese immigrants can succeed here in America. No wonder so many Chinese immigrants (22 percent of all those who arrived in the United States between 1965 and 1977) have poured into New York City as their final destination.

The Structure of the Enclave: A Duality

Chinatown's economy reflects a segmentation of the larger economy and a structural duality that operates principally by its own logic. This duality is made up of a protected sector and an export sector, both characterized by small businesses that are extremely competitive and susceptible to business succession. How can a small business conquer cutthroat competition and develop? How can an initially disadvantaged group move out of wage labor and into business ownership? These questions are important to our understanding of the enclave as an alternative path to ethnic incorporation.

The Enclave Protected Sector

The enclave protected sector arises within the ethnic community itself.[26] It represents a captive market, oriented toward ethnic-specific goods and services that are not easily accessible outside the enclave and toward solutions to various adjustment and settlement problems relating to immigration. These special demands for ethnic consumer goods and services provide a direct link between places of origin and the tastes and buying preferences of ethnic group members, and they substantially reduce the level of competition with larger, native-owned firms.[27]

This sector is protected from structural changes in the larger economy because it is secured by its own exclusive capital market, labor market, and consumer market. The two major economic activities in the enclave—production (of ethnic consumer goods and services) and trade—are specially targeted to and supported by the ethnic consumer market. In this way, they are able to maintain a relatively high level of control and economic independence. For example, the restaurant business is one of the basic businesses in the Chinese enclave economy, but not every Chinese restaurant falls into the protected sector of the enclave economy. The one in Chinatown is clearly more advantageous than the one outside of Chinatown, for the latter loses its ethnic clientele to the nonethnic one—a consumer market that is less predictable.

The enclave protected sector is dominated by small businesses specially targeted toward adjustment problems and the settlement needs of its group members. However, these economic activities are not necessarily confined to entry-level, low-prestige, and labor-intensive activities. With a sufficiently large ethnic consumer market, that is, population base, it gives rise to a wide variety of higher-level, white-collar, and knowledge-intensive occupations, ranging from top positions, such as doctors, lawyers and accountants, to other white-collar, service-oriented occupations, such as bankers, insurance and real estate agents, retailers, and wholesalers. Many of these occupations match the characteristics of those in the primary sector of the larger economy. In this way, the protected sector opens up a relatively independent opportunity structure that is less vulnerable to structural changes in the larger economy for ethnic members, particularly immigrants, who may otherwise be deterred because of their initial disadvantages. For instance, immigrants with remarkable educational and professional skills and experience would be able to pursue careers commensurate with their past human-capital investment in the enclave.

The advantages provided by Chinatown's protected sector resemble those provided by the monoethnic labor market described by Moshe Semyonov.[28] Through a careful examination of the role of the local opportunity structure and the effects of the local labor-market segregation on occupational and economic inequality between Arabs and Jews in Israel, Semyonov finds that Arabs participating in the biethnic labor market suffer the detrimental consequences of both occupational and income discrimination, while, by contrast, Arabs working in the mono-ethnic labor market are occupationally advantaged. Semyonov argues that the biethnic labor market is essentially discriminatory against minority groups. The increase in the relative size of the minority population, on the one hand, further intensifies antagonism and racial prejudice gener-ated by job competition, and on the other, enables superordinates to pass the least-desired jobs onto subordinates. By organizing a monoethnic labor market, subordinates can be protected from labor-market discrimi-nation and can possibly enjoy the advantages of those higher occupational positions that would otherwise be unavailable to them. However, China-town does not simply reflect the positive characteristics of a monoethnic labor market. It is also better able to expand its interface with the larger economy to exploit opportunities and resources that fit into the ethnic economic structure. Because it is partially dependent upon the larger economy, as is the case for the ethnic export sector, Chinatown's posi-tion in the larger economy appears stronger than that of a monoethnic structure.

The Enclave Export Sector

The enclave export sector contains a nonethnic market characteristic of leftover niches of the larger secondary economy, such as underserved or abandoned businesses and businesses that serve unstable or uncertain demands, that provide exotic goods, and that require low economies of scale.[29] Relative to the enclave protected sector, the export sector does not have a combination of the three ethnic markets, and thus it does not have control over the production process or business operations. Further-more, the export sector is often represented by jobs similar to those in the mainstream secondary economy.

The export sector is closely intertwined with the outside economy and is very sensitive to the fluctuations of the larger economic system; thus, it is as unstable and uncertain as the latter. For example, one major characteristic of Chinatown's garment industry is that it has a nonethnic consumer market and is largely subject to nonethnic manufacturers with whom the work is contracted. Before 1965, Chinatown's export sector was dominated by the laundry business. There used to be about twenty-seven hundred laundries in New York,[30] serving a non-Chinese clientele in the metropolitan area. Technological improvements in both machinery and fabrics caused the decline in the laundry industry. After the decline, the enclave found another niche to capture Chinatown's large pool of unskilled, low-wage labor. The growth of the garment industry in Chinatown also indicates another characteristic of the export sector—that it is highly subject to inter-ethnic competition in the larger structural context. For instance, New York City's garment industry was previously dominated by Puerto Ricans and later by recent arrivals from the Dominican Republic and Colombia, and the Chinese increased their ownership to a great extent only over the last ten years or so.[31] Now the garment industry has become a significant export sector in Chinatown. It stands out from the mainstream secondary economy by taking advantage of ethnicity and effectively utilizing the large pool of immigrant labor. Although protected by an ethnic labor market, ethnic entrepreneurs are dependent upon the demands of the larger consumer market and must compete with other ethnic groups for a share of the pie.

The formation of the enclave export sector seems to follow the notion of the filtering process. The large influx of a minority population increases the supply of cheap labor—a potential pool of replacement labor to fill the least desirable, lowest-paying positions—in turn, pushing members of the majority group one step up the occupational ladder and, hence, widening the gap between the majority and the minority groups.[32] The recruitment to ownership in the enclave economy also resembles this filtering-down process. As Roger Waldinger puts it, "Natives opt out of the supply of potential owners in a particular industry, perhaps because ownership in the industry generates too little status, perhaps because its economic rewards are insufficient to retain them compared to the alternative available. If this is the case, then there may be a replacement demand and immigrants could then enter the industry to fill the ownership positions vacated by the natives."[33]

The export sector in Chinatown's enclave economy somewhat fits into this filtering process, in the sense that the sector itself can find niches only at the narrow margins of the larger economy. However, unlike the larger peripheral sector, the ethnic export sector can show stronger competitiveness over other ethnic groups (which do not have an economic enclave), in that it can effectively take advantage of the social relations and ethnic solidarity that are so deeply embedded in the enclave economy. Immigrants themselves, even if they have a choice between the enclave export sector and the larger secondary economy, prefer participating in the enclave, for ethnicity often works to offset some of the exploitative aspects of the export industries located in the enclave.

The enclave has been repeatedly charged as highly exploitative of co-ethnic workers, more exploitative than the larger secondary economy.[34] This charge is misleading, in that it reinforces a negative stereotype of the enclave. Actually, the enclave helps to create employment opportunities for its group members who may otherwise be more likely to join the general population of unemployed and add pressure to the welfare system and government assistance programs. If not for ethnic business ventures, the large immigrant labor force would probably suffer the same fate as the native unemployed and welfare dependents.

The Success of the Enclave

How can ethnic businesses succeed and grow? Success depends on three things: the ability of the ethnic economy to mobilize capital resources; the ability to control the cost of labor and business operations; and access to the consumer markets. For an economic community to grow, reinvestment is necessary. The interaction of the two sectors reproduces a dialectical relationship between internal consumption and reinvestment, which plays an important role in the development of the enclave economy. On the one hand, the protected sector secures a steady circulation of capital within the enclave and effectively prevents economic resources from being drained out of the ethnic community. On the other hand, income generated from the export sector tends to strengthen the buying power of ethnic members and to accumulate savings for further investment in the protected sector. In this way, capital gets circulated from the broader society into the ethnic capital market, which in turn makes possible the expansion of the protected as well as the export sector.

Although enclave businesses are mostly small-scale and internal competition is sometimes intense, with a fairly high turnover rate, it is unlikely that the enclave protected sector will eventually lose to outsiders or be swallowed up by the larger economy. Intraethnic competition does not necessarily harm the enclave economy as a whole. Rather, a pattern of business take-over among co-ethnics prevails. That is, someone may be out-competed, but he or she is more likely to be succeeded by a co-ethnic than by someone from outside the enclave. For instance, when a Chinatown restaurant fails, for whatever reason, there is always another ambitious Chinese who takes over and tries to do a better job. In Chinatown, many restaurants, stores, and small businesses change hands frequently. However, the absolute number of restaurants and stores continues growing so fast that an outsider might wonder how they could possibly stay in business. Also, the high turnover of ethnic enterprises, which is common for ethnic economies and small businesses, may not necessarily mean failure for enclave entrepreneurs. It may very well be that the more ambitious entrepreneurs simply use their initial businesses as a long-term strategy to pursue more challenging ventures after a certain number of years of capital accumulation and career training.

How can an initially disadvantaged group move out of wage labor and into business ownership? Chinatown's consolidated social structure generates a particular form of social capital that helps immigrant Chinese surmount structural obstacles and raises them socioeconomically. *Social capital* refers to ethnic resources specific to ethnicity. It works for both ethnic entrepreneurs and workers, providing (1) a familiar environment in which they are effectively shielded from deficiencies in language, education, and general knowledge about the larger society; (2) an extensive kinship network that channels information; (3) a unique way of mobilizing capital resources, for example, rotating credit; and (4) a set of cultural values and norms that reinforce achievement orientation, work ethic, and the ability to postpone gratification. For example, achievement orientation or a middle-class value system—a strong work ethic, frugality, and future orientation—is necessary to develop entrepreneurship. Some minority groups may take a more "rationalistic and individualistic" approach, whereas others take a collective approach, drawing on the ties to the family, group, and community to fulfill their goals. Because of the relative disadvantages associated with immigration, immigrant Chinese are not on the same ground as native workers. They find it difficult to compete without the support of ethnic ties and Chinatown's economy. With this social capital, it is possible to overcome structural disadvantages.

Enclave employment is advantageous not only for entrepreneurs but also for workers. In Chinatown, low wages are compensated for by the savings of time and effort involved in finding a "good job" in the larger market, the possibility of working longer hours to help contribute more to family savings, a familiar work environment, and for some, the possibility of eventual transition to self-employment. Many business families earn decent incomes, and they earn more money than they would earn from nonbusiness occupations. Moreover, enclave workers can avoid many hassles and costs associated with employment in the secondary labor market, the most obvious one being labor-market discrimination on the basis of race and national origin. Thus, enclave workers often willingly accept exploitation. They choose to work in Chinatown because they view it as a better option. In this sense, being confined in the enclave does not necessarily mean the "failure" of assimilation. Employment in

Chinatown serves as a vehicle for ambitious immigrants to learn the skills of a trade and accumulate capital for their own businesses through various mechanisms within the ethnic community.

Conclusion

What has made Chinatown thrive in the past two decades? First, population growth has an impact. A large influx of immigrants with heterogeneous socioeconomic backgrounds provided a continuous supply of potential entrepreneurs and workers. Like many new arrivals of other ethnic groups, a good proportion of the recent arrivals have tended to know limited English and to have few of the marketable skills essential for competing in the open labor market. The availability of cheap immigrant labor, combined with the initial disadvantages of the immigrants, effectively reduces the labor cost, thus stimulating ethnic industries and businesses able to exploit this type of cheap labor. However, cheap labor has always existed in immigrant communities and in Old Chinatown; it may create a necessary condition for new business opportunities, but it does not inevitably lead to more jobs. In some cases, for example, Mexican immigrants and early Chinese immigrants, immigrants often find themselves competing with native workers in the same job markets.[35] This situation leads to only two possible options for immigrants: either they are out-competed by the native workers, or they are depreciated and limited to the lowest rung of the occupational ladder.

Second, Chinatown thrives because of shared ethnicity and a particular means of economic organization. The Chinese have a tendency to work with each other, especially within the family. They are able to mobilize resources through mutual-aid, clan (family), and trade and business associations. Yet, the traditional means of economic organization have long existed in Chinatown without producing the differentiated division of labor that is characteristic of the enclave economy.

The development of a structural duality in Chinatown's economy contributes to the community's current prosperity. Over the past three decades, Chinatown has developed into an economic enclave with a highly differentiated division of labor, organized around a structural duality: a protected sector and an export sector. While the protected sector is secured by an exclusive capital market, labor market, and consumer market oriented toward the ethnic population, the export sector generates income to be circulated back into the ethnic markets and reinvested in both sectors. In this manner, the size and vitality of the enclave economy is greatly expanded to generate a structure of job opportunities for immigrants with varied socioeconomic backgrounds. With the existence of such a structure, immigrants do not necessarily always have to start from the lowest rung of the occupational ladder; it is possible for them to achieve upward social mobility by participating in the enclave without extensive acculturation. Nevertheless, to say that the enclave protected sector reproduces some positive characteristics of the larger primary economy does not necessarily mean that it can simply be equated with it. Although the enclave protected sector is relatively autonomous in relation to the larger economy and less sensitive to its structural changes, it has never developed into the kind of monopoly evident in the larger economy. Thus, we must take care not to exaggerate the protective functions of the enclave.

On the other hand, with a strong differentiated enclave economy, immigrants are also differentiated into two classes: the entrepreneurial class and the working class, each having a different level of benefits from participating in the economic enclave. The entrepreneurs are able to take advantage of ethnic solidarity to compensate for occupational disadvantages. The immigrants can take advantage of ethnic solidarity to make up for whatever they would lose if they did not have such an option. Hence, both workers and bosses can profit from the advantages of the enclave economy when class relations are restrained by ethnic commitment. Conceptually, if immigrants are structurally denied employment in the larger labor market, those with advanced education and occupational expertise would be expected to have a better chance of participating in the enclave economy, particularly in the protected sector and in the ownership positions of the export sector. They would probably be better able to capture the enclave advantages and gain sufficient returns from past human capital than they would in the open economy. As a whole, the enclave cannot easily be viewed as an "extension of the larger secondary economy." [36]

In Chinatown, there is a familiar cultural environment in which workers can interact in their own language and observe common rites and practices. Culture creates a common bond between ethnic entrepreneurs and workers, making for a more personalized and humane environment than the highly alienated work conditions confronted in the larger labor market. For many enclave workers, spelling a tour of duty at low-paid menial work in co-ethnic businesses is part of the time-honored path toward family advancement and economic independence. Such efforts underlie, to a great extent, the recession-proof growth in Chinatown's economy.

However, the dual structure of the enclave economy is only a quasi duality relative to that of the larger economy. Relative to the mainstream economy, the enclave economy, as a whole, represents the basic characteristics of the broader competitive sector. Immigrant firms, even some of those in the protected sector of the enclave economy, operate in an environment of considerable economic uncertainty. Their markets are largely local or ethnic-specific; they do not generate their own technology; and they often depend on labor-intensive production processes. Most important, they lack a monopoly position in the larger economy.[37] In this sense, the enclave economy is susceptible to the disadvantages of the larger secondary economy. However, while the enclave economy may not always guarantee better-paying jobs for immigrants in a strictly calculated sense, its participants are able to reap benefits from ethnicity, a form of social capital that is absent in the larger economy.

6

The Ethnic Labor Force and
Its Labor-Market Experience

Chinatown's booming enclave economy has transformed the community from an isolated immigrant neighborhood into one that goes beyond its original boundaries. As an increasingly large number of Chinese immigrants continue to pour into New York City bringing ample human and economic resources into the enclave, ethnic Chinese residents and businesses are no longer restricted to Old Chinatown. They are much more spread out than their predecessors, into outer-borough neighborhoods and even into the metropolitan suburbs. However, the decentralization of the Chinese population and its business activities does not seem to be accompanied by diminishing ethnic coherence or a drain of human capital and economic resources from the community; rather, Chinatown has never been more capable of attracting a heterogeneous ethnic labor force and mobilizing its ethnic resources to expand its horizon and consolidate its economic base. This chapter describes some major characteristics of the enclave labor force, exploring particularly the human-capital characteristics, the occupational distribution, and the earnings of the Chinese immigrant workers.

The Enclave Labor Market

New York City concentrated about 16 percent of the nation's total Chinese population by 1980; it has been a major receiving city of Chinese immigration since the turn of the century, with the number of newcomers growing rapidly in recent years. Most of the recent immigrants entering New York tend to stay in the city to grasp opportunities provided by the booming enclave economy. They are more likely to participate in the ethnic labor market than in the larger labor market, whereas U.S.-born Chinese are more likely to participate in the larger economy. Immigrant Chinese who remain within the networks of Chinatown do not seem to be seriously penalized for the segregation. Rather, many of them often do better economically than those who accept entry-level jobs available in the open labor market. This evidence supports the enclave-economy model. However, there has been a controversy over findings from ethnic enclaves, using the census data.[1]

The original proposition of the enclave-economy model states that immigrant workers in the enclave labor market achieve greater returns on human capital than those who participate in the outside economy.[2] Based on research among recent immigrants in Miami's Cuban community, Alejandro Portes and his colleagues reported that those who worked within the enclave had a greater probability of becoming self-employed entrepreneurs. Compared to immigrants who were employed in the secondary labor market, those in the enclave had occupations that more closely corresponded with their educational attainment, and earnings that more closely corresponded with their occupational status.

Portes's interpretation of such findings has been questioned by Jimy M. Sanders and Victor Nee, who analyzed census data for Cuban immigrants in Florida and for Chinese immigrants in California.[3] They reasoned that if human-capital investments yielded greater returns to persons tied to the enclave, such returns should show up as effects of education and labor-market experience (and possibly English-language ability) on earnings. Portes did not find such effects on earnings in his research on recent immigrants in Miami or in parallel studies of recent Mexican immigrants, but this hypothesis was certainly consistent with the strong emphasis in his theoretical writings on the superior returns on skills and past human-capital investments of enclave workers. And one might reasonably expect to find such relationships in a sample that included immigrants from a wider variety of time periods.

Sanders and Nee distinguished ethnic group members who could be categorized as entrepreneurs from those who were employed by others. They found that among Cuban immigrant entrepreneurs earnings were positively associated with college education and labor-market experience, both within and outside of the Miami-Hialeah enclave. Among Cuban employees, however, there was a significant earnings return on education and labor-market experience only outside of the enclave economy.[4] The analysis for Chinese immigrants in California generally reproduced these results. Sanders and Nee concluded that the earnings return on human capital in enclave economies was mostly limited to those immigrants who became entrepreneurs.

In their published response to these findings, Portes and Leif Jensen criticized Sanders and Nee's study on theoretical and methodological grounds, concluded that the findings were "irrelevant" to the earnings-return hypothesis, and reported the results of their own analyses of census data, which, they said, contradicted those of Sanders and Nee.[5] The controversy, in fact, described two sides of the same coin: One emphasized the positive earnings returns for human capital among enclave participants; the other looked at the negative impact of the enclave as an extension of the larger secondary economy. The factual disparities were largely due to the operationalization of the concept of the enclave. The two teams of researchers disagreed because the results of the analysis depended on which indicator was employed.

If earnings returns from such human-capital investments as education and labor-market experience were limited to ethnic entrepreneurs, as reported by Sanders and Nee, the positive function of the enclave would be sharply circumscribed. In their critique, Portes and Jensen accepted the general strategy of comparing models of earnings for persons within and outside of the enclave (although Portes's previous work compared the enclave to the primary and secondary labor markets as distinct economic sectors) and comparing models for workers with models for entrepreneurs. But they criticized Sanders and Nee for incorrectly operationalizing the concept of enclave.

For Portes, "enclave entrepreneurs are owners of firms in an area where similar enterprises concentrate. Enclave workers are employees of these firms."[6] Portes and Jensen argued that Sanders and Nee, by defining the enclave in terms of "place of residence," missed the central element in the concept. Further, they asserted that the Sanders and Nee definition was inherently biased because the "place of residence" procedure excluded the better-off segment of enclave participants, who might have moved out of the residential enclave to more affluent neighborhoods or suburbs elsewhere, and overrepresented the worse-off segment of the population, who were more likely to reside within the geographical enclave.[7]

Portes and Jensen proposed that census data of the type analyzed by Sanders and Nee be organized according to "place of work," rather than "place of residence." But the two methods have one thing in common: They are both geographically bound. Neither is sensitive to ethnic ownership or to the ethnic composition of the labor force of the firm that employs it. Through a replication of New York City's Chinatown, I examine and compare three possible ways of defining the economic enclave: by place of residence, by place of work, and by industry. Each aspect partially captures the concept of the economic enclave. I simply use these measures as indicators of the likelihood that a person works in the enclave.

These three definitions require detailed discussion and defense. The place-of-residence definition assumes that Chinese immigrants who live in New York City are more likely to participate in the enclave economy than are those who live in surrounding areas. This assumption is justified by the concentration of the region's Chinese population in New York City. The 1980 Census showed that 84.5 percent of New York State's Chinese lived in New York City, and the majority of New York City's Chinese were concentrated in three counties—New York County (41.9 percent), Kings County (21.0 percent) and Queens County (31.8 percent). Further, 73 percent of New York County's Chinese lived within fourteen census tracts in the extended Chinatown area in Lower East Manhattan. Chinese immigrants, particularly recent immigrants, have tended to seek both residences and jobs in Manhattan's Chinatown or the newly developing satellite Chinatowns in Flushing, Queens, and Sunset Park, Brooklyn. The Public Use Microdata Sample (PUMS) showed that of those Chinese immigrant employees who lived in New York City, about 25 percent worked outside the city, and they tended to be restaurant workers (61 percent). Chinese immigrants who lived outside New York City were far less likely to work in the city; only 21 percent of the immigrant employees who lived outside the city commuted into the city to work. About 63 percent of the nonresidents who did work in the city were in high-ranking managerial, professional, and technical jobs in the core economy. This pattern is possible because New York City, especially Manhattan, is also a central business district for the metropolitan area.

Using a place-of-residence definition for a study of the New York Chinatown may be more defensible than the residence definition adopted by Sanders and Nee. The city of San Francisco accounted for only a little more than a quarter (82,480 of 322,309) of California's Chinese population in 1980, while other large concentrations could be found elsewhere in that state (for example, 18 percent of California's Chinese lived in Oakland and the surrounding communities, and 14 percent lived in the city of Los Angeles). Thus what Sanders and Nee defined as outside the enclave may well include residential enclaves other than San Francisco.[8]

Another way to define the enclave is by place of work. In using this definition, I delimit the enclave as Chinese immigrants working in New York City. In the previous chapter I showed that most of the Chinese-owned businesses were located in New York City, where thousands of ethnic jobs were provided for Chinese immigrants. The 1980 census also showed that 67 percent of the immigrant Chinese workers who lived in New York City and adjacent counties in New York and New Jersey, worked in New York City.

In contrast to the two geographical definitions, it is also possible to define the enclave by industrial sectors. Because ownership information is not provided in the PUMS data, I rely on information about the ethnic composition of particular industries. I assume that sectors in which Chinese immigrants are overrepresented constitute the enclave economy, and I regard all others as nonenclave. Recent studies of New York City's Chinatown indicate that the garment and restaurant businesses are the two basic Chinese industries. The 1980 PUMS data showed that 27 percent of the immigrant Chinese labor force in New York City worked in the garment and textile-related industries (as compared to 5 percent for all workers in New York City) and 25 percent worked in eating and drinking places, apparently restaurants (as compared to 4 percent for all workers). Finally, some 16 percent of Chinese immigrants worked in retail shops and service occupations likely to be ethnic-owned businesses (I included the wholesale and retail trades, business and repair services, personal services, and health services, except hospitals).

The 1988 *Chinese Business Guide and Directory for Metropolitan New York and Boston* further confirmed this distribution: the garment industry (a total of 437 entries) and restaurant business (781) alone made up 20 percent of the total number of entries.[9] Other Chinese-owned services catering predominantly to a Chinese clientele were also well represented, for example, barber shops and beauty salons (111); offices of herbal doctors (101); herbal stores (53); doctors (300); dentists (98); grocery stores (187); gift shops (65); jewelry stores (97); insurance and real estate agencies (320); restaurant equipment suppliers (92); bookstores, entertainment facilities, and video-rental stores (81); travel agencies (115); and so on. Thus, the enclave niches are the garment industry, the restaurant business, and the ethnic-oriented retail and service industries.[10] This definition is not precise, but no doubt a large proportion of the Chinese immigrant population works in those niches.

The census data are not sufficient to distinguish between the enclave labor market and the larger labor market. These data have at least two limits: the PUMS data limit details on place of residence, place of work, and other selected items to protect the confidentiality of the respondents. Thus, there is no way to determine accurately whether the individual concerned lives or works in the enclave. Moreover, the data are not sensitive to ownership of industries and thus do not capture the distinction between enclave industries and nonenclave ones, regardless of geographical location. It may be that certain types of ethnic businesses, particularly those serving a broader clientele, spread throughout the geographical area, rather than being confined to the physical enclave. Therefore, the boundaries of the enclave are fairly arbitrary. However, whether the economic enclave is defined by place of residence, place of work, or industry, there is a large amount of overlap among the three. Of those Chinese immigrants who worked in New York City, only 10 percent resided outside the city, while 54 percent of those who worked outside the city also lived outside. Further, 69 percent of those who lived and worked in New York City were employed in what I have defined as enclave industries, compared to only 33 percent of those who lived and worked outside the city. This empirical overlap encourages confidence in all three definitions of the enclave.

Human-Capital Characteristics
of the Ethnic Labor Force

Immigrant Chinese Workers in New York

Generally, an adult Chinese immigrant, who typically has limited knowledge of English and little information about the larger labor market, does not expect to participate in the large economy. Upon arrival, he or she is immediately introduced to the enclave labor market by family and kinship networks. Yun-guang's example is typical. Yun-guang was twenty-three years old when interviewed. He had come to the United States with his twenty-year-old brother in 1987 under the second preference category of the immigration law—unmarried sons and daughters of permanent residents. His mother came two years earlier to work on their petitions. Before he came, he had worked for a machine tool factory in Guangzhou for five years, and he expected that he would continue working as a mechanic. At the time of the interview Yun-guang was working as a plumber in a Chinatown firm, and his brother was working in a garment factory. When asked why he chose to work in Chinatown, he gave the following answer:

> It never occurred to me that I could work outside Chinatown. There may be a lot of opportunities which my mechanic's skill would fit; but I don't know much English and I don't know how to go look for jobs out there. Before I came, I knew a lot about opportunities in Chinatown from my mother and my sister's family who were already

here. They kind of guided me into Chinatown. So when I came, I was immediately introduced to a plumbing firm in Chinatown. I think people, in general, are eager to start working as soon as they arrive here. They've got to have a job to satisfy their basic needs and to save money for future plans. Since many of them don't know English, I guess it is natural for them to grab at anything that is immediately available, which is mostly found in Chinatown through your folks. I think that is the reason why people don't usually consider an outside opportunity when there are jobs inside. Also, it is not so bad working in Chinatown. I don't think you would get less pay if you have the skill needed, and are able to work longer hours for more money.[11]

The majority of the recent Chinese immigrants, regardless of place of origin (whether from China, Hong Kong, or Taiwan), often started working immediately upon arrival. Culturally they would feel ashamed not to work but to accept welfare and public assistance. This is a positive quality that plays a crucial role in the development of the economic enclave. Because of the strong drive to work, the enclave is continuously provided with a pool of ambitious entrepreneurs, well-qualified professionals, and goal-oriented workers. The labor-force participation rate for immigrant Chinese has been consistently high. The 1980 PUMS data showed that 77 percent of immigrant Chinese between twenty-five and sixty-four years old were active in the labor force, as compared to 68 percent of non-Hispanic whites. They also had a much lower rate of unemployment (3.9 percent versus 6.4 percent for whites). With job opportunities available in Chinatown, many Chinese immigrants simply stayed inside the community.

Table 6-1 shows the basic human-capital characteristics of immigrant Chinese workers and foreign-born non-Hispanic white workers.[12] In New York City, immigrant Chinese workers were younger than their non-Hispanic white counterparts. Chinese females made up a larger share of the labor force (44 percent) than white females (37 percent). Chinese workers were more likely to be married and to live with children under seventeen years old. Only 52 percent of the Chinese workers reported having good English skills, as compared to 86 percent of the foreign-born whites, and 96 percent of the Chinese spoke a language other than English at home. The Chinese workers were newer immigrants; close to three-quarters of them came to the United States after 1965, whereas the majority of the white immigrants came before 1965. Half of the Chinese workers were naturalized U.S. citizens. The Chinese workers were

Table 6-1. Labor-Force Characteristics of the Foreign-Born Population in the New York Metropolitan Area, Chinese and Non-Hispanic Whites, 1980

Characteristics	New York City		Outside N.Y.C.	
	Chinese	Whites	Chinese	Whites
Number of persons	2,188	12,050	531	12,382
% Females	43.8	37.3	38.4	36.2
Mean age	41.7	44.3	39.8	44.8
% Married	79.5	72.4	87.2	82.9
% With children under 17	61.5	59.7	68.9	59.9
% Immigrated after 1965	72.4	41.4	66.5	32.2
% U.S. citizens	49.5	65.2	57.4	70.3
% Speak English well	51.6	86.2	87.0	87.7
% Speak a language other than English at home	96.2	73.5	94.7	65.3
% Some college	29.3	33.7	72.9	32.1
% Some high school	33.3	38.1	18.1	40.0
% Elementary or no schooling	37.4	28.2	9.0	27.9
Mean years of school completed	12.1	13.8	17.7	13.7
Class of workers				
% Private sector	84.9	77.4	77.4	77.2
% Public sector	5.4	9.1	11.7	9.3
% Self-employed	9.7	13.5	10.9	13.5
% Worked over 40 hours per week	73.5	67.1	71.4	73.1
% Worked in enclave industries	64.4	34.1	29.9	28.9
Occupation				
% Managerial and professional	19.0	25.6	53.0	25.6
% Technical and precision production	8.2	18.4	14.3	20.9
% Sales, services, and administrative support	42.3	39.5	24.4	32.5
% Laborers	30.5	16.5	8.3	21.0
% Lived in owner-occupied housing	32.5	39.5	76.0	74.8
Mean individual income in 1979	$9,780	$15,332	$18,543	$17,584

Table 6-1. (Continued)

Characteristics	New York City		Outside N.Y.C.	
	Chinese	Whites	Chinese	Whites
% Earned over $15,000 in				
1979	18.3	41.9	55.4	49.3
Mean family income in 1979	$19,756	$21,685	$31,252	$28,748

Source: U.S. Census of Population and Housing: 1980 PUMS.

Note: Including all foreign-born Chinese and non-Hispanic white workers between 25 and 64 years of age who worked at least 160 hours and earned a minimum of $500 in 1979.

more disadvantaged in their educational attainment. Some 30 percent of them had some college education, but the undereducated or uneducated made up 37 percent. Non-Hispanic whites showed much stronger educational credentials; they had a higher percentage of college education, a lower illiteracy rate, and a higher average number of years of school completed. Immigrant Chinese workers held predominantly private-sector wage-earning jobs (85 percent versus 77 percent for whites). They were much less likely to work in the public sector. The Chinese males also showed a high self-employment rate (10 percent), though not as high a rate as that of the whites (13 percent). Immigrant Chinese tended to work longer hours; 74 percent of them worked over forty hours per week on average. More than 60 percent of them were engaged in enclave industries. Both individual earnings ($9,780) and family income ($19,756) were lower than those of whites. Only 18 percent of the individual Chinese immigrant workers earned more than $15,000 in 1979 (as compared to 42 percent for whites).

For immigrant Chinese who lived outside New York, the situation is much better. Obviously, immigrant Chinese who have stronger human-capital credentials tend to reside in the suburbs. Although the majority of them (67 percent) are recent immigrants, they show a much better English proficiency than their co-ethnics living in New York City, and similar to that of the white immigrants. A much higher percentage of them have some college education (73 percent versus 32 percent for immigrant whites). They are less likely to be engaged in enclave industries than their co-ethnics in New York City. More of them are managers and professionals. Both individual income and family income are higher than those of immigrant white workers and substantially higher than those of their co-ethnics in New York City.

These results show that recent immigrant Chinese have varied levels of human-capital credentials. They are not just uniformly uneducated and poor laborers like the sojourning Chinese of earlier years. Their drive to work and succeed contribute to a very high labor-force participation rate for both men and women. However, compared to immigrant whites, the Chinese are clearly disadvantaged in terms of citizenship status associated with recency of immigration, English-language ability, and education. Fewer of them are executives, managers, and professionals, and more are laborers. Their income is much lower. These disadvantages are mainly related to their immigrant status, lack of sufficient English, lack of transferable education and skills, lack of information concerning the larger society, and the length of stay in the United States. First-generation immigrant Chinese still have a long way to go to achieve parity with the white majority. Many of them may never be able to catch up; they are so occupied with work that they can hardly find the time and energy to improve their individual human-capital characteristics. Yet, they believe that their children can make progress. Someday they will see their children surpass them and watch their families move up the socioeconomic ladder.

U.S.-Born Chinese Workers in New York

How well are the children of immigrant Chinese doing? Only 10 percent of New York City's Chinese labor force and 15 percent of the ethnic labor force elsewhere in the New York metropolitan area were born in the United States. Compared to their foreign-born co-ethnics, native-born Chinese living in the city have much better human-capital credentials and occupational and socioeconomic achievement. But outside the city, their immigrant co-ethnics did just as well, and they display no clear advantage other than in being native-born (see Table 6-2). Influenced by the immigrant family background, native-born Chinese tend to be bilingual; close to 60 percent of them still speak a language other than English at home. Compared to their white counterparts, only those who resided outside New York City appeared superior in socioeconomic achievement. For those who lived in the city, despite their stronger human-capital credentials and occupational achievement, income levels were lower. Although 67 percent of them had some college education (as compared to 50 percent for whites) and 44 percent of them were managers or professionals (as compared to 38 percent), only 43 percent of them earned over $15,000 in 1979, compared to 53 percent of whites.

The diversity of human-capital characteristics in the ethnic labor force

Table 6-2. Labor-Force Characteristics of the U.S.-Born Population in the New York Metropolitan Area, Chinese and Non-Hispanic Whites, 1980

Characteristics	New York City		Outside N.Y.C.	
	Chinese	Whites	Chinese	Whites
Number of persons	257	51,846	97	113,384
% Females	40.5	43.2	40.2	38.8
Mean age	35.4	41.9	37.9	42.8
% Married	48.6	56.4	75.3	75.7
% With children under 17	52.9	56.7	54.6	55.8
% Speak a language other than English at home	65.0	15.1	52.6	5.7
% Some college	66.9	49.8	67.0	44.9
% Some high school	22.6	41.7	24.7	46.0
% Elementary or no schooling	10.5	8.5	8.3	9.1
Mean years of school completed	16.6	16.1	17.2	15.7
Class of workers				
% Private sector workers	68.9	71.5	78.4	70.4
% Public sector workers	20.6	19.1	16.4	19.6
% Self-employed	10.5	9.4	5.2	10.0
% Worked over 40 hours per week	63.8	60.3	61.9	67.4
% Worked in enclave industries	27.6	20.5	17.5	21.5
Occupation				
% Managerial and professional	43.6	38.2	43.8	35.4
% Technical and precision production	9.3	5.7	20.8	7.6
% Sales, services, and administrative support	41.2	50.7	28.2	46.7
% Laborers	5.9	5.4	7.2	10.3
% Lived in owner-occupied housing	35.9	36.3	75.3	77.9
Mean individual income in 1979	$14,052	$17,523	$19,833	$18,940
% Earned over $15,000 in 1979	43.2	52.8	60.8	54.9
Mean family income in 1979	$21,081	$22,799	$31,534	$30,697

Source: U.S. Census of Population and Housing: 1980 PUMS.
Note: Including all U.S.-born Chinese and non-Hispanic white workers between 25 and 64 years of age who worked at least 160 hours and earned a minimum of $500 in 1979.

reflects greater progress for the group as a whole: recent immigrant Chinese have shown much stronger labor-market credentials than their predecessors, and the second-generation Chinese have already surpassed their non-Hispanic white counterparts in average educational attainment. The next question is: How do Chinese workers fare in the labor market as opposed to their non-Hispanic white counterparts, or does higher educational attainment diminish the significance of structural, cultural, and racial barriers to social mobility for the Chinese? I first examine the case of male workers.

Returns on Human Capital: Male Workers

The significant educational achievement among second-generation Chinese has been celebrated as a model for the successful assimilation of immigrants. As a natural consequence of this success we should expect that the Chinese would overcome structural, cultural, and racial barriers that used to limit their labor-market options and block their upward social mobility, to achieve parity with the majority in occupation and income. In Chinatown, education has indeed been emphasized as the single most important means of status attainment. Families have invested a large amount of economic and social resources in their children, hoping that their children's upward mobility would eventually pull the family a step up on the socioeconomic ladder. In fact, Chinese children attending public schools and colleges have been doing exceptionally well, and upon graduation, they seem to be able to obtain fairly good employment.

Education, Occupation, and Earnings

It has generally been taken for granted that improvement in the overall levels of human capital increases the chances of economic assimilation, that there are positive occupational and earnings returns on human capital, that education enhances and permits a wider choice of occupation. Therefore, because of the significant improvement in education among the Chinese, particularly the second-generation Chinese, it has been believed that the Chinese are as "successful" as native whites in the U.S. labor market.[13]

But does education positively affect occupational mobility for the Chinese? According to the 1980 census, among New York City's foreign-born Chinese males with at least some college education, 52 percent were in top-ranking positions as managers and professionals, just a little lower than that for foreign-born non-Hispanic whites (55 percent). Native-

Table 6-3. Average Individual Income, by Education, Place of Birth, and Ethnicity, for Male Workers, New York City, 1979

Ethnicity	Elementary School	Percent[1]	High School	Percent[1]	College	Percent[1]
U.S.-born white	$14,293	100.0	$17,616	100.0	$24,043	100.0
U.S.-born Chinese	$ 7,105	49.7	$10,930	62.0	$16,395	68.2
Foreign-born white	$13,929	100.0	$15,993	100.0	$23,075	100.0
Foreign-born Chinese	$ 7,708	55.3	$ 8,519	53.2	$17,017	73.7

Source: U.S. Census of Population and Housing: 1980 PUMS.

Note: Including all Chinese and non-Hispanic white men between 25 and 64 years of age who worked at least 160 hours and earned a minimum of $500 in 1979.

[1] Individual income of Chinese as a percentage of the income of their non-Hispanic white counterparts.

born Chinese males with at least some college education did a little better in comparison with their co-ethnics, but still lagged behind native-born whites in their occupational distribution: 54 percent of them were in those top-ranking positions as compared to 61 percent of whites.

These findings support the general assumption that education positively affects occupational distribution. Although male Chinese still have some difficulty in obtaining executive and managerial positions, overall, the Chinese, despite their minority status, are able to move up the occupational scale by means of increased educational attainment. It is natural to expect that education will bring equal earnings returns as well. A look across each row of Table 6-3 reveals a positive linear relationship: all individuals, regardless of place of birth and ethnicity, consistently earned more with increased education. That is, the higher the education, the higher the income. These descriptive data indicate that improved education pays off. They also imply that educational attainment is associated with occupational achievement.

Nonetheless, a look up and down each column in Table 6-3 unveils another pattern. Surprisingly, economic rewards of education vary substantially according to place of birth and ethnicity. Native-born non-Hispanic white males had the highest average income at every level of education, and the incomes of foreign-born white males at every level of education were very close. However, Chinese males, regardless of place of birth, did not fare as well. Native-born Chinese males with some college education made only about 68 percent as much as native-born white males and 71 percent as much as foreign-born white males. They even

Table 6-4. Average Individual Income, by Occupation, Place of Birth, and Ethnicity, for Male Workers, New York City, 1979

Ethnicity	Blue-Collar	White-Collar Services	White-Collar Professionals	White-Collar Managers
U.S.-born white	$15,901	$18,238	$24,326	$26,516
U.S.-born Chinese	$ 9,956	$11,060	$18,874	$16,060
Chinese income as % of white income	62.6	60.6	77.6	60.6
Foreign-born white	$13,931	$15,441	$23,736	$25,108
Foreign-born Chinese	$ 7,632	$ 8,870	$19,909	$14,701
Chinese income as % of white income	54.8	57.4	83.9	58.5

Source: U.S. Census of Population and Housing: 1980 PUMS.
Note: Including all Chinese and non-Hispanic white men between 25 and 64 years of age who worked at least 160 hours and earned a minimum of $500 in 1979.

made less than their foreign-born co-ethnics: $16,395 versus $17,017. Clearly, Chinese men with the same educational credentials still did not earn as much as non-Hispanic white men. The implication is that ethnicity may influence socioeconomic attainment more strongly than does education.

In terms of occupation, Chinese men, both immigrants and natives were able to move on to higher occupations, but not quite to the top executive and managerial level. The income discrepancies within each level of education may be due to occupational differences. In Table 6-4 a similar pattern can be seen.

For the non-Hispanic white men, the higher the occupational level, the higher the income across every row of the table. But for the Chinese, a disturbing pattern indicates that top executive and managerial positions occupied by the Chinese offered lower returns than the professional positions did. For example, differences in average individual incomes between top executive occupations and professional occupations were $2,814 lower for native-born Chinese men, $5,208 lower for foreign-born Chinese men. Furthermore, the Chinese, regardless of place of birth, consistently earned considerably less than their non-Hispanic white counterparts, no matter what occupational category they were in.

In sum, marked differences in individual and family income still exist between Chinese and whites. In New York City, there is still a large earnings gap between the Chinese and the majority group. Of the foreign-born Chinese living in New York City, 26 percent had an income under $5,000, and 39 percent between $5,000 and $10,000. If we divide earnings over $15,000 into increments of $5,000, in every category the Chinese had a smaller percentage of members than did whites. For example, only 5 percent of the foreign-born Chinese and 5 percent of the native-born Chinese made between $20,000 and $24,999, as opposed to 14 percent of the foreign-born whites and 11 percent of the U.S.-born whites. In the higher income levels, over $30,000, there were even fewer Chinese—3 percent of both foreign-born and native-born Chinese, versus 8 percent of foreign-born whites and 11 percent of native-born whites.

The case of Chinese male workers in New York apparently contradicts the success story often told about the Chinese. These results suggest that disadvantages related to ethnicity or race continue to play a crucial role in the labor market and to affect the mobility patterns of the Chinese. New York City's Chinese are still more disadvantaged than the majority group.

Even the second-generation Chinese, most of whom have been incorporated into the larger economy, still encounter difficulties similar to those faced by their immigrant parents in moving up the socioeconomic ladder. Despite a higher rate of college education, a much lower share in manufacturing or blue-collar jobs, and certain similarities in labor-force characteristics to those of whites, native Chinese do not seem to fare better. They consistently make less than their white counterparts at every level of education and occupation. They often express dissatisfaction with this state of affairs and frustration with the stereotyped view of the Chinese as strictly technical professionals lacking leadership or managerial skills. Mr. Lam, an American-born Chinese working on Wall Street, noted: "People here often think of the Chinese as brilliant at numbers and formulas but incapable of comprehensive planning and management. You are okay as long as you stay where you are and do a good job, and you will also get promoted when the time comes. But wherever you go, there is always a limit, some kind of a threshold that you can't cross. When it comes to leadership or management positions, forget it."[14]

Returns on Human Capital in the Enclave Economy

A key proposition in the theory of ethnic enclave economies is that the enclave opens opportunities for its members that are not easily accessible in the larger society. The enclave labor market, capital market, and consumer market partially shelter ethnic group members from competition with other social groups, from discrimination and abuse on account of their ethnic origins, and from government surveillance and regulations. In many respects these boundaries around the enclave provide tangible benefits to group members and offer a positive alternative to assimilation.

Does Chinatown provide positive earnings and occupational returns to education and other human capital? I used a multivariate model to measure the independent effect of human capital on earnings and occupation, based on 1980 PUMS data.[15] The analysis was done separately for male Chinese immigrant workers and entrepreneurs working in or out of the enclave.[16]

For the earnings-returns models, the dependent variable was the logged value of personal earnings in 1979. For employees, earnings included only income from wages and salaries (INCOME1 in 1980 PUMS); for entrepreneurs, earnings included the sum of salaried income, self-employment income, and other incomes (INCOME1, INCOME2, and INCOME3 in 1980 PUMS). For the occupational mobility models, the dependent variable for occupation was coded according to the 1970 National Opinion Research Center's two-digit occupational prestige scores.[17] There were a large number of independent variables. Those that had clear meaning in terms of human capital include labor-market experience, education, and English-language ability. Marital status, the number of hours worked in 1979, U.S. citizenship, year of immigration, and occupation categories were included as control variables. In the occupational mobility models, log hours worked in 1979 and the occupational dummy variables were deleted as control variables.[18]

Table 6-5 summarizes the model that used the industrial sector as the definition of the enclave. Among male Chinese workers who lived in New York City and worked in the enclave industries, college education conferred significant positive effects. Hours worked and occupation, as control variables, had statistically significant and strong effects. Labor-market experience, elementary education and college education were related to earnings for workers who lived in New York City but worked in the nonenclave industries. It is curious, however, that English-language ability had no effect in this latter group. One would expect from the enclave model that this variable would have greater effects outside the enclave than within. Moreover, U.S. citizenship and hours worked had strong positive effects, but immigrant status had a negative effect on earnings for those working outside the enclave, as expected. For enclave workers, the occupational predictors had strong negative effects on earnings, indicating that those in sales, administrative support, business and service occupations and those who worked as laborers earned signifi-

Table 6-5. Regression Equations Predicting 1979 Earnings (ln) for Male Immigrant Chinese Employees in New York City

	Enclave Industry B^1	Nonenclave Industry B^1
Intercept	5.078**	3.281**
Labor market experience	−.352[2]	.054**
Labor market experience squared	.036[2]	−.911**[2]
Elementary education	.006	−.052**
High school education	−.005	.012
College education	.053**	.063**
English-language skills	.042	.027
U.S. citizen	.054	.146*
Immigration 1975–1979	−.084	−.376**
Immigration 1965–1974	−.032	−.197**
Married	−.017	−.031
Log–hours worked–1979	.525**	.795**
Sales, administrative support, and precision production	−.223**	−.088
Business, protective, and household services	−.414**	−.006
Operators and laborers	−.459**	−.263*
R square	.322	.498
N of cases	666	343

Source: U.S. Census of Population and Housing: 1980 PUMS.

Note: Including only private-sector employees aged 25 to 64 who worked at least 160 hours and earned a minimum of $500 in 1979.

[1] Unstandardized regression coefficients.

[2] The decimal point is moved three places to the right.

*Significant at .05 level, one-tail (the t-ratio is greater than or equal to 1.65).

**Significant at .01 level, one-tail (the t-ratio is greater than or equal to 2.33).

cantly less than the managers, professionals, and technicians. But among nonenclave workers, only the laborers earned significantly less than the managers, professionals, and technicians. The analyses using the place of residence sample and the place of work sample produced similar results for male immigrant Chinese employees.[19]

Table 6-6 presents regression equations for male immigrant Chinese entrepreneurs in the New York metropolitan area. For enclave entre-

Table 6-6. Regression Equations Predicting 1979 Earnings (ln)
for Male Immigrant Chinese Entrepreneurs in the New York
Metropolitan Area

	Enclave Industry B^1	Nonenclave Industry B^1
Intercept	5.555**	−3.456
Labor market experience	−.037	.102*
Labor market experience squared	−.497[2]	−.001*
Elementary education	−.006	.087
High school education	−.010	−.105
College education	.106**	.112*
English-language skills	.334**	.437
U.S. citizen	−.093	−.183
Immigration 1975–1979	−.458*	−.336
Immigration 1965–1974	−.057	−.181
Married	.138	.302
Log–hours worked–1979	.357**	1.312**
Sales, administrative support, and precision production	−.204	−.319**
Business, protective, and household services	.023	−.400**
Operators and laborers	−.195	.191
R square	.264	.545
N of cases	193	72

Source: U.S. Census of Population and Housing: 1980 PUMS.
Note: Including only those who were self-employed or employees of their own firms,
aged 25 to 64, who worked at least 160 hours and earned a minimum of $500 in 1979.
[1] Unstandardized regression coefficients.
[2] The decimal point is moved three places to the right.
*Significant at .05 level, one-tail (the t-ratio is greater than or equal to 1.65).
**Significant at .01 level, one-tail (the t-ratio is greater than or equal to 2.33).

preneurs, college education and English skills had significant effects on
earnings. Hours worked and immigration between 1975 and 1979 (showing a strong negative effect) were significant control variables. The effect
of college education for nonenclave entrepreneurs was similar to its effect
for enclave entrepreneurs. Labor-market experience had a significant
effect; so did hours worked and occupation. However, English skills had

no significant effects. Unlike the results reported for California Chinese by Sanders and Nee, it appears that these human-capital variables were important for both workers and entrepreneurs in the New York enclave.

These results differed from those that might be predicted from a reading of the existing literature. Unlike Sanders and Nee, I found positive returns on human capital for workers both inside and outside the enclave. And unexpectedly, English skills did not have a significantly positive effect for workers and entrepreneurs outside the enclave. Finally, unlike the portrait of the enclave as a place where cultural assimilation was unnecessary, I found positive returns on English language for entrepreneurs within the enclave but not outside. The analyses for entrepreneurs using the place of residence and place of work to define the enclave also showed significant earnings return on human capital in the enclave.[20]

In terms of occupational returns, I found that labor-market experience had a significant but slightly negative effect on occupation for Chinese immigrant workers in the enclave but not for workers outside the enclave. High school education added an average of 2.7 points to the occupational scale for outside workers but nothing for enclave workers. However, college education was a significant coefficient for both groups of workers; it added one point more to the occupational scale for enclave workers than for outside workers. English-language ability brought significant returns for nonenclave workers. U.S. citizenship did not bring returns in either group. For immigrant entrepreneurs, regardless of how the enclave was defined, labor-market experience and college education had significantly positive effects on occupational scores in the enclave.[21]

Chinatown: A Better Option

One consistent finding is that college education has positive returns for the earnings and occupations of male enclave workers, regardless of how the enclave is defined. My overall findings show that, among New York's Chinese immigrant men, enclave workers are able to take advantage of human-capital resources to increase earnings (although not consistently more than workers outside of the enclave) and to achieve occupational prestige. Further, there is no consistent evidence that entrepreneurs in the enclave or outside of the enclave have greater returns on human capital than do similarly situated workers. These findings support the enclave economy model in the sense that the enclave serves as a segmented sector of the U.S. economy and provides a positive alternative for immigrant incorporation. However, hypotheses of this sort require more comparative studies of enclave labor markets. In such research, my experience suggests that the PUMS is a useful source of information on labor markets, particularly if the researcher has enough other information on which to base judgments about enclave definitions. But I emphasize that census data are only a proxy for more direct measures, which require information on the ownership and labor-force composition of the firms in which respondents are employed.

My fieldwork data, that is, extensive interviews and participant observation, supplement and further explain these empirical findings, particularly in three aspects. First, there is a greater possibility of self-employment in the enclave; second, education has an effect on socioeconomic attainment in the enclave as much as outside the enclave; third, English has a stronger effect on socioeconomic attainment in the enclave than outside the enclave; and fourth, there are both material and symbolic reasons for immigrant Chinese to choose Chinatown as their point of departure.

Self-employment as an Indicator of Social Mobility

Statistical data show that people who work in the enclave are more likely to become self-employed. Among immigrants in Chinatown, there are two overwhelming goals: to own a business and to own a house. Owning a house is like putting money in a safe place and, at the same time, generating a much higher profit than interest on a bank account. Owning a business is like making a dream come true. For most of the immigrants, a "boss" always seems to enjoy higher prestige and make more money than a worker, and the boss always has the power to control things.

Many enclave workers are excited about the opportunities in the enclave. Mr. Liang, an immigrant store owner, commented:

> In Chinatown a growing demand for goods and services, with the resulting development of the local economy, provides ample opportunities for self-employment. Chinatown workers learn to work hard and save money to become a boss, because they know the opportunity is there. If they didn't see this, they might not be so motivated. A couple of my former employees have taken off to start a business similar to mine. They acquired all the necessary tricks to operate the business while working for me and have now turned out to be my competitors. It doesn't matter that much to me, since I always anticipate competition.[22]

Mr. Kuang, a waiter in Chinatown, who had saved money for nearly six years and was about to open a fast-food takeout store in Long Island, shared Liang's idea of self-employment in Chinatown:

> Although I have been working at least sixty-six hours per week for all these years, and the hourly pay has not been so good, only about $4 dollars per hour, I have been able to accumulate enough to make a significant move. I am not sure whether I could have done it if I had been employed outside of the Chinatown economy; maybe I could, but I just would not have even thought of trying.
>
> In Chinatown, I always have a sense of security around people of my own kind, whereas outside, I would be scared simply because I would feel like I look foreign and sound foreign.
>
> To own a small business in New York City is all I want and all I could possibly achieve. Being a boss, I can enjoy more economic freedom and be more in control. I don't think I could get any farther if I left Chinatown and the city.[23]

Young Li, an immigrant who obtained his master's degree in engineering in New York, worked for one of the import-export firms in Chinatown, trading between Chinatown and the Orient. I asked whether he had chosen to work in the enclave. "Yes," he replied:

> I can give you reasons why I did. It is quite simple. There is a lot of potential in doing business with China, Hong Kong, and Taiwan. There are so many immigrants here who need ethnic consumer goods and foodstuff imported from the Orient. Also, the Americans have started to compete for a share of the market in the Orient, particularly China. Doing business here in Chinatown, you can take full advantage of ethnicity. Just being a Chinese, with a smart brain of course, will help you a lot. You are familiar with the culture, the mentality and the ways of doing business in China. That is the advantage of trading with China. I could get a job outside without much difficulty if I wanted. But then I would have lost this advantage.[24]

Young Li was traveling back and forth between the United States and China frequently and was doing very well. He seemed to enjoy his work. He was confident in his career in the trading business and had plans to start his own firm.

"Everything is good here," said Mr. Lee, a native of Hong Kong who arrived in New York's Chinatown in 1980, starting to work as a waiter.

If you work hard and focus straight, you can make it no matter what you do or where you are. However, Chinatown, to me and probably to most of the newcomers, is a good place to start. People keep saying that jobs in Chinatown are worse and pay less. But when they go out, they find comparable jobs which do not pay much higher; and most of the time, they find that their weekly pay is much less than the take-home cash of the Chinatown workers. So they come back here, by choice. There are many different kinds of jobs available outside of Chinatown, jobs that pay much more. The question is, Can you get one?

Lee worked as a waiter for seven years. He had now become the owner of two restaurants, one in Manhattan's Chinatown, the other in Sunset Park, Brooklyn. "It feels good to be a boss." [25]

Being a boss is certainly the primary goal for many immigrant Chinese, and in Chinatown, the chances of moving up to self-employment are better. Some of those who cannot make it to the entrepreneurial class choose to work in Chinatown to fulfill their other goals—to accumulate enough money to buy a home and to support their children through college. Apparently, within the enclave workers are inspired by the success of their bosses and motivated to work hard and spend less in order to accumulate capital for self-employment. This is possible in Chinatown, because of the continuous influx of cheap labor and the growing demand for a wide variety of goods and services by the Chinese population in particular and the larger population in general.

The Effect of Education on Social Mobility

Despite the fact that the enclave is dominated by low-wage and labor-intensive jobs, education pays off in Chinese men's socioeconomic attainment in the enclave economy as much as in the open economy. It is misleading to say that within the community one does not need much education to move ahead. This is probably true for most of the low-wage, labor-intensive work. Yet, today's Chinatown has developed a far wider range of economic activities than before. Poor education could mean a reduction of income and a loss of upward mobility.

One example comes from my direct observation of Chinatown's employment agencies. Most of the jobs listed in these agencies are restaurant jobs, and thus, those who come in to the agencies are mostly uneducated immigrant men (except for a few foreign students who are not eligible to work and come to seek temporary off-the-books jobs). Once I sat in an agency for just fifteen minutes, and I heard an agent lecture a young man, apparently a newcomer, loudly and impatiently: "You must be crazy! Go look at yourself in that mirror! How much education have you got? How much English do you know? You don't look like you have either, and you are asking for a $1,500 monthly salary? I only have a dishwashing job that pays $800 per month. If you don't like it, you do not have any job here." [26] The poor man was quite embarrassed, and people around me told me that the well-educated people are less interested in restaurant jobs and are not likely to drop by the agencies in the first place. Even if they have to take restaurant jobs, they are better able to read the ads, to get around by themselves, and to bargain directly with the bosses, and they tend to get the front-house and supervisory positions that pay higher. "When you come here, people assume that you only want a job of any kind. They don't expect you to bargain for wages, because you do not know what's going on."

Mr. Chen's experience provided another example.

> I immigrated three years ago. I first worked as a dishwasher for half a year and then changed to my present job as a mechanic in a fortune cookie factory. Before immigration, I was trained in a vocational school as a mechanic and had a few years of work experience. Education and work experience did not count in the dishwashing job, but they did in my present job. If I hadn't had the skills and experience, I would have been confined to operative work in the factory, and I would have been paid at least one-third less. [27]

Mr. Chen had to start working the day after his arrival. A dishwashing job, which paid $200 per week, was immediately available for him through the help of his friend. Then he found a mechanic's job by himself, which paid $350 per week. However, it should be noted that, as Chen said, many jobs in Chinatown required long working hours. Chen worked ten to twelve hours a day, six days a week on his present job, as he had in the first one.

Many enclave workers shared similar views of the effect of education. Mr. Chiu, who started a Chinatown garment factory after completing his college education, felt very strongly that education played an important role in running a business,

> In Chinatown, everybody talks about opening a garment shop. It seems that the garment industry can bring easy and quick cash for whoever invests in it. This is not true. People are overly optimistic about the industry and do not see the high turnover rate and the

cutthroat competition within the industry. In such a severely competitive business environment, if you do not know the business well enough, if you do not know English, if you do not have enough education, your chance of success will be a lot slimmer, and you could barely make ends meet, let alone making a surplus.

I have three years of college education. My wife also has a degree in dress design. Our education helped us a lot in our business start-up and operation. I feel that if you are well educated, you are better able to plan, budget, and control your business both at present and in the long run. Moreover, education can enable you to avoid unnecessary operating costs, allow you to bargain for prices with the manufacturers more effectively and become more flexible. In a word, your business will not survive the competition if you do not have a good brain. I believe experience and education can make a difference in succeeding in business.[28]

Mr. Lee, another worker, shared Mr. Chiu's view. Mr. Lee was twenty-five years old. He had immigrated with his family twenty years before and had had his degree in mechanical engineering for three years. After graduation from college, he chose to take over his father's garment factory on Elizabeth Street in Chinatown. When asked why he did not try to look for a job in the big companies outside Chinatown, and how important his college education was to the business, he replied:

First of all, I am lucky because I have my father's business. But even if I hadn't, I still think I could have taken a job somewhere temporarily just to save enough money to run my own business. Suppose racial discrimination does not have an effect in the larger economy (I think it does), I would still prefer to take over my father's business, because being somebody's boss is far better than being supervised by somebody else.

Economically, if you have a good education, if you work hard and manage well, you will have a much better chance to increase your income than a wage earner will. The starting salary for junior mechanical engineers in many of the large firms is from $20,000 to $24,000 a year. I made more than that in the first year in my business. Indeed, I am doing much better than my father, because my education helps. For example, my father used to hire a mechanic for the factory and a middleman to negotiate with the manufacturers, both of which I do myself. That saved a lot of the operating cost. My father did not know the benefits of the "laws" and how to deal with the labor unions, the workers and the government, whereas I can turn these around to work to my benefit. My father did not make long-term plans for business expansion and was content with what he had, whereas I know better how to plan for the future. Instead of saving money in the bank, I reinvest it back into the business.

Now I do not only have this garment shop but also a restaurant. I am thinking of opening a noodle factory. I am not saying that my father failed the past ten years because he did not achieve what I have done in the last three years. His poor education only led him that far. In Chinatown, there are two types of businessmen: One is conservative and narrow-minded like my father, and the other is ambitious and adventuresome like myself. The level of education determines, to a large extent, what category one would fall into, and it certainly makes a difference in business.[29]

The positive effect of education, particularly college education, on socioeconomic status is important both in and out of Chinatown. The implication is that those who are better educated have choices, whether in the enclave or outside. However, it does not necessarily mean that a well-educated immigrant is not affected by racial discrimination and structural difficulties if he is outside. Presumed racism is, perhaps, one of the reasons (other than economic) why the well-educated choose to participate in the enclave. Education enables one to deal better with environmental constraints that have been mentioned. In this sense, enclave participation is both economically rational and emotionally understandable.

The Role of English Proficiency in the Enclave

Generally, English-language ability is among the most important factors for assimilation, and the main reason why immigrants keep to Chinatown is because they do not know the language. However, particularly for ethnic entrepreneurs, English skills significantly affected earnings in the enclave but not outside it. Why does English pay off in the enclave, where it seems less essential, but not in the open economy, where it seems so important? There are probably two explanations, one related to the goals of immigrants and the other to the effects of racial discrimination. In an interview, Mr. Chin, a second-generation Chinese-American, who was the program director of the New York Chinatown History Project, gave some explanation.

From my personal experience, this has to do with different mentalities and goals of the pre-1965 and post-1965 Chinese immigrants.

Before 1965, Chinatown was dominated by a sojourning mentality and a short-term goal. People always had the idea that someday, ten, fifteen, or twenty years later, they were going to return home. Even long after they had decided to stay or knew intellectually that they could not go back, they still held on to that mentality, unconsciously and emotionally.

Their goal, thus, was nothing but to make enough money to bring home. They did not see any necessity and did not intend to learn English, for the kind of jobs they were engaged in required little English. There was no reason to leave Chinatown. If you didn't speak Chinese, you would be looked down upon, because the mentality was still based in China.

Why after 1965 did things begin to reverse so that people who spoke English well were suddenly looked up to? I think the estimation depends on what your goals are and what you think is going to happen. If the goal is to stay here, to make money and develop things here, then English becomes very important and you will try to speak English as fluently as possible in order to become integrated into the mainstream.

Economically, Chinatown is really a passing-through point; it is not a settling point. Chinese immigrants come to Chinatown, because they do not have to speak English right away and the transition is easier. As they proceed with their dreams, they will realize that they can be part of the society and that certain things can be done only if they know the language. They also realize that if they speak English with more fluency, everything is possible. The first priority is to survive, but beyond survival, the goal is to do better. Doing better requires better English. Within the enclave, everybody speaks Chinese or Cantonese. The more English you can speak, the better the chances are for interfacing with people outside the community and taking advantage of opportunities outside the community.

Mr. Chin expressed his feeling that, in Chinatown, better English skills usually mean more money.

Why? Because you can interact with people outside Chinatown. I can give you an example from my personal experience from a bartender to a manager in a restaurant. In the restaurant business, there is a big separation between the front and the back of the house. The front deals with people—for example, bartenders, waiters, managers— and English skills are crucial if the restaurant is located outside of Chinatown. If you communicate with your customers better and more efficiently, you tend to make more in tips and you help expand the restaurant's clientele. On the contrary, at the back of the house—for example, cooks, dishwashers—English is not necessary, the back-house workers have fixed wages. The reason why everybody admires English, wants to speak English, and has an interest in learning English is not because English is a beautiful language. It is a necessity and an economic opportunity.[30]

While Chin stressed the effect of English in Chinatown, Mr. Chow, a young computer specialist in a large, mainstream electronics company, talked about it from a different perspective. When asked why English did not have a greater effect on socioeconomic mobility outside Chinatown, he said,

> The reason why English does not yield returns on income and occupation is not that it is not essential in the open economy; on the contrary, it is indispensable. The point is that you are assumed to have equally good English skills as the native Americans when you compete with them for jobs outside the enclave. If you don't know English, it is just impossible for you to get anything. For those who are able to obtain jobs outside the enclave, they must have fairly good English skills.
>
> Thus, it is not so much whether your knowledge of English counts. A lot of immigrants, particularly those who go to school here, have a very good command of English. Rather, it is a matter of how you are perceived by employers, and racial prejudice often influences this perception. You always sound foreign and look foreign. For example, no matter how good your English is, you always tend to speak with an accent, plus you cannot change your looks. Going through job interviews can be frustrating, because the interviewers do not know you at all, and they are more likely to perceive you as a foreigner because of your different look and strange accent, and base their judgment on a stereotype or racial prejudice. You may get a job all right; but when it comes to promotion, especially to managerial positions, you are more likely to be out-competed when your rival is a non-Hispanic native white, even if you both have similar credentials. Whereas in Chinatown, everybody looks the same, and ethnic identity helps to bridge the gap between employers and employees.
>
> Moreover, English is a special asset in Chinatown, because this is not something everybody in the community has. Chinatown is not

totally isolated, it has a lot of linkages to the outside world. You can't move far without English.

Mr. Chow immigrated when he was a baby, and he spoke perfect English. He had a well-paying job, and yet he was still thinking of going back to Chinatown to start his own electronics business. When I asked why, he answered:

> This is simple. Working in Chinatown, I have the advantages both of a Chinese and of an American. As a Chinese, I have access to all the ethnic resources and am protected by ethnic solidarity. As an American, I have a level of English, U.S. education, and work experience which is superior to that of most of the immigrants. On the one hand, I am sheltered from racial prejudice, and on the other hand, I am still able to succeed in Chinatown and do whatever can be done in the open economy.[31]

These fieldwork accounts in many respects confirm the findings from the PUMS. That is, there are significant earnings and occupational returns within the economic enclave in New York City.

Material and Symbolic Compensations of the Enclave

Another reason that immigrant Chinese tend to stay in Chinatown is that ethnic solidarity keeps immigrants together. First, immigrants feel good about working for co-ethnic bosses, who tend to be more understanding than nonethnic bosses. For instance, many garment workers who had once worked for *lofan* (meaning "whites" in Cantonese) eventually turn back to the enclave partly because they are frustrated at not being understood. Many workers complain that their *lofan* bosses showed no concern for the language problem of the workers. Second, immigrant Chinese tend to have the desire to make quick money and are used to the long working hours. Thus, they prefer to be able to work longer hours. In Chinatown, most workers work six days a week and a ten-hour work day is typical. Back in China, they used to work six days a week, but got very little pay. Here, they feel that even if they must do the same amount of work, they are paid much more. So, if they are allowed to work more, they can make more. Further, immigrants think in terms of the absolute exchange rate with *renminbi* (the Chinese currency in the unit of yuan). Their average wage in China was about thirty dollars per month. In their calculation, they can make that amount in a day here, even with the worst-paying jobs. Thus a three-dollar per hour rate, below the minimum wage, does not seem so bad to them.

Immigrants are well aware that they are perceived as low-wage labor; only in ethnic firms can they possibly make up for the low wages by working long hours. They do not know much about federal and state labor laws and are certainly unlikely to sue their bosses for legal violations. Moreover, many immigrants have little concept of taxes and tax-related obligations, because they are not used to having taxes directly deducted from their pay. They feel that they are being swindled if money is withheld from their paychecks. In some ethnic firms, the bosses pay taxes for the workers, paying the workers in cash instead of giving them a check listing a tax deduction. With hard cash to take home every week, they care little about the long-term negative affects of this illegal but culturally accepted practice.

Second, immigrant firms usually tolerate a very flexible work schedule. Workers, especially women, can choose to work a few hours in the shop and go home (often nearby) to take care of the housework. Some of the mothers are allowed to bring their small babies to the garment shops and to have their older children come to the shop to wait for them after school. As long as the job gets done, it is fine with the boss. But wages in these factories are usually lower.

Third, the enclave economy does not follow the typical business cycle of boom and recession in which a large number of workers have to be laid off at some point in the period of recession. It guarantees jobs for immigrants; one way or another, one can find something to do, though for less pay in hard times.

Fourth, ethnic discrimination and prejudice still play a role in the open labor market, effectively blocking upward mobility or access to the larger economy for immigrants. The large, unexpected influx of immigrants from Asia and the Caribbean since 1965 has created tremendous pressure on the U.S. labor market and caused a lot of racial resentment from the white working class. The "unintended" effect of the immigration reform, interacting with existing racism, places non-European immigrants in an unwelcome situation upon arrival, and it is exacerbated by the language and skill disadvantages they brought along with them. Most of the time, new immigrants are confronted with the discriminatory hiring practices of native employers. A recent study by the New York State Inter-Agency Task Force on Immigration Affairs found that the Immigration and Reform Act of 1986, which offered amnesty to eligible illegal aliens, led to three specific forms of discrimination.[32] Employers refused to accept legally valid proof of residency, denied employment to those who experienced minor delays in gathering necessary documentation, and screened out those applicants who looked or sounded foreign. Frustrated and harassed by discriminatory employers in the larger labor market, immigrants would rather turn back to the enclave for employment whenever possible.

Ethnic solidarity produces a reciprocal relationship between immigrant workers and entrepreneurs that makes it possible for both to achieve what they want. The class relations between the two are, to a great extent, moderated by a common ethnic commitment. Lower wages and the willingness to accept low wages are, perhaps, part of the secret of economic success for many small-scale entrepreneurs, because lower wages are the only effective way to keep labor costs down and so retain market competitiveness. The reason low wages could be maintained successfully and labor union control could be prevented is that ethnic entrepreneurs are also bound by ethnic commitment. They offer flexible work hours for their co-ethnic workers, show cultural understanding, and guarantee jobs even during periods of recession. Ethnic workers, in return, show their loyalty by working hard and covering up legal violations. They are glad of the opportunity to gain experience and save money by working hard and long. Many of the garment contractors and shop owners worked their way up as sewing machine operators and restaurant workers.

Some Pitfalls in Chinatown

To argue that the enclave economy provides positive returns on human capital for immigrant Chinese workers does not deny that the absolute earning gap between workers within and outside the enclave is large. Many of the jobs in the enclave are characterized by low wages and long hours, making them seem highly exploitative from the outside. Yet the availability of a reliable low-wage ethnic work force represents an important condition for the survival and success of many ethnic small businesses.

In Chinatown, downward social mobility for some recent immigrants is not uncommon. In addition to immigrant disadvantages, newcomers are often intimidated by the unfamiliar conditions in the larger economy. They often assume that racial discrimination blocks their access to the open labor market. Thus, some Chinese immigrants, like their predecessors, are forced into the enclave as a means of survival. Some of them are forced to take jobs that actually depreciate their past human-capital credentials.

Mr. Hu, who immigrated from Hong Kong four years before I interviewed him, was working as a clerk in a Chinatown bookstore. Before emigration, he had a college degree in finance and a good-paying, professional job at the Hong Kong and Shanghai Bank. When asked why he did not try to look for jobs in the financial sector in Manhattan, he sighed,

> What can you do? You come here with broken English; you don't know what is going on outside [Chinatown]; nobody seems to care much about your education and credentials; and every single piece of job information you can possibly get is associated with Chinatown.
>
> I got this job through a friend who happened to know the boss. At first, I felt very depressed because this job suggested downward mobility for me. Yet, people thought I was lucky to get such a nice clean "white-collar" job. I guess I have to be satisfied.
>
> Now, I have decided that I like the job. When you escape the 1997 uncertain future in Hong Kong, you should also be prepared to lose something from immigration. You can't get both, can you? [33]

Unlike Mr. Hu, who seems to have adjusted well in Chinatown, Mr. Li had a different story. Before emigration he had been a full professor in political science from Guangzhou. At the time of the interview, he was fifty-eight years old and was working in a food-processing factory in Chinatown. He was angry and frustrated about the demotion. Yet he made a comment similar to Mr. Hu's:

> I never expected to end up making tofu in Chinatown. I feel as if I am deprived of all the prestige and achievement I worked so hard for over my lifetime when I was in China.
>
> I can't teach here, because my English isn't good enough. People around here seem to recommend nothing but menial jobs to you. When I got this job making tofu, they told me that this was the right job for an old person like me. It is a bad job, but I have to take it. I have three children at college and I have to work until they graduate from school. [34]

Mr. Li went back to China a year later to resume teaching at the university. For him, working in Chinatown was not anywhere close to the American dream most immigrants had in mind.

Conclusion

The economic enclave has begun to develop into a structure of opportunities for Chinese investors, entrepreneurs, and immigrants to make their way up the socioeconomic ladder; it helps them adjust to their new country socioeconomically. Indeed, for many Chinese immigrants in New York, Chinatown's enclave economy does not simply satisfy their survival needs but also opens opportunities for social mobility.

However, one should be careful not to overplay the romantic perception that one does not have to leave the enclave in order to do well. In reality, Chinatown's enclave economy has two faces. It is true that it shields ethnic workers, particularly immigrants, from interethnic competition and from discrimination on account of their ethnic background. This by no means suggests that they cannot obtain jobs in the larger labor market. For immigrant Chinese, the larger labor market is "open," and ethnic discrimination is much more covert than before, especially in entry-level, low-income industry. Because of their poor English language ability and other initial disadvantages as immigrants, they can only reach jobs in the open market that pay minimum wage, about the same as those in Chinatown. Taking ethnic advantages into account, Chinatown has been a better place for them to start. Therefore, they choose to work in the enclave not simply because they fear being out-competed or discriminated against but also because they want to take advantage of their ethnicity.

Moreover, Chinatown's economy is not as isolated as many think. While the protected sector remains relatively stable, the interface with the outside has greatly expanded the export sector of the enclave economy. For self-employment, an important indicator of socioeconomic achievement, immigrants have a better chance in Chinatown. Thus cultural adaptation has become more important in the enclave than outside, where racial prejudice still obstructs social mobility.

The second face shows a conglomeration of small businesses and low-wage jobs, whose characteristics resemble those of the larger secondary economy. Many Chinese immigrants participating in the enclave are in more disadvantaged positions. To a large extent, the survival and success of many small enterprises in Chinatown depend on the availability of cheap labor. Chinatown's economy can support only so many ethnic entrepreneurs. Cutthroat competition may drive many small businesses into bankruptcy. Furthermore, immigrant workers who have access to the enclave labor market through ethnic solidarity may become entangled in a web of ethnic obligations that interferes with their rational pursuit of economic opportunities.[35] Their adaptation in the host society may be confined to ethnic segregation.

For the immigrant Chinese, however, there are material and symbolic compensations in the enclave that cannot be calculated exclusively from wages or by mainstream standards. In this respect, Chinatown works on the basis of ethnic solidarity and social relations, channeling its ethnic members to achieve a more successful transition into the American society.

7

The Other Half of the Sky: Socioeconomic
Adaptation of Immigrant Women

"Women hold up half of the sky." This saying describes what is true of Chinatown's enclave labor force. More often than not, when people think of the Chinese in the United States, they imagine railroad workers, hand laundrymen, or restaurant waiters. Women are seldom seen, or heard of, in Old Chinatown. Past studies of Chinese immigration and immigrant incorporation have often depicted female immigrants as invisible or stereotyped, even after 1965 when women began to come in large numbers. These studies have emphasized the experience of men or examined the research with little recognition that the experience of immigrant women may be different from that of men. More recently, studies of the enclaves of Cubans in Miami and Chinese and Koreans in New York and Los Angeles have begun to show interest in women's position in enclave labor markets.[1] Some researchers consider the ethnic enclave highly exploitative of women.[2] Others perceive it not simply as an adaptive response to the new environment but also as a continuation of ethnic social and cultural patterns.[3] Contrasting arguments highlight the exploitative aspects of the enclave and the cooperative family orientation of ethnic entrepreneurship.

In Chinatown, women constitute a major share of the ethnic labor force, and their position in the labor market is not the same as men's. Thus, patterns of socioeconomic adaptation of men are not applicable to women. In this chapter, I describe how these patterns are related to the labor-market experience of immigrant Chinese women in the enclave. I begin with an overview of Chinese women's traditional roles. I then examine the socioeconomic impact of female immigration on Chinatown. Finally, I look at the multiple roles and labor-market experience of women after immigration and examine the importance of their experience for immigrant adaptation.

Traditional Role Expectations

New York's Chinatown was a bachelors' society for the greater part of this century.

Not until after 1965, when U.S. immigration policies were revised to favor family reunification, did Chinese women enter New York in large numbers, changing the Chinatown bachelors' society forever. In the 1940s, there were six times as many Chinese men as women in New York State; by 1980, the ratio had declined to 106 men per 100 women. The primary motive of immigration of Chinese women has been family reunification. Between 1982 and 1985, more than ninety thousand women (54 percent of the total new arrivals from China, Hong Kong, and Taiwan) entered the United States either to join their husbands or to reunite with their children or parents who had immigrated earlier. In the absence of a close family relationship, immigration is almost impossible unless one falls into the third preference category (the talented with exceptional ability), the sixth preference category (skilled and needed labor), or the category of refugees. Immigrant Chinese women have constituted more than half of the total Chinese influx in recent years, and this trend will continue in the near future.

Along with family reunification, there is reason to believe that women share a motive similar to that of immigrant men—to seek better opportunities for themselves, their children, and their families. The socioeconomic characteristics of Chinese women are shaped by a different set of conditions from those of Chinese men or even non-Hispanic white women. Thus, it is necessary to understand the social, cultural and economic conditions under which these women have lived.

Traditionally, the status of women in China was low. Their subordinate position both in the family and in society has long been taken for granted. By and large, women had little control over family economics and enjoyed few equal rights with men. In the past, when Chinese women were born, their families did not recognize them as permanent members but rather as "belonging to other people" because they would eventually marry out of their natal families.[4] Until a woman was married, becoming a wife and a mother, she was a daughter and, as such, a dependent obliged to obey her parents. Once she was married, she would belong to her husband's family. For her natal family, thus, she was simply "water spilled on the ground"; any time, effort, and money spent on her education and training would be a sheer waste.

There were two traditional ways to assure that the family would not lose much in raising a daughter: one was to turn her into unpaid family labor; the other was to request a considerable sum of money (a dowry) from the family she was about to marry into. As a result, an unmarried woman—a daughter—was obliged to work as much as she could both inside the home and in the fields. Her labor was never rewarded in a monetary form. Furthermore, since the parents-in-law went to great expense to bring home a wife for one of their sons, the daughter-in-law (literally bought into the family) was expected to continue working without pay not only as a daughter but also as a wife and mother, taking care of her husband and producing children, especially sons, for the husband's family. The only security for the daughter-in-law was her ability to produce children. Moreover, although a woman was economically cut off from her natal family by marriage, she always owed her parents a debt, which she was obliged to repay by acts of filial piety that would continue through her lifetime. The primary purpose of marriage was for the interest of the family, either her natal or her husband's family or both, rather than for love.

In traditional China, women's subordinate position in the family and the traditional roles allotted to them rendered them economically dependent and powerless. Women had no control over their own fate, let alone anything else. They could not decide at what job they would like to work, to whom they would like to be married, or how many children they wished to have.

The gender roles of Chinese women were not simply confined to the home. Women in China were always involved in work outside the home. In the traditional agriculture-based economy, their work was essential for the subsistence of the family unit. Besides domestic work—child rearing, tending the animals, fetching water from the well or river, grinding rice or wheat into flour, cooking, cleaning, and many other household chores—they were engaged in income-generating work. They either took up the kind of work that could be done at home—silk reeling, weaving, spinning, embroidering, or knitting—or worked alongside their husbands in the fields, especially during the busy seasons. Thus, traditional Chinese women have always worked to help support the family, though they were never part of the wage-labor force.

The traditional Chinese family structure and the roles of women changed after the Communist government took control in 1949. One significant step was the constitutionalization of women's civil rights. Moreover, as the country attempted to become industrialized, many agricultural workers were pushed off the farmland and drawn into cities. Many women in rural areas, particularly those between sixteen and twenty-five years of age, poured into cities to look for jobs. The opportunity, and the necessity, to earn a regular income outside the home somewhat increased women's ability to control their own futures. However, traditional perceptions and expectations of women still prevailed. A woman had to work because her husband's wage, or her family income, was not enough to support the family; her income was, thus, necessary, but it was often treated as supplementary, not essential, to the family. Although women became part of the paid labor force, their multiple roles as daughters, wives, and mothers remained unchanged. After long hours of work outside the home, the man could go home and relax, while the woman, be she a daughter, wife, or mother, had to attend to the cooking, cleaning, child care, and all sorts of household chores.

In general, Chinese women are still totally responsible for domestic work and child care even when they work for wages. They struggle to fulfill their duties as daughters, wives, and mothers while also earning wages. The traditional role expectations and the experiences of women before immigration have an enduring impact on immigrant Chinese women in the United States. Although some women may conceive of immigration as a way to escape the patriarchal tradition that has oppressed them for so long in their home society, many of them still carry with them the traditional values and roles. Immigrant women do wish for some basic changes in women's status in their new country, but their wishes are not so much for themselves as for their children. Mrs. Li, a fifty-eight-year-old former librarian from Canton, commented:

> In today's China, it is unconstitutional to deny women equal rights to education and jobs. However, in reality, the traditional female subordination still holds tight. One obvious evidence is that in people's minds, they still think that it is not necessary for a woman to receive higher education or get into managerial positions. If a woman got too high up in her career, she would be regarded as too aggressive and assertive to live with, she would be stereotyped as militant and unfeminine, and she would have a hard time finding a husband. Men do not seem to like the idea of equal rights when it comes to challenging their traditionally established position. So, there are still many men who are not comfortable working with independent, aggressive, and intelligent female coworkers and do not want to choose those women as wives.

I am one of the few lucky women of my age who have higher education. But in order to conform to the traditional values and appear to be virtuous, I have always suppressed my independent ideas and my intellectual part. I do not really expect any change myself, since I have gotten used to it; but I do hope that my children will be able to live in a less repressive and more liberal world.

I thought here in America, there would be less gender discrimination, and women could enjoy more rights. But in Chinatown, things turn out to be worse. Changes have not come to this isolated world as they have in China.[5]

Indeed, Chinatown seems to be frozen in tradition. While China has gone through a lot of revolution and change, Chinatown still maintains the very essence of patriarchal dominance. Immigrant women only hope that this situation will change when their children grow up.

Moreover, upon arrival in their new country, these women are immediately tied to a social structure of family relations. They are expected and they themselves expect to fulfill their family obligations and help their family members to make their American dreams come true. When they immigrate, women often have two major objectives in mind—to get rich for their families and to help their family members (particularly those from their natal families) immigrate. Mrs. Li recalled,

I decided to come mainly because that was the only way I could get my three grown children out of China.[6] In fact, I did not benefit from immigration at all. My husband, who was a university professor, could not find a job commensurate with his education and experience because of his poor English skill and age. He ended up working for five dollars an hour in a food-manufacturing company in Chinatown. I had to work in a garment factory. I was very slow because of my poor eyesight and had little experience in operating a sewing machine. I was paid by the piece. No matter how hard I worked, twenty dollars a day [for at least eight hours] was about the most I could make. What else could we do? We had to pay the rent, the food and all the basic expenses. We could not afford just to stay home. We simply had a difficult time adjusting to the life here.

I came because I wanted my children to come. Immediately after I arrived here, I filed a petition for immigrant visas for my three adult children. Shortly after they came, my husband went back to China to teach and I stayed to take care of my children. Now all my children have worked their way through college, and now they have all settled down and gotten married. I feel that I have done enough for them, and that it is now time to think about going back to China to join my husband for the rest of my life.[7]

Mrs. Li immigrated to the United States in 1983 to join her mother under the fourth category—married sons and daughters of a U.S. citizen. When her mother came to join her father here in the late 1950s, Mrs. Li could not come because she was already married; moreover, she did not want to immigrate, for she had small children, a good job, and a simple but happy life. Over the years, however, she had gone through all kinds of political turmoil, particularly the Cultural Revolution in the 1960s and 1970s, when both she and her husband were sent to labor camps for "re-education". Although she and her husband were later rehabilitated, those bitter experiences changed Mrs. Li's view of immigration. She started to consider the possibility not so much for herself as for her three adult children. Mrs. Li continued to stay and work in the United States after her husband went back to China only because of her children.

Mei Chao told a story that reflects the way women feel about family obligations:

I was from a village in Taishan. My husband came back to the village to marry me and get me out here. Almost every family in my village had relatives in the Gold Mountain. People called them "the guests from the Gold Mountain," and they used to boast about having one, because they regularly received remittances from abroad that significantly enhanced their living standard in the village.

All of a sudden, these guests of the Gold Mountain came home and took their wives and children with them back to the United States. Many of my friends and coworkers left, and they managed to help their families get rich and help their relatives out in a short period of time. Emigration, then, became a heated topic everywhere in the village. I wanted very much to go, too, because that was the only way I could help my family get rich. But I was not qualified to emigrate under any of the relative preference categories. In order to go, I decided to marry out, like many other girls. The procedure was surprisingly easy and fast; through a kin connection, after a year or so, I came here married to a man I had met only once before.

Marriage is only a matter of convenience. As a woman, I think a village man is as good a worker as a Chinatown man. But the fundamental difference is that the latter is in the Gold Mountain where he can make a lot more money than the man in my home village. Also,

I could help my brothers out of China. I never expected to have a romantic relationship, but I am very grateful to my husband because he got me out.

As the eldest of four children, Mei Chao had worked very hard both in the fields and at home before coming to America. She accepted her simple life until the late 1970s when China and the United States normalized diplomatic relations and the families of the Chinese immigrants from Taishan began to emigrate. Mei Chao, now Mrs. Cheng and the mother of two children, had two expectations of her marriage: One was to secure her family life here, and the other was to get her natal family out of China. Soon after she came, she started to work outside the home. With little education or English, she did not even think of going out of Chinatown. She found a job in a garment shop and has worked as a sewing machine operator ever since. She worked for more than fifty hours a week and, at the same time, managed to take care of the two young children and the housework. Mei Chao seemed quite satisfied with her decision to marry out, and with what appeared to be a busy life here. She added,

> I don't see my husband often since both of us work very hard and he works in a restaurant at a different shift. I don't really have to work since we stick to the simple lifestyle in Chinatown. But I want to work as much as I can to help save money. I feel my work is rewarding, though I am paid $4.50 per hour [above average in Chinatown]. I know that a woman like myself, uneducated and not speaking English, cannot go beyond Chinatown, hoping for anything else other than a garment job. I have never had very high expectations. However, when I first arrived, I had two wishes: One was to work hard and help my husband save enough money to own a business; the other was to get my parents and my brothers out of China.[8]

Mei Chao's two wishes are shared by many other immigrant Chinese women; they view immigration as one of the most effective ways to fulfill their family obligations. Once they come, they work quietly and diligently, side by side with their male counterparts, to make their American dream come true.

Furthermore, many immigrant women view emigration as a form of upward social mobility and often base their value judgments on comparison with their past experience. Mei Chao had to quit school in the fourth grade to work with other women in the fields to help support her family, making less than $125 a year. Compared to that pay, her wages of $4.50

per hour seemed like a fortune.[9] Today, as she wished, she has finally quit the garment job and works with her husband in their own fast-food takeout restaurant, recently established in Brooklyn. Her mother and one of her brothers have immigrated and the other two brothers are about to come. Mei Chao seems very happy. She never felt that she was exploited or deprived by working in the garment shop. Instead, she viewed her hard work as rewarding in the sense that she could contribute to the economic gain of her family—almost half of the initial capital for opening up the restaurant came from Mei Chao's garment work—and that she had fulfilled her responsibility as a daughter by helping her natal family to emigrate.

Several implications can be drawn from the experiences of these immigrant women. First, immigrant Chinese women hold to traditional values and expectations and are bound by family obligations after immigration. Thus, their American experience is different from that of men. Second, working outside the home is nothing new; it has always been part of their way of life. Their incomes, though still considered secondary, are indispensable for the well-being of their families. Third, their goals are linked to their families. Their work, including both wage labor and unpaid family labor, has become a common family strategy for social mobility in Chinatown. They work side by side with their husbands or family members to push their family up the socioeconomic ladder.

Immigrant Chinese Women in New York

The Impact of Female Chinese Immigration

As more and more Chinese women have immigrated, the exclusively male demography of Chinatown has been transformed. Now the community is bustling with young families. In the 1940s, there were six times as many Chinese men as women in New York State; and in the 1950s, Chinese men still outnumbered women by nearly 300 percent. Now the ratio is nearly balanced. Immigration statistics show that from 1982 to 1985 more Chinese women than men entered the United States—53 percent women and 47 percent men from mainland China; 53 percent and 47 percent from Taiwan; and about 50 percent and 50 percent from Hong Kong. In fact, women immigrants have outnumbered men almost every year since then, especially since the mid-1970s, when China finally opened itself up to the West. Not only do women dominate the immigration trend, but the majority (65 percent) are in the working ages of twenty to fifty-nine (67 percent for immigrants from China, 50 percent for those from Hong Kong, and 68 percent for those from Taiwan). By the 1980s, 79 percent of the Chinese households in New York were family-type households, and 87 percent of the Chinese families were married-couple families (compared to the state's average of 70 percent family-type households and 78 percent married-couple families). The average number of persons per family was 3.73 for the Chinese, a little higher than the state average (3.30).

As Chinatown's social nature has changed, the pressure on the community's physical capacity has become enormous. Chinatown's limited housing, aging and deteriorated, is simply not capable of accommodating the demands of the incoming families. In fact, this strategic piece of turf has become a battlefield on which investors and businessmen compete for economic opportunities, and it is no longer primarily a residence for new immigrants. Consequently, families are spread out in other areas of the city, depending on easy subway access to Chinatown. Visible Chinese populations are seen in Flushing, Elmhurst, Corona, Jackson Heights, Astoria, and Rego Park in Queens; Borough Park, Flatbush, Bay Ridge, Park Slope, Midwood, Sheepshead Bay, and Sunset Park in Brooklyn.[10]

Residential out-migration of the Chinese population in recent years can be partially attributed to the entry of women. Mr. Chan tells a two-generation story that well illustrates this trend. Mr. Chan, who came with his mother from Hong Kong in 1967 to join his father in Chinatown, recalled what he saw as a teenager:

> Father lived with two bachelor workers in a small unit on the top floor (the sixth) of a large old walk-up brick building on Mott Street. There was only one bedroom, about thirteen square feet, just enough to lay three twin size mattresses. The kitchen was very small; next to the stove, there was a bathtub but no shower. If somebody was taking a bath, the others would have to stay in the bedroom, and nobody was able to get in or out of the house.
>
> When mother and I came, father's roommates volunteered to move into other bachelors' houses so that we had a place to sleep. Father got a queen-size bunk bed, and the whole family crammed in the same room. It seems unbearable, but I know a lot of immigrant families in Chinatown live like that.
>
> Why didn't we move out? At that time, not many Chinese lived outside of Chinatown. Without knowing English well, we did not even know where to move, and there were a lot of inconveniences outside the community. Here in Chinatown, people can all walk to

work and shop, and conduct their daily activities with ease. Moreover, the rent was low, only fifty dollars a month for our room [because the apartment was rent controlled], and the landlord could not raise the rent as long as we stayed. We were used to that kind of crowdedness in Hong Kong anyway. We would rather save money and time by staying in Chinatown.

Mr. Chan now lives in Bay Ridge, Brooklyn. When he was asked what made him move out of Chinatown, he replied:

Because my wife came. Eight years ago, I went back to Canton to get married. A few months later, my wife came. I could not possibly find an apartment in Chinatown, though I wanted very much to. I looked into a couple of possibilities there, but I was instantly scared away, the rent had climbed up to four hundred dollars per month plus four thousand dollars or more key money[11] for just a tiny unit like my parents'.

   Through a friend who had relatives living in Bay Ridge, I got this pretty decent one-bedroom apartment for five hundred dollars per month. Both my wife and I work in Chinatown, and we have to spend a considerable amount of time and money daily on transportation to and from work. Chinatown will have less and less space for residents. Living elsewhere will become the only choice for new immigrant families.[12]

Large-scale immigration of women has two major effects on Chinatown's economy: First, through sheer numbers and by promoting a family-centered society in which most adults are living with a spouse, it has expanded the market for Chinese goods and services that are inaccessible in the larger society, thus developing the enclave protected sector. Second, by providing a large additional pool of cheap and low-skilled labor at a critical time in the city's overall economic restructuring, it has promoted the rapid development of a Chinese garment industry, which serves as a backbone of the enclave export sector in Chinatown. Women's concentration in the garment industry is extraordinary: more than 55 percent of all immigrant Chinese women who worked at least 160 hours and earned over five hundred dollars in 1979 were employed in the garment industry.[13]

Characteristics of Immigrant
Chinese Women in New York

Table 7-1 displays some of the basic characteristics of New York State's Chinese female population, as compared to the state's non-Hispanic white female population. In 1980 the foreign born composed nearly three-fourths (74 percent) of the total female Chinese population in New York State. The age distribution shows that more than half of the female Chinese were between twenty-five and sixty-four years old, with a much smaller group on both ends—7 percent aged under five years and 8 percent aged sixty-five or over. On the average, as compared to New York State's non-Hispanic white women, Chinese women were younger. They were more likely to be married (60 percent versus 52 percent) and less likely to be divorced or separated (3.2 percent versus 7.9 percent). The educational achievement of Chinese women went to both extremes. On one end, they constituted a fairly large percentage of the illiterate or semiliterate (21 percent, as compared to only 3 percent for non-Hispanic white women); on the other end, they had a higher percentage of college education compared to white women (21 percent versus 15 percent). Chinese women had a much higher rate of labor-force participation (59 percent versus 45 percent and for immigrant Chinese women the rate was much higher). Occupationally, female Chinese were very segregated. They were disproportionately concentrated in positions as operators and labors and fewer of them were administrators, managers, and technicians than was the case among non-Hispanic whites. They were underrepresented in administrative-support jobs, which were regarded as female-dominated occupations.

Data on immigrants' socioeconomic status upon arrival were not broken down by sex, and statistics were not available to show the socioeconomic characteristics of women before immigration. Yet ethnographic data indicated that the majority of the adult immigrant women came from rural areas in south China, and the rest came from cities all over China. They were from various socioeconomic backgrounds. Many young adult women aged twenty to thirty-five from mainland China immigrated through marriage, taking advantage of the 1965 immigration laws.

In China, particularly in villages around the Pearl River delta in the south, where emigration originated, many young women tend to prefer marriage abroad as a way to come to America. They perceive immigration as the only way to upgrade their socioeconomic status and that of their families. Marriage abroad is possible because many Chinese immigrant

Table 7-1. Characteristics of Chinese Women and Non-Hispanic White Women in New York State, 1980

	Chinese	Non-Hispanic White
Total	71,365	7,323,204
% foreign born	74.2	12.7
Age		
% Under 5 years of age	6.9	5.4
% 5 to 24	32.2	29.4
% 25 to 64	53.1	49.0
% 65 and over	7.8	16.2
Median age	30.2	35.0
Marital Status		
Persons 15 years or over	57,020	5,955,919
% Married, except separated	59.5	52.0
% Single	28.1	25.7
% Divorced or separated	3.2	7.9
% Widowed	9.2	14.4
Education		
Persons 25 or over	43,529	4,774,050
% 0 to 4 years elementary	21.1	3.1
% High school graduates	51.8	67.8
% 4 or more years of college	21.0	15.4
Labor force status		
Persons 16 or over	55,435	5,864,611
% In labor force	59.0	44.6
% Of civilian labor force unemployed	3.5	6.4
Occupation		
Employed persons 16 years or over	32,679	2,617,611
% Administrative, managerial, and executive	18.6	25.0
% Technicians	3.7	2.9
% Sales	6.4	11.1
% Administrative support	19.2	35.7
% Business, household, and protection services	6.0	14.1
% Precision production, repair, and crafts	2.7	1.8
% Operators and laborers	43.2	9.0
% Farming	.2	.4

Source: *U.S. Census of Population*: 1980.

men, already in the United States, have difficulty finding a Chinese wife in Chinatown. They often depend on the ethnic or kinship networks in their home villages in seeking a wife. For example, Mei Chao's husband, Mr. Cheng, originally immigrated from Hong Kong with his family and became a naturalized citizen. For him, the primary purpose for getting married was to carry on the family name. Since he had limited choice in finding a Chinese wife here, he decided to "import" one, as many of his coworkers did. He met Mei Chao in Taishan through a relative and managed to get her out a few months after their wedding in China.

Younger women from rural China, particularly those who married into the country, usually had limited education, English-language ability, and marketable skills. They did not have very high aspirations for themselves; rather, they tended to work for the benefit of the family as a whole. Despite these initial disadvantages, they seem to have had fewer adjustment problems than older or better-educated women. First, life in America was regarded as absolutely better than life in the backward villages in China. Long before immigration they knew that, if they were willing to work just as hard as in China, they could make a lot of money in the Gold Mountain. So they were ready and eager to work, either to save money to send back to their natal families or to help bring in additional income and accumulate capital for their own families. Second, they were accustomed to working outside the home. The low-wage jobs and long working hours in Chinatown did not seem to bother them at all, for these rural women were used to doing backbreaking menial farmwork in the fields for very little pay. Third, despite the fact that they were uneducated and unskilled, they could quickly learn the minimum skills required to operate a sewing machine. Therefore, the initial disadvantages, on the one hand, kept women dependent on Chinatown's economy and, on the other hand, helped them withstand the social and psychological pressures associated with immigration.

Middle-aged women made up another portion of the incoming female population. Most of these immigrant women are wives and mothers who had immigrated with children under twenty-one to reunite their families. After 1943 wives of the Chinatown sojourners began to immigrate. Some of these middle-aged women, who could have come years earlier, in the 1940s and 1950s, delayed their American trip primarily because of the need to take care of their families and small children or their parents-in-law, who were too old to immigrate. This group of women is the most altruistic. They came mainly for their children, not for themselves. They did not really immigrate for the comfort and freedom of the American life, for they often look on themselves as too slow to adjust to the new country and too old to learn English and to establish a career of any sort. All they wish for is the success of their children. Without knowing English, without comparable skills and training, and without youth their options in the labor market are limited. Jobs in Chinatown become their only option. (This is true even for some women who had a higher level of education and professional skills because of both ethnic and gender discrimination.) Some choose to stay home to help with the housework and to care for their small grandchildren. Those who work outside the home are almost uniformly employed in private household service and the garment industry. Even if most know they will not go back to China, their mentality is still based in China. They do not seem to have socioeconomic aspirations for themselves.

Yet another portion of the female immigrant population is composed of well-educated and professional women. Many women from this group also immigrated under relative-preference categories. Some were students who attended U.S. colleges and decided to stay after completing their education. The American-trained women tend to refuse to identify themselves with Chinatown. They are more likely to find jobs in the mainstream economy. In contrast, those not educated in the United States mostly depend on the economic enclave because of their poor English ability (and, for some, lack of transferable skills). However, the better-educated and professional immigrant women do not seem to benefit from the enclave as much as immigrant men with similar socioeconomic backgrounds. Most of the jobs commensurable with their past professional experience and education are taken by men. Therefore, the human-capital characteristics of women do not seem to generate as great economic returns as those of men. The male supremacy that dominates the Chinese culture also reinforces gender discrimination in the enclave labor market—good jobs are simply not open to women in Chinatown. Thus, some of these female immigrants often feel more disadvantaged, disappointed, and deprived than other immigrant women.

However, those who are ambitious and motivated can often succeed through self-employment. In many cases, their efforts are combined with their husbands' in family economic pursuits. In Chinatown, female entrepreneurs are more likely to run businesses with their husbands. Mrs. Tan, for example, who obtained a bachelor's degree in economics in China, came here to join her husband in 1983. Because of her limited English skills, she could not possibly get a job in the larger economy. Like many women in Chinatown, she worked as a sewing machine operator in her sister-in-law's garment shop. After several years of hard work, she and her husband had saved enough money to open their own shop in Brooklyn. At the time I met her, she was running the garment shop while her husband managed a neighborhood store they had just recently opened in Brooklyn. Miss Hua, an immigrant herself and a young, ambitious, and educated woman, was one of the successful female entrepreneurs in Chinatown. She entered the garment trade in the mid-1970s, not simply to make a few more dollars but to prove that Chinatown could make good garments. Miss Hua's sportswear company, occupying a third-floor loft at Lafayette Street and employing about eighty Chinese immigrants, was one of hundreds of garment factories in Chinatown. She dealt with Marty, a fashion manufacturer for whom nobody in Chinatown had ever worked. Her thriving business and quality operation won her recognition in the garment trade. As a woman, she took fierce pride in her entrepreneurial skill and her success.

From whatever background, all Chinatown women share a common characteristic: They are all, in one way or another, performing multiple roles as daughters, wives, mothers, and wage earners. As immigrants, Chinese women (like men) bear all sorts of disadvantages associated with immigrant status—ethnic visibility, weaker educational credentials, poorer English and occupational skills. In addition, they also carry with them a set of traditional roles that have been internalized into their value system at an early stage of life. They continue to assume these roles when uprooted from their country of origin because Chinatown, though surrounded by the world's most advanced civilization, has long maintained the most traditional Chinese culture and values. However, what is special about these women is that they have a strong work ethic and family commitment. They believe that, together with their family members, they can "make it" in America. The high rate of labor-force participation for immigrant women indicates that they are committed to work outside the home. Although the economic contribution of women has enhanced their status in the family and the community, there is still a long way to go before women can achieve equal rights with men in Chinatown. As wage earners, they are limited to jobs in the low-wage sector of the economic enclave.

Labor Market Performance

Women made up nearly half of the Chinese immigrant labor force in New York. Table 7-2 compares characteristics of males and females in the

Table 7-2. Labor-Force Characteristics of the Foreign-Born Chinese in the New York Metropolitan Area, 1980

	New York City		Outside N.Y.C.	
	Female	Male	Female	Male
Total	846	1,011	224	385
% Married	77.3	81.0	86.2	85.7
% With 2 or more children	62.2	—	48.7	—
% Immigration after 1965	74.7	74.5	70.5	68.3
% U.S. citizen	48.8	45.9	58.0	55.8
% Speak English well or very well	38.8	53.5	86.7	89.0
% Some college education	25.7	31.5	70.3	84.4
Mean years of education	11.0	12.4	16.5	18.7
Occupation				
% Managerial, professional, and technical	12.6	22.3	47.3	76.2
% Administrative support and precision production	23.4	17.4	29.0	9.0
% Sales and services	5.2	47.9	9.4	12.1
% Laborers	58.8	12.4	14.3	2.7
Mean hours worked per week	38.309	42.788	36.585	40.860
Mean 1979 earnings	$7,812	$10,200	$11,065	$22,012

Source: U.S. Census of Population and Housing: 1980 PUMS.

Note: Including only private-sector employees aged 25 to 64 who worked at least 160 hours and earned a minimum of $500 in 1979.

ethnic labor force in the New York metropolitan area. The statistics reveal a disadvantaged picture for immigrant women who lived in New York City in 1980. Female Chinese immigrants showed similar percentages to males in marital status, years of immigration and U.S. citizenship, but their educational levels were lower: they completed only eleven years of schooling on average (compared to twelve for males), and only 26 percent of them had some college education (as compared to 32 percent of the men). Their English-language ability was weaker than that of men; less than 40 percent of them spoke English well (as compared to 54 percent of Chinese men). Occupationally, immigrant women in the city leaned toward jobs at the lower end of the occupational scale, and close to 60 percent of them were garment workers. Immigrant Chinese women living outside New York City fared much better. They had much better knowl-

Table 7-3. Average Individual Income, by Education, Place of Birth, and Ethnicity, for Female Workers, New York City, 1979

Ethnicity	Elementary School	Percent[1]	High School	Percent[1]	College	Percent[1]
U.S.-born white	$8,978	100.0	$10,695	100.0	$15,559	100.0
U.S.-born Chinese	$4,122	45.9	$11,464	107.2	$15,528	99.8
Foreign-born white	$7,864	100.0	$ 9,923	100.0	$14,498	100.0
Foreign-born Chinese	$5,741	73.0	$ 7,215	72.7	$13,142	90.6

Source: U.S. Census of Population and Housing: 1980 PUMS.
Note: Including all Chinese and non-Hispanic white women between 25 and 64 years of age who worked at least 160 hours and earned a minimum of $500 in 1979.
[1] Individual income of Chinese as a percentage of the income of their non-Hispanic white counterparts.

edge of English, and their educational achievement was remarkable, not better than that of immigrant Chinese men but much better than their female white counterparts. They showed higher proportions in better occupations.

Immigrant Chinese women in or out of New York City tend to be full-time workers, but marked differences in individual income exist between Chinese men and women workers. The average individual income in 1979 was $7,812 for Chinese women in New York City, only 76 percent of the income of their male counterparts, reflecting the effects of lower educational attainment, lower English skills, and also gender discrimination. However, women living outside the city earned only half as much as their male counterparts, despite their much-improved human-capital characteristics and occupational attainment. It seems that, relatively, immigrant women were better off in the city.

Education, Occupation, and Earnings

The disadvantaged position of immigrant Chinese women seems to reflect their generally low human-capital credentials. How do they fare in the labor market if they obtain higher level of education? Table 7-3 compares Chinese women with non-Hispanic white women, showing the relationship between education and income. U.S.-born Chinese women with at least some high school education had incomes higher than those of non-Hispanic white women, and those with college education had incomes similar to their counterparts'. They seem to have fared relatively better relative to white women than the rest of the group.

Table 7-4. Average Individual Income, by Occupation, Place of Birth, and Ethnicity, for Female Workers, New York City, 1979

Ethnicity	Blue-Collar	White-Collar Services	White-Collar Professionals	White-Collar Executives
U.S.-born white	$7,765	$11,661	$15,682	$18,145
U.S.-born Chinese	$2,705	$11,071	$18,918	$13,812
Chinese income as % of white income	34.8	94.9	120.6	76.1
Foreign-Born White	$6,961	$10,059	$15,593	$17,513
Foreign-Born Chinese	$5,363	$ 9,321	$15,354	$15,328
Chinese income as % of white income	77.0	92.7	98.5	87.5

Source: U.S. Census of Population and Housing: 1980 PUMS.

Note: Including all Chinese and non-Hispanic white women between 25 and 64 years of age who worked at least 160 hours and earned a minimum of $500 in 1979.

Chinese women who had lower income returns on their education may be in occupations that generally pay less. According to the 1980 census, almost half of the U.S.-born Chinese women occupied the top-ranking white-collar occupations (49 percent as compared to 37 percent of their white counterparts). Immigrant Chinese women, however, did not fare quite as well. Only 15 percent were in the top-ranking occupations, while more than half were concentrated in the entry-level menial jobs typical of enclave economies. Table 7-4 illustrates the relationship between occupation and income. U.S.-born Chinese women did much better than their white counterparts in white-collar professional occupations, and immigrant Chinese women did just as well as whites in those occupations. However, Chinese women were disadvantaged at managerial positions as well as on menial jobs.

Returns on Human Capital in the Enclave

The majority of immigrant women participate in the enclave labor market. A major part of Chinatown's economy depends on the availability of female immigrant labor. While the enclave seems to take advantage of women, it also creates jobs for these women, who otherwise would not be able to find work or would have to go back to China. The specific question here is whether participation in the enclave economy affects immigrant women's ability to reap earnings returns on human capital, as hypothesized for men.

For comparison purposes, I applied the same set of multiple regression models of earnings and occupational returns to human capital for men to female Chinese immigrant workers.[14] Separate analysis was done for female workers within and outside the economic enclave, based on the three definitions—place of residence, place of work, and industrial sector. For female Chinese immigrant workers, results from regression analyses based on the three definitions overlapped in a similar way to that of men. In 1980 about 67 percent of female Chinese workers lived and worked in New York City, and 21 percent lived and worked outside the city; only a small percentage lived in the city but worked outside or vice versa. Of those who lived and worked in the city, 68 percent were in the enclave industries.

Female immigrant Chinese workers were concentrated in the enclave industries, particularly in the garment industry. Close to 70 percent of the female immigrant workers in New York City worked in the enclave industries. Of those enclave workers, 85 percent were garment workers. Table 7-5 reports equations for female workers in New York City's garment industry and nonenclave industries. Among women who worked in New York City's garment industry, the most consistent effects on earnings were for hours worked and occupation. Similarly, among women living in the enclave, the strongest predictors of earnings were hours worked and occupation. The surprise here was the total absence of human-capital effects: neither labor-market experience nor education nor English-language skills nor citizenship had any significant effects. Analyses based on defining the enclave by place of residence and place of work generally reproduced these results.

However, results from multivariate models predicting occupational prestige were quite different.[15] While none of the human-capital measures showed significant effects on income for female immigrant workers in the enclave, they did have significant effects on occupational attainment, measured by occupational prestige scores.[16] No matter whether the enclave was defined by place of residence, place of work, or industrial sector, college education and English-language skills both had significant positive effects on achieving higher occupational prestige in the enclave as well as outside.

The inconsistent results of the earnings-return and occupational-return equations pose difficulties in interpretation. Generally, occupational success should be closely related to higher earnings return. If human capital did not bring a significant return in income, as is the case

Table 7-5. Regression Equations Predicting 1979 Earnings (ln) for Female Immigrant Chinese Employees in New York City

	Garment Industry B[1]	Nonenclave Industry B[1]
Intercept	4.304**	6.542**
Labor market experience	.017	−.002
Labor market experience squared	−.228[2]	−.052[2]
Elementary education	.008	−.031
High school education	.843[2]	.018
College education	.005	.759[2]
English-language skills	.026	.136
U.S. citizen	.072	.025
Immigration 1975–1979	−.160*	−.220*
Immigration 1965–1974	.031	−.087
Married	.030	−.027
Fertility	−.013	−.006
Log–hours worked–1979	.595**	.448**
Sales, administrative support, and precision production	−.326	−.365**
Business, protective, and household services	−.786*	−.497**
Operators and laborers	−.584*	−.743**
R square	.348	.331
N of cases	496	262

Source: U.S. *Census of Population and Housing:* 1980 PUMS.

Note: Including only private-sector employees aged 25 to 64, who worked at least 160 hours and earned a minimum of $500 in 1979.

[1] Unstandardized regression coefficients.

[2] The decimal point is moved three places to the right.

*Significant at .05 level, one-tail (the t-ratio is greater than or equal to 1.65).

**Significant at .01 level, one-tail (the t-ratio is greater than or equal to 2.33).

for the Chinese female workers in the enclave economy, we should expect that it would not bring a return in occupational attainment. Nevertheless, in New York, I found that Chinese immigrant women within the enclave have no measurable earnings returns on previous human capital but that human capital has helped them achieve higher occupational prestige. These results did not stem in any obvious way from the personal characteristics of these women; they are not unusually low in education, nor are they predominantly part-time workers.

What accounts for the fact that the earnings of immigrant Chinese women are unrelated to their experience, education, English-language ability, and citizenship? In Chinatown, women workers face two sorts of disadvantages. The first, which they share with men, is the set of disadvantages associated with immigrant status. The second is a set of cultural obstacles within the enclave: occupational segregation by gender (particularly in the garment industry) and the traditional multiple roles of daughters, wives, mothers, and wage workers. Data on the census and fieldwork research on women in the garment industry provide more insight.

Chinatown's Garment Workers

Chinatown's garment industry took root and grew at a time when New York City's manufacturing sector was declining. According to a report by the International Ladies' Garment Workers' Union and the New York Skirt and Sportswear Association, in 1969 there were about fifty-eight thousand industrial jobs in the downtown industrial district, south of Houston Street and east of Broadway; but in 1980 industrial employment had shrunk to forty-five thousand. Jobs in nonapparel manufacturing, of which this area had once been a leading center, dropped off abruptly by more than 40 percent. Apparel jobs also fell sharply, from forty thousand to twenty-five thousand. However, the growing Chinatown garment sector more than doubled, from eight thousand to sixteen thousand.[17]

Chinatown's garment industry sprang up basically in response to a new wave of immigration, which supplied not only a large pool of cheap female labor but also a group of entrepreneurs who were willing to invest in and manage the garment trade. Moreover, declining manufacturing left vacant many loft buildings in which the garment industry could develop. Between 1975 and 1980, the number of Chinese-owned garment factories grew by an average of 36 a year, reaching a peak of 430 in 1980. In that year Chinatown contained one-third of all the jobs in Manhattan's women's outerwear industry and a much larger share of the production jobs.[18] As a result, Chinatown's garment industry has grown into one of the two basic sectors (the restaurant industry being the other) of the enclave economy. Immigrant women have played a crucial role in the community's economic development.

Table 7-6. Characteristics of Female Immigrant Workers
in the Garment Industry, New York City, 1980

	Chinese workers	All workers
Total	496	4,244
Median age	45.0	45.3
% Married	86.1	60.6
% With 2 or more children	78.4	58.1
% Immigrated after 1965	86.0	38.0
% U.S. citizen	41.3	67.1
% Spoke English well or very well	13.5	39.1
% Some high school	34.5	40.5
% Some college education	2.4	9.2
Mean years of school completed	8.2	11.2
% Operators and laborers	94.6	73.1
Mean hours worked per week	38.8	36.9
Mean 1979 earnings	$5,321	$7,509
Mean family income	$17,152	$17,325

Source: U.S. Census of Population and Housing: 1980 PUMS.
Note: Including only employees in the garment industry (1980 PUMS Standard Industry
Codes 132–152), who worked at least 160 hours and earned a minimum of $500 in 1979.

Female workers are not different from men in regard to their immigrant status—poor English-language ability, lack of transferable work
skills, and limited information concerning the larger employment market.
They are forced to take low-paying, long-hour, menial jobs in Chinatown. However, as women, female workers have encountered more barriers than men in their new country. Gender discrimination both in and
out of Chinatown; the traditional roles of women as daughters, wives,
and mothers; the denial of equal educational opportunities to women in
the Chinese culture; and their dependent status as immigrant wives leave
women almost nothing but one option—to work in the garment industry.

The large number of women who have flooded the ethnic labor market in Chinatown has exacerbated the effect of the rigid gender division,
turning the entire garment industry into a female occupation. In Chinatown's garment industry, more than 80 percent of the Chinese immigrant
workers are women. Table 7-6 lists the characteristics of New York City's
female garment workers in 1980. Comparing characteristics of all female

workers in the industry, the Chinese were more likely to be married and live with children (86 percent of them were married, and 78 percent had at least two children). They arrived more recently (86 percent entered the United States after 1965). About 41 percent of them were naturalized U.S. citizens. Furthermore, they displayed relatively lower human-capital characteristics. Most were poorly educated (the mean years of school completed was only eight); only a few of them (2.4 percent) had some college education. They knew very little English (less than 15 percent of them spoke English well). But most of them took up full-time jobs (they worked for average of thirty-nine hours per week in 1979). Ninety-five percent of the Chinese in the garment industry were sewing machine operators.

Chinese female garment workers were extremely low paid. Their average annual salary in 1979 was only a little more than five thousand dollars, at an average hourly pay of only $2.80, far below minimum wage (though it is also possible that many of the workers underreported their income). Interviews with the garment workers revealed that most of the factories set the hourly rate according to experience. For new hands, it was below or about minimum wage. For more skilled workers, the rate varied from $4.00 to $5.50. But many workers, mostly older women, who did miscellaneous work in the factory (e.g., cleaning, cutting thread, wrapping) were paid between $2.50 and $3.00 per hour.

Why should Chinese women be so disproportionately engaged in the garment industry? Some may think that women are particularly good at certain jobs, which are hence defined as women's jobs. Our society has always taken for granted the common assumption that the gender division of labor is natural and generally beneficial for women. The reality is that jobs that are defined as women's work invariably entail lower rates of pay, status, and skill, whereas higher-paid skilled jobs tend to be the preserve of men.[19] The making of garments has been traditionally accepted as women's work because of the rigid gender divisions within the labor market. The garment industry, long before the Chinese entered it, was supported by a large pool of cheap female labor from the European immigrant groups—the Jews, Italians, Greeks, and others. Nowadays, as immigrants of European origin are gradually being accepted into the American mainstream, the industry has been taken over by the newer immigrant groups, particularly the Chinese and the Hispanics.

According to the common assumption, women enter the garment trade because they are good at it. However, history shows that men once held those jobs. Chinese men used to dominate laundry work, and the coat and suit industry used to be dependent on male European immigrants. Why then does the gender division of labor remain so rigid? It is not because of the particular skills that women or men possess but because of the association of the occupation with women's principal roles and their subordinate status.

As immigrants, both men and women experience racial or cultural subordination, which acts to confine them to certain types of work and reinforces their disadvantaged status as wage workers. But for immigrant women, immigrant disadvantages are shaped in a particular way because they share with all women subordination as a gender. Thus, wherever a woman comes from, whether she works or not, whether she is married or has children, her principal role in life is defined not as a wage worker first but as a wife or mother. It is this definition that is replicated and reinforced through the creation of whole sectors of low-paid, low-skilled women's work.[20]

The negative consequences of the stereotyped definition of women's role can also be understood from another perspective. Confinement to the low-wage, labor-intensive sector implies that women can afford to take such jobs because their paid work is only "secondary" or "supplementary." Their role is still defined as an actual, or potential, wife or mother; they still have to depend, economically and socially, on a male breadwinner.[21]

In Chinatown, women are disproportionately engaged in the garment industry while men are concentrated in restaurants. This gender division is closely associated with women's traditional roles. First, as a principal breadwinner, a man is expected to have a stable full-time job; as a dependent and a wife, a woman is expected to perform her principal role as wife and mother, and a stable job is not her primary concern. Chinatown's restaurant industry is relatively more stable, in the sense that it is basically supported year-round by an ethnic market, whereas Chinatown's garment industry is highly seasonal and unstable. Because of rising labor costs, a lot of apparel manufacturing, particularly for the standardized portion of the demand, has been transferred to the Third World—Southeast Asia, particularly Hong Kong, Taiwan, and even China—where the cost of labor is low. New York's manufacturing sector retains only that portion of the demand that is transient, unstandardized, and susceptible to the quick-changing vagaries of fashion. This portion of the demand is unpredictable. Chinatown's apparel orders are mostly for lower-priced women's sportswear and the stylish products that are made to fill in mass-consumption lines that stores leave open to take advantage of unpredictable and late changes in demand.[22] The uncertainty and unpredictability make Chinatown's garment work highly seasonal.

Unlike the restaurant business, which is more independent, the garment industry falls into the export sector of the enclave economy, and it depends largely on the fluctuating demand of the larger consumer market and the production decisions of apparel manufacturers who are not Chinatown insiders. Lack of control over the consumer market and production renders Chinatown's garment industry vulnerable to competition from producers of low-priced standardized lines that are located abroad and to market changes. When demand declines, fewer orders are contracted into Chinatown, and more workers have to be laid off. Thus, a man, as the head of the family, tends to head for the relatively more stable restaurant jobs, leaving the garment jobs for women. An interview with a restaurant waiter provides support for this point. Asked whether he would like to work in the garment factory, he answered: "No, I would not want to work in the garment factory. You know, in Chinatown, the garment job is a woman's job. How could one support his family with a woman's job? I have a couple of kids to raise. What would happen to my family if the factory did not get enough orders and I got laid off?"[23] Apparently, this waiter was implying that a man did not work in the garment factory because he was the breadwinner. Men, thus, are less likely to enter the sweatshop.

Another reason that women flock to the garment industry is that it offers full-time and part-time jobs to them, regardless of their prior labor-market experience. Although most of the women have not worked in the job before immigration, they learn as they work because the required skills are minimal. Within a short period of time, many become experienced sewing machine operators.

Moreover, wages for sewing machine operators are generally lower than the wages and tips waiters can earn. Chinatown's garment industry is highly competitive. In order to survive the competition, the Chinese garment contractors have to offer low prices for orders and make marginal profits by pushing wages down as low as possible. Half of the garment workers earned less than $5,000 in 1979. As for men, about 42 percent of all male workers were in the restaurant business, and more than 70 percent of them were waiters. In 1979, male restaurant workers earned an average of $1,200 more than female garment workers; and men who were in the garment industry earned an average of $2,000 more than women.

Moreover, because women are still given total responsibility for the household work, the working wives or mothers tend to prefer jobs that leave them time for taking care of their housework and children. Thus, they are not suitable for restaurant jobs, which require a rigid work schedule, particularly the evening shift. Garment work does not need to be done on a fixed schedule, and many Chinese garment contractors offer flexible work hours and favorable locations to their workers, in part as a way to compensate for the low wages. Workers can take the time off during the day to drop off and pick up their children at school or to nurse their babies. They are even allowed to bring their babies to the workshop.

Most of the garment factories are firmly anchored in the extended Chinatown area despite the increasingly tight commercial space, rising rent, and Chinatown's residential dispersion. The main reason is that Chinatown has a large pool of cheap female immigrant labor. Many garment workers live in the enclave and walk to work, but even those who live in Queens or Brooklyn still prefer to go back to Chinatown to work, because there they can fulfill some of their household duties at the same time—shopping and picking up groceries and ready-cooked food on their way home. It would not be as convenient for women to work in factories in outer boroughs, because they would still need to go back to Chinatown to shop and therefore would have to spend more time outside the home. Many women commute to Chinatown to work at the jobs available to them, therefore. Even if their families move out of the area, they must continue to work, for their contributions to the family's income are essential to fulfill the goals of self-employment and home ownership.

But the farther the families move away from the garment center, the longer the journey to work, and the greater the pressure on women in performing all the expected roles. The following story reflects the busy life of these garment workers. When I interviewed her, Mrs. Chow was a recent immigrant with a four-year-old daughter and an eighteen-month-old son. She lived in Woodside, Queens, and worked in a garment factory in Manhattan's Chinatown. She and her husband, who worked in a restaurant in the Bronx, were on different work schedules, and they rarely had time together.

Every day, Mrs. Chow got up at five o'clock in the morning to prepare breakfast for the children. She left the house with her two children at six-thirty while her husband was still sleeping. She fed the children on the subway train. Getting off the subway, she dropped the older child off at the Chinatown Daycare Center and left the smaller one at the baby-sitter's home not far from the factory. Mrs. Chow started to work at eight o'clock and got off at five o'clock. She went to see her baby during the midday break. After work, she hurried to pick up some ready-made food and groceries nearby. Then she picked up her kids. The three got home around seven o'clock. Then she prepared dinner for the children and herself. She bathed the children and put them to bed at eight-thirty. She went to bed around nine-thirty, while her husband was still at work.

Mrs. Chow worked about thirty-five to forty hours a week but was laid off about three months a year when there was not enough work at the factory. She was able to take the time off during the day to go to the baby-sitter's house to see her baby. When the kids were sick she could take a day or two off or take the garment work home. She wanted to work as much as she could so that her family could save money to open up a small family business. Because of the two children and the long working hours of her husband, she could only manage a job with a flexible schedule. When asked how she felt about working, she said: "I lead a very busy life, but I feel happy working with other women in the factory and making money for the family. Although I have to spend more than half of my wages on child care, I still can save about one-third. During the time I was laid off, I had too much housework to do and I felt even busier than when I worked. Sometimes I get frustrated if I am confined at home and don't see my coworkers." [24]

Many women workers who lived in Chinatown could manage both work and household responsibilities more efficiently because they could save at least two hours on traveling to work. They were thus able to work more hours than Mrs. Chow. But Mrs. Chow's story makes the point that no matter whether a woman works or not, no matter how much traveling she must do, she is expected to do most of the housework and child care.

In Chinatown garment workers must rely on family members and others in the community for child care. The majority of the China-town garment workers are mothers of small children, desperately juggling work with the household chores, shopping, cooking, and arranging for baby-sitters. Child care is an especially burning issue for many of these working women. In Chinatown in 1988 there was only one subsidized day-care center for garment workers and a few home day-care services that were sponsored by the city government and some of the quasi-governmental organizations. Miss Kwan, a union activist, said that the immigrant mothers "cannot believe that when they get here, there is nobody to take care of their kids." In China many workplaces had day-care facilities for their own employees, or some women could leave the kids with the grandparents. Here in Chinatown only a few young mothers can ask their parents to take care of their children. The rest have to take their small children along to work or leave them with paid baby-sitters.

The New York City Chinatown Daycare Center, located at 115 Chrystie Street, was opened in 1983 in a unique cooperative effort involving the ILGWU, the Great Blouse, Skirt, and Undergarment Association, individual manufacturers, and the Agency for Child Development, Human Resources Administration of New York City. The center had space for about eighty children and always had a full enrollment. All the enrolled youngsters were children of the garment workers, from two and a half to five years old. These children were chosen by lottery from among the families of the approximately twenty thousand members of the ILGWU, who worked in Chinatown's garment industry. Besides the day-care center, there were some government- and community-sponsored projects— home day-care services—to help the working women. The fee for the subsidized day care in the late 1980s ranged from eight to ten dollars a week for each child from a low-income family. However, the formal means of support and the subsidized day-care services were not sufficient to meet the pressing needs of the garment workers. Many working women had to turn to family or private day-care services to solve their problem. In Chinatown a lot of older, retired women take care of their grandchildren as older women are traditionally expected to do. Women in Chinatown usually find their baby-sitter through kinship networks, and baby-sitters do not have to put up ads to get a job. Also, some mothers choose not to work, to stay home with their children instead. Many of these women usually baby-sit two or three more children, in addition to their own, in order to make some extra money and to provide playmates for their own children. Mrs. Chang is one of the luckiest. In 1988, when I interviewed her, she was able to leave her two children, one of them two and a half and the other eight months old, with her own parents, whom she had helped to immigrate a year before. She told me:

> Thanks to my parents, my kids do not have to go to inexperienced baby-sitters and I can concentrate on my job without worry. I am lucky, because my parents agree to do this for me. Some parents would rather go to work than baby-sit.
>
> It has worked out pretty well. I give $800 to my parents each month and leave my kids with them in their apartment. I only take my kids home during the weekend. Money is not a big problem. I have to support my parents anyway. The difference is that with my parents' care, I am sure my kids are okay and I don't feel guilty while I am at work. My parents also take care of two other babies at the same time, so that they can have a little more money themselves.[25]

Private day care is available in individual homes. The costs ranged from fourteen to twenty dollars per day in 1988, and the services were reliable and flexible. These places became an effective means to solve the child-care problem. The working mothers usually spent half of their wages on child care. They also needed support from their bosses, who would allow children to come to the garment shop to wait for their mothers. Younger children could be left in private care all day, but older kids had shorter school hours. Mothers usually dropped them off at school before they went to work. If kids went to schools in Chinatown, they simply walked to the garment shops and stood by the sewing machines while their mothers worked. Older children might help their mothers hang up finished garments, turn belts, or prepare garments for sewing, but the young ones generally just stood by waiting.[26] But if children were not in Chinatown schools, mothers had to arrange pickup and extended day care for their children.

The garment industry thrives, taking advantage of women's willing acceptance of low wages. The stiff competition in the industry also leads to poor working conditions. In Chinatown there is evidence of growing numbers of garment shops with many fire and safety hazards, paying wages below the federal minimum. The U.S. Labor Department has repeatedly raided and filed charges against some of the Chinatown garment factories over the past ten years.[27] However, these actions are only a minimal deterrent to garment owners intent on keeping wages low and paying their workers off the books. For these employers, as Ms. Fung, a staff attorney for the Asian-American Legal and Education Fund, pointed out, such actions—imposition of fines and closing of factories—were considered only a routine business expense; most shopowners quickly reopened their shops, knowing that the Labor Department officers would not be returning soon after their press conferences. In Ms. Fung's opinion, shared by many Chinatown leaders, such raids on the garment industry would hurt only Chinese garment workers.[28] These were primarily poor immigrant women with limited education and restricted occupational options. Many of them were willing to work long hours at low wages and without overtime pay, so long as they had some sort of job that could bring in income to support themselves and their families. These workers would simply lose their jobs following a raid. They then blamed the government, rather than the law-breaking employers, for depriving them of a livelihood. Unaware of their rights and taking a different stance toward this work, these women would try to obtain jobs in other garment factories that might also engage in illegal practices. In Chinatown today, the garment industry provides jobs to immigrant women who would otherwise not be able to work. As a result, three out of five women workers are low-wage garment workers.

When asked about the benefits and drawbacks of working in Chinatown, many women would reply like Mrs. Wu, a recent immigrant who came from one of the villages in Taishan to join her husband. Mrs. Wu was one of those women who got married merely for economic necessity and barely knew her husband-to-be before the wedding. She had only three years of schooling, knew no English, had no occupational skills, and yet, she was more than willing to work and make money. The second week after she came, she got a job in a garment factory through her relative who was also a sewing machine operator. When asked whether the long working schedule had bothered her, she said,

> It does not bother me at all. I even wish I could work more. I am a semiliterate country girl. I have nothing but labor. As long as I have a job, I will be satisfied because I have a chance to make money. Here I am paid by the piece and I can make an average of three dollars per hour. A lot of my coworkers can make more than this; some make five dollars per hour. By the end of the week I can bring home about $180 to $200 [for sixty hours of work]. If I work for *lofan,* I can only bring home about $140 with tax deductions and I can't work extra hours. What do you think I would do with a two-day weekend? I do not even dare to go out of Chinatown alone.[39]

The garment industry may appear highly exploitative of women, but from the point of view of these women workers, the industry is their only opportunity. They all seem to be satisfied that they have a job at all, whatever it may be. As Mrs. Chen put it, "I would have to go back to China if there wasn't a garment industry in Chinatown." The willingness of immigrant women to accept substandard working conditions and wages is certainly a problem in that it can exert pressure on other enclave workers to reduce what they are willing to work for. However, for these women, getting a job and being paid fairly still remain two separate issues. They are more concerned about having a job of some sort to help their families move ahead than about their own rights. Some people would argue that it is all right for a woman to take a low-wage job, since she only works for pin money and her husband is supporting them. Others expect a woman's work and earnings to affect household norms and behavior. Chinatown's reality is that a woman works out of economic necessity, and her income is added to her husband's as a family income. However, her employment and income do not seem to change household behavior and norms. This pattern is also evident for non-Hispanic white working women in the larger economy.[30] A woman's expected duties as a wife and a mother do not change much when she becomes a wage earner; rather, they hinder her from seeking higher-paying jobs. As a result, women's equal rights with men remain as distant as they were before immigration. However, the roles women play are indispensable for the social mobility of the family as whole, and this state of affairs is taken for granted by women workers in Chinatown.

Conclusion

Results from multivariate analysis show considerable evidence of positive earnings returns for male enclave workers from education, labor-market experience, and English-language ability, but none of these human-capital variables is positively related to the income of female enclave workers. There are two ways to interpret these results. Viewed from an individual or economic perspective, the enclave labor market appears to be clearly exploitative of women. However, women's positions are contained in ethnic social networks that are built into the structure of social relations and cultural values. Their role in the enclave is not just secondary but crucial in status attainment for the family.

Fieldwork data strongly support this latter view. The socioeconomic gains of the family, as commonly evidenced in entrepreneurship, housing ownership, and social-capital investment in their children, are the payoff for stints of wage work. Many female immigrant workers are expected (and themselves expect) to earn wages in ways that do not conflict with their family obligations. Sewing at piecework rates fits these expectations well because working hours are flexible and women can make more money simply by working faster and longer—even if the pay per piece is low. Many middle-aged women, those who immigrated at age forty or fifty, accept a short-term orientation toward work: their purpose (even for many who had professional occupations in China) is not to develop a career but to contribute immediately to the household income for the benefit of younger members. Thus, they are usually content with what they have in Chinatown.

Better-paying jobs in the enclave economy tend to be reserved for men because male supremacy that dominates the Chinese culture (and the Western culture) reinforces gender discrimination in the enclave labor market. However, women workers' human capital helps them to gain higher occupational prestige because occupations in the enclave have the same prestige scores as those in the open economy. An enclave female worker in an administrative-support position might not make the same income as one in a similar position in the open economy, but the two will have the same occupational prestige scores. In this respect, education and English-language ability can be an asset for female immigrant workers. Even if immigrant women are limited to the enclave, they may still be able to take advantage of their past human capital to achieve similar occupational returns. Whatever the results, one has to remember that Chinese culture gives priority not to individual achievement but to the welfare of the family and the community. Female labor-force participation is part of a family strategy for social mobility.

Women have always worked, but their economic role and performance has often been ignored: Their work has been unappreciated and their contribution was devalued and unnoticed.[31] In reality, women's participation in the labor force is an economic necessity to maintain a household. A breadwinner's income in Chinatown is not enough to support a family of three or four. Families with dreams of buying a home or starting a business—which is true of most—definitely need the income of women. For immigrant women, family is always the priority. The family—the husband and the children—comes first. Although they are in worse jobs and earn less, their labor-force participation has been indispensable as a family strategy to achieve social mobility.[32] The results of this analysis imply that immigrant incorporation is not a simple, unilinear process from community to individuality. The social mobility of women, as well as that of their male co-ethnics, is deeply embedded in the social structure of the ethnic community.

The increasing number of working women in Chinatown has dramatically altered the economic and social fabric of the community. The most obvious change is seen in the booming garment industry, in which women have constituted a large pool of cheap labor. Their labor is cheaper than men's not only because of the initial disadvantages associated with immigration but also because of the tradition of male dominance in the Chinese culture and the multiple roles women are expected to perform. In Chinatown there is a big gap between perception and reality. Chinese women are still perceived as subordinate; their economic contribution is still perceived as secondary. In reality, however, they have played a crucial part in the subsistence of the community and the family. Many households could not possibly survive, or get ahead, without women's incomes. In fact, women themselves are well aware of this reality, because they are the ones who handle the rent, bills, and everyday expenses, and they are the ones who know exactly how much is required to meet the basic household needs. But they do not see themselves as victims of gender inequality and discrimination. Rather, they use their past work experience as a point of reference to justify their current position in the enclave labor market. They accept their struggle between home and the workplace as part of the struggle to achieve the American dream. Women workers set their priorities on status attainment for their families and are willing to sacrifice to achieve their family goal. Chinatown, in this respect, provides them with ethnic support, opportunities, work flexibility, and a viable path for their adaptation to the new country.

8

Residential Mobility
and Ethnic Segregation

Manhattan's Old Chinatown has always been a definable, contiguous geographic locality in which the Chinese are concentrated. However, today's Chinese are much more spread out than their predecessors. More than half of New York City's Chinese now live in Queens and Brooklyn in growing Chinese neighborhoods. The rapid residential dispersion of the Chinese population does not seem to have been accompanied by the decline of the original enclave, however. While other ethnic enclaves, such as Little Italy, have dispersed and then dwindled in significance Chinatown has survived for more than 140 years and has retained a strong ethnic economy and a full-fledged ethnic community. Immigrant Chinese continue to have an enormous incentive for self-segregation, being so totally alien to the culture and ways of life in the United States and with only a minimal number of predecessors available to help them. Patterns of in- and out-migration within the Chinatown boundaries often involve not dispersal but construction of new ethnic enclaves, where the Chinese, particularly immigrants, continue to cluster together and tie themselves to Chinatown.

This chapter provides an analysis of the residential patterns and segregation of Chinese residents in and around New York City. The analysis is based on the assumption that residential mobility can serve as an indicator of the social position of ethnic groups.[1] It attempts to show how unique characteristics of the enclave economy, kinship ties of new immigrants to the ethnic community, and ethnic segmentation of the housing market work together to structure the pattern of residential mobility for New York City's Chinese.

Growth in Chinatown: Neighborhood Take-Over

In the 1860s when Chinese laborers began to be shipped in large numbers across the Pacific to the West Coast, there were not many Chinese in New York. The census of 1860 showed that only 120 Chinese lived in New York City, 0.2 percent of the total Chinese population in the United States, which then totaled 63,199. The first group of eastbound Chinese immigrants settled in a three-street area (Mott, Park, and Doyer) on the Lower East Side of Manhattan.[2] During the first few years of Chinese exclusion in the 1890s, New York City gained a few thousand Chinese, increasing the community by 147 percent, while the total U.S. Chinese population dropped by 16 percent from the previous decade. The city's Chinese population experienced some decline at the beginning of the twentieth century, but it increased steadily in the following decades. As a direct effect of the repeal of the Chinese Exclusion Act and more liberalized immigration laws, New York City's Chinese population increased by 73 percent in the 1960s, 111 percent in the 1970s, and 79 percent in the 1980s. Before 1965, most of the Chinese immigrants were concentrated in Manhattan's Chinatown. Although decentralization of the Chinese population began as early as the 1950s, substantial out-migration was not common until much later.

Significant neighborhood take-over and population spread around Chinatown occurred only after 1965, when an unprecedentedly large volume of immigrants started to pour into the community. As a result, by 1970 about 26,770 Chinese were concentrated in the "extended Chinatown" (Table 8-1 and Figure 8-1).[3] In the 1980s, this number increased to 37,917, a 42 percent increase. Some tracts, such as 2.01 and 15.01, had only a few Chinese a decade before; by 1980 more than ten times as many Chinese had settled there. Tracts 2.02, 6, 16, 22.01, 25, and 43 increased by half or more of the 1970 population. Tracts 8, 18, 27, and 41 all experienced growth in the decade between 1970 and 1980; the proportion of Chinese living in tracts 8, 16, 29, and 41 increased by more than 60 percent from 1970 to 1980.

Close to sixty thousand New York Chinese were believed to live in Chinatown in the 1980s, compared to fewer than twenty-five thousand during the 1960s. But, in fact, Chinatown has always sustained a much larger number of residents than reported. The discrepancy is due to the reluctance of the Chinese to cooperate with the census officials and also possibly to the presence of a considerable number of illegal immigrants.[4]

Table 8-1. New York City's Chinese Population within Extended Chinatown, by Census Tract, 1980 and 1970

Tract	1980 Total	1980 Chinese	1970[1] Total	1970[1] Chinese
2.01	3,357	638	2,226	52
2.02	8,019	645	9,311	299
6	10,638	5,086	8,322	2,506
8	9,220	6,322	9,609	4,262
14.02	2,620	326	2,753	396
15.01	3,816	342	497	34
16	8,085	6,688	6,357	3,763
18	6,961	3,227	7,735	2,233
22.01	6,487	759	8,147	378
25	6,369	1,795	5,471	842
27	1,410	689	1,692	670
29	6,016	4,931	9,412	5,938
41	8,669	5,523	9,294	4,930
43	4,230	946	5,104	468
Total	85,897 (100.0)	37,917 (44.1)	85,930 (100.0)	26,771 (31.2)

Source: U.S. Census of Population: 1970 and 1980.
[1] Adapted from B. L. Sung 1974.

Over the years, Chinatown has not experienced community decline, as predicted by theories of immigrant assimilation, which hold true for neighboring Little Italy and the Jewish community. Instead of diminishing in significance, both the population and the physical boundaries of Chinatown are growing at accelerated speed as the tremendous influx of Chinese immigrants brings life to the decaying area surrounding Chinatown. According to a news report from the *New York Times* in 1985, in what used to be the Jewish Lower East Side, a Chinese-American church occupied the building that once housed a Jewish Theological Seminary; a Chinese Buddhist association moved into a vacated synagogue; a fully occupied Chinese condominium development of $150,000-plus units took the place of a former Jewish school. As the city's most densely populated neighborhood, Chinatown has necessarily spilled beyond its traditional boundaries, spreading over southeastern Manhattan,

Figure 8-1. Residential Concentration of the Chinese in Extended Chinatown, Defined by 1980 Census Tracts

Source: U.S. Census of Population: 1980 Tracts.

moving out to neighborhoods once solidly Jewish and Puerto Rican and all but smothering Little Italy, which is now but a two-block relic amid a jumble of Chinese apartments and businesses.

Canal Street used to divide Chinatown from Little Italy. There was a time when the Chinatown residents did not dare to venture north of the street, even for a stroll. Now the borderline no longer exists. The Chinese have not only crossed the street but also set up shops and bought houses there as far north as Fourteenth Street. Because of the increasing number of immigrants seeking to rent apartments close to where they work, the demand for housing in the Chinatown area is very great, far exceeding available housing.

The increasing demand for housing and commercial space has stimulated real estate transactions in the extended Chinatown area, as well as other areas of Asian concentration in outer boroughs. Sensing a profit, real estate companies and wealthy individuals started to buy up properties around the Chinatown area. Although purchasing prices skyrocketed, real estate investments continued to increase because people speculated that the rental price of properties in or close to Chinatown would also be higher than that in the most desirable locations in Manhattan and that tremendous returns would be generated whenever the property changed hands.[5] The New York City property statistics show that in 1988, 83 percent of the total lots and 90 percent of the condominiums in the ten-block Old Chinatown area were Chinese-owned. Of the sales made in the area between 1975 and 1988, 86 percent of the purchasers were Chinese. In Little Italy and areas as far north as Houston Street between Bowery and Lafayette, once solidly Italian and Jewish, now about 34 percent of the total lots (602) are owned by the Chinese; and 41 percent of the total of lots sold after 1975 were purchased by Chinese (Table 8-2). It is estimated that a hundred thousand Chinese now live in a forty-square-block extended Chinatown area bounded by Grand Street, East Broadway, Worth Street, and Broadway.

Population and development pressure from recent Chinese immigration has pushed the community out further: satellite Chinatowns have fanned out along the subway lines into other neighborhoods in Queens and Brooklyn. In New York City, there is no longer a single Chinatown; satellite enclaves have boomed in Flushing, Queens, and Brooklyn's Sunset Park and Bay Ridge.

Mr. Yip, branch director of the Chinatown Planning Council, described the outgrowth of Manhattan's Chinatown into Queens as a satellite Chinatown with a "different twist."[6] Queens in the late 1960s was a

Table 8-2. Real Estate Statistics and Chinese Ownership
in Old Chinatown and Little Italy in New York City, 1988

	Old Chinatown	Little Italy[1]
Total lots	207	602
% Chinese-owned	83.1	33.6
Total condominiums	146	52
% Chinese-owned	90.4	9.6
Total lots sold after 1975	94	373
% purchased by Chinese	86.2	41.0
Total condominiums sold after 1975	146	52
% purchased by Chinese	90.4	9.6

Source: New York City Real Estate Corporation 1988.
[1] Refers to areas north of Canal Street up to Houston Street between Bowery and Lafayette Street.

bedroom community whose residents commuted to Manhattan to work. As a large wave of Chinese immigrants poured into New York, Old Chinatown simply became saturated. The so-called uptown Chinese, particularly the more affluent Taiwanese, found it hard to be crowded in with the poor and culturally different Cantonese group. They found a home in Flushing and soon established another enclave. Flushing's Chinatown is relatively new, inhabited by immigrants mainly from Taiwan. More recently, new immigrants from Hong Kong and mainland China and older immigrants from Manhattan's Chinatown have also begun to move into this new enclave. More than half of the Chinese in Queens speak Mandarin and other northern dialects.

The Chinese enclave in Flushing is a more affluent residential enclave. Immigrants who settle there are usually better-off. Many new arrivals from Taiwan and Hong Kong have brought with them big or small fortunes. The richer, well-established Chinese-American families have also moved out of Manhattan's Chinatown and bought homes in Flushing, though most of them still commute to Old Chinatown to work. According to the 1980 census, Chinese immigrants in Flushing had a median family income of $18,650 as compared to $13,230 for Chinese families in Manhattan. Also, they were more likely to own their houses and they generally lived in newer houses. Forty-eight percent of them lived in owner-occupied housing, and only 23 percent of the housing they lived in was built before 1939, whereas 95 percent of their counterparts in Manhattan lived in rental housing, and 63 percent of the housing for this group was more than forty years old.

With sufficient capital and a strong population base, the ethnic economy in Flushing is booming. By 1986, according to the Flushing Business Association, Hong Kong Chinese alone owned about 40 percent of the more than four hundred Chinese businesses in Flushing, including real estate agencies, restaurants, import/export companies, and retail shops. On the main avenues and side streets, there is also an abundance of barber shops, beauty salons, and teahouses that use their strong ethnic appeal to attract Chinese customers.

Brooklyn's Chinatown is more of an outlet or extension of Old Chinatown than a newly founded Chinatown with a unique character like the one in Flushing. It mainly houses new arrivals and many working-class immigrants. The chief attraction of Brooklyn's Sunset Park/Bay Ridge area is its relatively affordable housing and easy access to the workplace in Manhattan through the subway lines. By the early 1980s, feeling the squeeze of rising rents and overcrowding in Manhattan, both former Chinatowners and recent immigrants began to move to Brooklyn along the convenient subway lines. In 1987 the number of Chinese in Brooklyn had more than doubled since 1980, from twenty-six thousand to about sixty thousand, as estimated by the Chinatown Planning Council.

As increasing numbers of immigrant workers moved into Brooklyn, so did ethnic businesses. The increasing number of garment factories and other ethnic service-oriented businesses, such as restaurants, grocery stores, beauty salons, and herbal medicine stores, is self-evident. Brooklyn's Chinatown is not as well-developed as Flushing's but is certainly better than Old Chinatown in terms of median family income and housing. The 1980 census revealed that Chinese immigrants in Brooklyn had a median family income of $18,492 as opposed to $12,000 in Old Chinatown. They were more likely than those in Old Chinatown to live in owner-occupied housing (40 percent versus 7 percent); and the housing they occupied was not as old as that occupied by those in Old Chinatown—39 percent of the housing they occupied was built before 1939 as compared to 61 percent in Old Chinatown. Mr. Fu of Brooklyn's Community Planning Board estimated that in 1988 at least thirty garment shops were operating in the old warehouses within a ten-block area of Sunset Park. On Eighth Avenue, between Fifty-second and Sixty-first streets, more than half of the mailboxes had Chinese surnames. "With an immigration quota of twenty thousand per year for China, and the Hong Kong quota increased to five thousand per year, more and more Chinese will be coming to New York. There is no more room in Manhattan, and Queens is too expensive for newcomers. Brooklyn, being affordable and easily accessible, is the logical place to be," Mr. Fu predicted.[7]

Today, Chinatown is no longer merely a fixed residential neighborhood; its growth has been accompanied by the development of an enclave economy, which has perpetuated the community by transforming it into a more progressive, socially determined, and dynamic immigrant society.

Segregation of the Chinese in New York

Prior research has developed various models to explain the residential integration of ethnic minority groups into the mainstream society. These models often treat residential segregation as an indicator of general shifts in the relative positions of the group.[8] The assimilation model, perhaps the most influential perspective on ethnic segregation, posits that all ethnic groups tend to be drawn into the economic mainstream, gaining social acceptance through their educational and occupational achievements. The initial establishment of an ethnic enclave—ethnic segregation—is regarded primarily as an adaptive strategy to enable ethnic group members to survive and overcome initial disadvantages and constraints in the early stages of the assimilation process. Segregation is said to be only temporary and to diminish as group members, having improved their labor-market position and absorbed mainstream values, choose residences in new areas.

These hypotheses have gained credibility from research on European ethnic minority groups such as Italian-Americans.[9] Their application to more recent immigrant groups has not been fully tested. The best published evidence has been offered by Douglas S. Massey and Nancy A. Denton.[10] They report that suburbanization is strongly predictive of lower residential isolation and segregation for both Asians and Hispanics, serving as a "key factor" in spatial assimilation. More recently, Richard D. Alba and John R. Logan have analyzed microdata from the 1980 census to estimate individual-level models of suburban residence for various racial and ethnic groups across the nation.[11] For the Chinese as well as some other groups, they report significant effects of marriage and the presence of children, English-language ability, and socioeconomic status. Alba and Logan find that there is a considerable amount of between-group variation in the process of spatial assimilation. The key predictors of location—socioeconomic status and acculturation—do not operate the same way for all minority groups. Further, their effects depend on the distinct social contexts in which group members live.

The experience of adaptation for some immigrant groups suggests contrasting paths that do not agree with the assimilation model. The model of the enclave economy emphasizes the crucial role that an ethnic economy and ethnic social networks can play in the mobility and status attainment of ethnic group members.[12] However, this model understands enclave participation as an alternative to assimilation for the labor market but not for housing. It specifically argues that the enclave does not block the residential mobility of its members. Evidence from the Cuban enclave in Miami has shown that higher-ranking enclave participants tend to reside in more affluent neighborhoods or suburbs, leaving behind the worse-off segment of the ethnic population in or around the geographical enclave.[13]

Models

Are the Chinese being residentially assimilated? Does residence outside the original Chinatown coincide with socioeconomic mobility and cultural adaptation? Is participation in the enclave economy and the ethnic social networks on which it is based no obstacle to decentralization? I approach these questions through three kinds of quantitative analysis. The results of these analyses are supplemented by fieldwork reports.

For these quantitative analyses, I rely on a sample that includes New York City and adjacent counties in New York and New Jersey and is divided into three subareas.[14] The first is Manhattan (New York County), the location of Chinatown. The second is the remaining counties (or boroughs) of New York City. The third is counties outside of New York City in New York and New Jersey. These different subareas are used because an individual may not necessarily achieve residential integration by simply moving out of Chinatown; perhaps those who move out of the city altogether are more likely to live in an ethnically mixed neighborhood. Certainly the outer boroughs are not the same as communities outside the city, in terms of racial composition, socioeconomic standing, and proximity to Chinatown's enclave economy.

The first quantitative analysis measures the overall degree of segregation of the Chinese from other groups.[15] Segregation across census tracts is measured as evenness of distribution, indicated by the Index of Dissimilarity (D). I calculate D for the segregation of the Chinese from three major groups: non-Hispanic whites; Hispanics; and non-Hispanic blacks. I also include segregation scores between major Asian groups: the Chinese, Japanese, Koreans, and Filipinos.

The second quantitative procedure addresses the characteristics of the individual Chinese that are linked to decentralization, using a logit regression model.[16] In its most common form, logit regression models predict a dependent variable with only two categories. My analysis therefore first examines whether the household head lived in New York City or outside the city. In the second form, the analysis is limited to city residents and the dependent variable is whether or not the household head lived in Manhattan or the outer boroughs. Both models predict socioeconomic status, as measured by years of education, household income, and occupational prestige;[17] sectoral employment, indicating whether or not the household head was employed in enclave industries that are disproportionately Chinese (restaurants, garment factories, etc.);[18] acculturation, represented by English-language ability and U.S. citizenship and year of immigration; age; and family situation variables, which include marital status and the presence of children.

The third quantitative analysis is to examine what type of neighborhoods the Chinese tend to move into, using a multivariate model.[19] The purpose is to estimate the independent effects of various neighborhood characteristics (percentages of non-Chinese Asians, non-Hispanic blacks, and Hispanics; median household income; percentage of top-ranking occupations; percentage of rental housing; and residential stability) on the percentage of Chinese.

Results: Residential Segregation of the Chinese

How segregated are the Chinese as compared to other ethnic and racial groups, and does residential mobility reduce the tendency toward ethnic segregation? The index of dissimilarity, D, measures how differently the Chinese and members of other selected racial/ethnic groups are distributed among census tracts across the area. According to prior research,[20] dissimilarity indices between 0 and .30 generally suggest a low degree of residential segregation, those between .30 and .60 a moderate degree, and those above .60 a high degree. Results from this analysis show that the Chinese are fairly highly segregated from other racial and ethnic groups in New York City, where the values of D range from .545 to .838. They are least segregated from Asian Indians, and most segregated from non-Hispanic blacks.

The data from comparisons among Asian subgroups and measures of segregation among them confirm that Asians of different national origins tend to live in segregated areas. For example, the Chinese are as segregated from the Japanese (.668) as they are from Hispanics (.654) and more than from non-Hispanic whites (.574). Further, the Chinese are not an extreme case. They are less segregated from Hispanics and blacks than are Koreans and Japanese but more segregated than Filipinos or Indians. Their segregation from non-Hispanic whites is toward the high end: not as high as that of the Japanese but higher than that of other Asian groups.

Moreover, the segregation of the Chinese from non-Hispanic whites is much higher in Manhattan (.740) than in the outer boroughs (.501) or outside the city (.376). Decentralization, particularly into the suburbs, is clearly associated with decreasing segregation for the Chinese. Other Asian groups, however, display a different pattern. Unlike the Chinese, segregation of Koreans, Japanese, Filipinos, and Indians from non-Hispanic whites is highest in the outer boroughs. For these groups, it is in Manhattan that the segregation scores are the lowest, even lower than outside the city. Chinese settlement in New York created a Chinatown located in Manhattan, the central core of the metropolis. Why did other groups not establish similar neighborhoods in the core area? Why did other groups not develop the same levels of concentration, even in the outer boroughs where they were most segregated? Here enclave theory makes a contribution, by demanding that attention be given to the specific character of the labor markets in which minorities are involved.

Most of the Chinese immigrants entered New York to join their families, and they came disproportionately from rural areas of south China, bringing little education and few industrial skills with them. These immigrants provided the labor force for an ethnic economy, traditionally based in the restaurant business, which has penetrated into different parts of the city and its suburbs; and in the garment industry, which has recently developed in Manhattan's Chinatown.[21] By contrast, Korean immigrants came in large numbers much later than the Chinese. They had no initial economic enclave in the core area, and about 60 percent of them lived in Queens County. Moreover, they have been concentrated in a few occupations, for example, the grocery trade (12.0 percent in grocery and food stores), garment manufacturing (6.8 percent), and the medical sector (11.4 percent), which are spread widely through the city.[22] But they do not tend to live in the same neighborhoods in which they work or set up their shops. For example, Korean-run grocery stores are often located in poor black neighborhoods throughout the city, but few Koreans reside in those areas. A "Koreatown" is being established in Manhattan, and yet only about 13 percent of New York City's Koreans live there.[23] Many recent Japanese immigrants have been recruited to work in subsidiaries of Japanese firms, located in Manhattan as well as in suburban areas. But the Japanese, especially recent immigrants in New York City, are concentrated in Brooklyn (40 percent) and Queens (44 percent), with only 3 percent of them living in Manhattan.[24] These findings imply that residential concentrations depend on locationally and ethnically distinct labor markets, and that the location of the most segregated ethnic neighborhoods depends on the specific social contexts into which immigrants entered at the time of settlement.

Results: Place of Residence

To what extent do characteristics of individual householders affect decentralization? Do the residential patterns of the Chinese respond to the same kinds of individual and family characteristics that affect the location of members of the non-Hispanic white majority? Table 8-3 reports the general characteristics of Chinese householders (aged twenty-five or over) in three parts of the metropolis—Manhattan, the outer boroughs, and outside the city—in 1980. Manhattan accounts for about 47 percent of New York City's Chinese householders, most of whom were highly segregated in the extended Chinatown area on the Lower East Side. The remaining 53 percent of the city's Chinese lived in the outer boroughs. Only a fifth of the Chinese householders in the entire area lived outside New York City.

Typically, where there were differences among areas, they fell along a continuum with Manhattan at one end, outside the city at the other, and the outer boroughs in between. There were no differences in the gender composition of the total Chinese population in these three areas, but close to or more than three-fifths of the householders were males. The Chinese living outside the city received an average of seven years' more schooling than those living in Manhattan, and the percentage with some college education was nearly triple that of Manhattan's Chinese (74 percent versus 25 percent). There were also large differences in socioeconomic status. The median household income of the Chinese living outside the city was more than double and the median individual income was almost quadruple that of Manhattan's Chinese. The differences in household income are partly mitigated by the smaller average number of wager earners in suburban households.

Concerning occupations, the Chinese living outside the city were pre-

Table 8-3. General Characteristics of the Chinese Householders
(Aged 25 and Over) in the New York Metropolitan Area, 1980

	Manhattan	Outer Boroughs	Outside N.Y.C.
Total (aged 25 and older)	868	992	456
Percent Male	78.0	86.6	87.7
Education			
Mean years of school completed	10.6	13.5	17.8
% Some college education	25.3	37.9	74.6
Income			
Median household income 1979	$11,000	$16,000	$27,000
Median individual income 1979	$5,442	$8,185	$20,005
Occupation			
% Managerial and executive	8.4	13.4	16.0
% Professional and technical	10.9	15.7	48.0
% Sales and services [1]	49.8	50.6	24.1
% Operators and laborers [2]	16.0	12.8	5.9
% Persons without occupation	14.9	7.5	6.0
Mean occupational prestige scores	35.3	38.4	51.0
Sectoral employment			
% Working in enclave industries	55.9	52.2	25.7
Year of immigration			
% Foreign born	90.8	90.4	85.4
% Immigrated 1975–1980	17.4	17.9	13.4
% Immigrated 1965–1974	35.9	41.6	38.0
% Immigrated before 1965	46.7	40.5	48.6
Citizenship			
% U.S. citizen	49.7	54.7	62.8
English ability			
% Speaking English well	44.5	65.6	89.3
Median age	50.0	43.0	41.0
Percent married	66.6	81.5	83.1
Percent with children	34.2	52.2	57.9

Source: U.S. Census of Population: 1980 PUMS.

[1] Including sales, administrative support, business and household services, precision production, and crafts.

[2] Including operators, transportation workers, and laborers.

dominantly engaged in managerial-executive, professional, and technical positions, while Manhattan's Chinese were more likely to work in business services or as operators. This pattern is closely related to the existence of the Chinese enclave economy centered in Chinatown. More than half of those working in Manhattan were employed in enclave industries (restaurants, garment factories, etc.), compared to only about a quarter of those outside the city.

The majority of the Chinese in all areas were foreign-born, close to 90 percent in the whole sample. There were no major differences between areas in this respect, nor were there substantial differences between areas in the period of immigration for those who were foreign-born. It appears that Manhattan's Chinatown is no longer the main area of first settlement for immigrants. On the other hand, there were some differences in citizenship (63 percent of those outside the city were citizens, compared to 50 percent of those in Manhattan). More striking differences were shown in English-language ability (89 percent living outside the city spoke English well, compared to only 45 percent in Manhattan). Manhattan's Chinese were somewhat older than those in other areas. Family composition and family life cycle therefore seemed to play a role in residential location. The percentage who were married ranged from a low of 66.6 percent in Manhattan to a high of 83.1 percent outside the city. Similarly, the percentage of persons with children under age seventeen ranged from only 34 percent in Manhattan to 58 percent outside the city.

The logit models predicting the likelihood of living in the suburbs (outside New York City versus inside the city) for the Chinese and non-Hispanic whites generate the following findings:

1. The three socioeconomic status variables all significantly increase the likelihood of living outside the city for the Chinese. For whites, however, household income has a positive effect, but education and occupational status have negative effects on living outside the city.

2. Sectoral employment does not show any significant effect on the Chinese group, but employment in these same industries (which, of course, do not constitute an "enclave" for whites) has a significant negative effect for whites.

3. The acculturation variables—English-language ability, citizenship, and year of immigration—show different patterns for both groups. For the Chinese, only English makes a difference in place of residence. For whites, only year of immigration has a signifi-

cant effect; U.S.-born and earlier immigrants are more likely to live in the suburbs than recent immigrants.
4. Age is not significant for either group, but the family situation variables are statistically significant for both.[25]

The equation predicting outer borough residence (living in outer boroughs versus living in Manhattan) is very similar to the one for suburban residence for the Chinese. For the non-Hispanic whites, however, the positive effects of household income, U.S. birth, and earlier immigration on residential decentralization disappear. Only education (negatively) and family situation have significant effects on outer-borough residence for whites. These findings do not point toward a simple interpretation: the predictors for the Chinese are not uniformly the same as or different from those for whites.

The findings for whites are only partly consistent with the assimilation model. The effect of immigration status on city/suburban residence is as predicted by cultural assimilation, but there is no parallel effect on location within the city. Similarly, higher household income is associated with suburban residence, but among those who live in New York City, household income does not distinguish between those who reside in Manhattan and those who live in the outer boroughs. Having children and being married are clearly related to residential decentralization. Some of these effects may reflect gentrification by whites, as well as the existence of exclusive white neighborhoods in parts of Manhattan.

The positive effects of most socioeconomic status variables for the Chinese suggest a strong relationship between social mobility and residential decentralization—more consistent with assimilation theory than those for whites. The absence of an effect of enclave employment for the Chinese supports Alejandro Portes's view that enclave participation does not restrict residential mobility, but the significant negative effect of sectoral employment for whites indicates that the residential mobility for whites who worked in the industries defined as enclave industries is limited. The effects of marital status and children are the same for the Chinese as for whites.

A curious difference concerns acculturation measures. For the Chinese, the only significant influence on location is English-language ability. The insignificance of the effects of U.S. citizenship, year of immigration, and age in these equations suggests that recent and young Chinese immigrants often bypass the enclave. This pattern represents a departure from the experience of earlier immigrant groups. Some more direct evidence on this point comes from a cross-tabulation of residence in 1975 with residence in 1980 at the county level.[26] The majority of the Chinese lived in the same residence and in the same subarea in 1980 as in 1975. Only about 8 percent of outer-borough Chinese and about 5 percent of those outside the city had moved into their present residence from Manhattan in the previous five years. By comparison, nearly 20 percent of the residents of the outer boroughs or outside the city had lived abroad only five years before. This finding does not prove that the immigrants came directly to outer areas, but it does appear that outward movement by longtime Manhattan residents accounts for only part of the growth of the Chinese population in the outer boroughs and suburbs.

Results: Neighborhood Characteristics

So far my analysis suggests that the Chinese tend to be segregated from other racial/ethnic groups in Manhattan or in New York City, and unless they are able to move out of the enclave or the city, their chances of interracial contact do not increase substantially. The next logical question is, In what kind of neighborhoods are the Chinese most likely to reside? Are they as likely as non-Hispanic whites to be found in neighborhoods with favorable characteristics? I employ multiple regression techniques to estimate the independent effects of various census-tract characteristics on the dependent variable—percentage of Chinese. I have also included two other equations—predicting the percentage of non-Hispanic blacks and the percentage of non-Hispanic whites—for comparison purposes. I suspected that segregation patterns for the Chinese might not be the same as those for blacks and whites.

Table 8-4 lists the selected characteristics of census tracts. Overall, tracts located outside the city had more desirable characteristics than those in the city. Within New York City only a little more than half the residents were white. In neighborhoods outside the city whites made up a much higher percentage of residents (81 percent). The concentration of immigrants tended to be much higher in the city. On average, close to a quarter of the city's population was foreign-born. Further, the city had an older housing stock, more rental housing and multifamily housing, and a lower level of residential stability. A similar pattern holds for Manhattan versus the outer boroughs, except that in Manhattan the percentages of the foreign-born, those with a college education, and those with top-ranking occupations are much higher.

Results from multivariate analyses for the Chinese showed that in New

Table 8-4. Selected Characteristics of Census Tracts in the New York Metropolitan Area

	N.Y.C.	Outside N.Y.C.	Manhattan	Outer Boroughs
Total number of tracts [1]	2,148	2,396	289	1,859
% Chinese	1.5	.3	3.0	1.3
% Non-Chinese Asians	1.4	1.0	1.5	1.4
% Non-Hispanic whites	53.6	81.1	50.3	54.1
% Non-Hispanic blacks	24.2	10.7	23.5	24.2
% Hispanics	18.8	6.5	21.0	18.4
% Other races	.5	.4	.7	.6
% Foreign-born	22.7	11.3	22.4	22.7
Median household income	$14,845	$22,794	$14,012	$14,973
% College education	26.0	33.5	43.3	23.3
% Top-ranking occupations	23.9	29.8	38.2	21.7
% Houses built before 1940	52.3	32.0	57.5	51.5
% Rental housing	68.6	34.4	92.8	64.9
% Multi-family housing	81.3	38.9	99.6	78.5
% Same residence as in 1975	54.8	58.8	49.4	55.7

Source: U.S. Census of Population: 1980 STF3A.
[1] Tracts with a total population of 50 or more.

York City, the Chinese were most likely to share a tract with other Asians and least likely to be in the same tract with either non-Hispanic blacks or Hispanics. They were found in tracts where the percentages of top-ranking occupations were lower. Tracts with larger percentages of Chinese were more likely to be found in Manhattan. However, none of the other tract characteristics seems to have significantly affected the residential patterns of the Chinese. Median household income, which is generally believed to be an important predictor, did not have a significant effect.

In suburban areas, the Chinese were located in better tracts. Median household income, top-ranking occupations, the percentages of other Asians and Hispanics all had significantly positive, though moderate, effects on where the Chinese lived. Moreover, the Chinese were more likely to live in newer neighborhoods outside the city. The percentage of non-Hispanic blacks, residential stability, and rental housing did not have significant effects. Compared to non-Hispanic blacks, the Chinese were doing better in residential mobility. Nevertheless, they still did not seem to live in neighborhoods with similar characteristics to those of whites.

For non-Hispanic blacks and non-Hispanic whites, the results were consistent with the existing literature on patterns of residential segregation.[27] Blacks were segregated from the majority and other minority groups, and they tended to be disproportionately concentrated in disadvantaged neighborhoods in central cities or in poor suburbs. Manhattan tended to concentrate tracts with a larger percentage of non-Hispanic blacks. Either in New York City or in the suburbs, blacks tended to reside in tracts with fewer Asians and fewer Hispanics, fewer persons with top-ranking occupations, and newer housing stocks. In addition, the city's non-Hispanic blacks were also found in lower-income tracts with fewer longtime residents and less owner-occupied housing. Outside the city, median household income did not affect where blacks lived, and residential stability and rental housing were significantly positively related to the percentage of blacks. Results for non-Hispanic whites are almost exactly the opposite of those for the non-Hispanic blacks.

The overall explanatory power (R^2) of the multivariate equations for the Chinese was very weak contrasted to those for non-Hispanic blacks and non-Hispanic whites, but it contributed to my growing knowledge about the dynamics of segregation and residential patterns. The segregation pattern for the Chinese was, in fact, different. On the one hand, residential movement of the city's Chinese was highly selective and moved toward relatively disadvantaged tracts; thus residential mobility might not necessarily be associated with status achievement. Unless the Chinese moved out of the city altogether, they would still have a high probability of being segregated from the majority or from other minority groups if they simply left Chinatown. On the other hand, the poor performance of median household income as a predictor suggested that ethnicity might dominate social class in determining residential patterns for the city's Chinese—that is, higher-income and lower-income households were possibly mixed in the same neighborhood.[28]

Residential Mobility and Resegregation

At first glance, residential mobility seems to be strongly associated with socioeconomic factors. Suburbanization seems a key step to spatial assimilation for the Asians. Perhaps the Chinese have a much better chance to assimilate into the mainstream if they move farther away from the city. It may also be true that the Chinese, like many other Asians, are less segregated compared to blacks and Hispanics if they reside somewhere outside the city.[29] Ever since they decided to stay in the United States, the Chinese have always wanted to convert their economic gains into residential ones by buying nice homes and settling down away from, but accessible to, Chinatown. They have been pursuing this strategy on a small scale for a long time, and it is, thus, not a unique phenomenon.

My analyses have revealed a number of contradictions and pointed to a more complex reality beyond what a simple reading of the assimilation model can account for. The unique issue for New York City's Chinese is why they are so overwhelmingly concentrated in the city and why they are so inclined to cling to each other. There are certain mechanisms that enforce or reinforce ethnic segregation within the Chinese community that classical measurement and statistical numbers cannot always sufficiently document. What has actually happened to Chinese residents in New York seems to reflect three factors: developmental pressures in Chinatown during the first half of the 1980s, reliance on family and kinship networks to obtain housing, and the impact of a growing ethnic housing market. All of these factors are better understood in the light of findings from fieldwork conducted within the Chinese community.

Development of the Enclave as a Determinant

An obvious reason why Chinese immigrants are so concentrated in New York City is that there is a Chinatown there. Chinatown, in this sense, does not simply refer to a residential enclave; rather, it indicates economic opportunities—jobs. Jobs that have been generated in the economic enclave are accessible to Chinese immigrants. Indeed, they are almost the only means through which immigrants can make their American dream come true. The majority of immigrant men and women work in restaurants, garment factories, and a wide range of ethnic businesses in Chinatown.

Workers who work in Chinatown but live elsewhere rely on the subway for daily transportation. Even some of the Chinese, particularly restaurant workers, who do not work in Chinatown, still have to go to Chinatown by subway first and then be transported elsewhere by company vans to work in Chinese restaurants that are scattered all over the city and in the New York metropolitan area. Every day, between nine and ten in the morning, the vans, some with restaurant names on the side, are seen lining up to pick up workers in such places as Confucius Plaza in Old Chinatown and in front of a Woolworth's store on Main Street in Flushing.

As might be expected, the relationship between job location and residence is reciprocal. To some extent, the ability of enclave industries to expand outside the city is limited by the shortage of Chinese workers in suburban areas. A restaurant owner, Mr. Yung, who ran a restaurant in Port Washington, Long Island, had to turn to Chinatown to recruit workers. He said:

> I run a Chinese restaurant and prefer Chinese employees, in part because I can easily communicate with the workers, and also my patrons would expect to see Chinese waiters serving the food. But it is hard to find Chinese workers in the local area. So I have to rely on one of about twenty Chinatown employment agencies to hire workers.
>
> The problem is that since these workers live with their families in the city, transportation to work by train is expensive and time-consuming. If we did not provide transportation, we simply could not get the workers. So I have to send a van every day to Chinatown to pick up workers to work.
>
> Nowadays, Chinese restaurants have sprung up in the suburbs, where it is hard to find ethnic workers. Some restaurants have set up dormitory-type facilities in apartments, and the ones that have not have to take the workers back and forth every morning from Chinatown or from Flushing. I also have a dormitory for my workers, but they do not want to stay there, they want to be with other Chinese. So this type of transporting of workers to work has become a pattern.[30]

For Chinese workers who do not live in Chinatown, access to dispersed job opportunities requires them to go to Chinatown by subway first. Mr. Lin, a waiter in Mr. Yung's restaurant, said:

> I live in Corona. Every morning I go to Flushing to wait for the company van to take me and other co-workers to work in Long Island. It usually takes about forty-five minutes each way, the same amount of time as it would take one from Corona to Chinatown by subway train. If the restaurant provides transportation, I would prefer to work outside the city. Working in the suburbs, I get higher pay, because suburb restaurants usually have more affluent patrons, and we get more tips. But I definitely do not want to move out to live near that restaurant, because I am not sure when I would switch jobs again.[31]

Therefore, the residential pattern of the city's Chinese is largely deter-mined by the ties to Chinatown's economy. It has become very important to find a place to live near the subway lines, just for job access. In fact, neighborhoods elsewhere in the city that have concentrated a consider-able number of Chinese are all accessible and convenient to the subway. For example, residents in Woodside, Elmhurst, Jackson Heights, Corona, and Flushing, Queens can take the number 7 subway train to Manhattan; Rego Park is accessible to the E, F, and G lines; Ridgewood is close to the L line; and residents in Sunset Park, Bay Ridge, Borough Park, and Brooklyn can take the B, N, R, or M trains to Chinatown. In sum, it does not matter where the Chinese live as long as there is easy access to where their jobs are.

The enclave economy provides jobs for immigrant Chinese, helps them adjust to the new country, and smooths barriers in the path of incor-poration. Meanwhile, however, the economic growth itself has created a tremendous demand on the limited space; and, as a result, residential space has had to give way to commercial development.

A growing local economy and an influx of foreign money gave a boost to the real estate market in much of Manhattan, particularly in the early 1980s. Chinatown clearly shows the economic boom that has resulted from tremendous foreign capital inflow from the Chinese communities in Hong Kong, Taiwan, and parts of Southeast Asia and from recent immigrants. The reason for such a large capital influx is partly the politi-cal uncertainty in Hong Kong, Taiwan, and Southeast Asia, particularly the unpredictable future of Hong Kong after the 1997 take-over by the Chinese Communist government, and partly the worldwide recession in the early 1970s that forced U.S. financial markets to offer higher inter-est rates.[32] Foreign investors have been especially interested in low-risk, nonliquid assets, that is, real estate development in Chinatown. They have either gradually bought old buildings, renovated them, and con-verted them into commercial space to yield much higher returns in rent or simply waited and speculated on higher resale to make a profit.[33] Partly as a result, residential space has given way to commercial development. Moreover, the desire of Chinese retailers to locate in the heart of China-town has further boosted the price of property. According to a study by the Real Estate Board of New York, the annual rent per square foot for commercial space in the core of Chinatown ($275) was far higher than on Wall Street ($175), it was also higher than the most desirable commer-cial locations in Manhattan's Central Business District, for example, on

Madison Avenue above Forty-second Street ($255).[34] During the 1970s
and early 1980s, real estate investment in Chinatown was on the rise.
John Wang, former director of the Chinatown Planning Council in New
York, was startled by the pace of change in the enclave during that period.
He talked about it in an interview:

> I can't keep up with it! I mean, I work here and the next day I come
> to work—Boom! What is that? Stores and buildings seem to change
> faces everyday.
>
> In the past ten or fifteen years, because of the tremendous influx
> of immigration and foreign capital, Chinatown has become a battle-
> field for developers and investors. According to a recent survey, it
> is estimated that real estate purchases in New York City by Chinese
> and Chinese-American investors were close to $150 million in 1983,
> with transactions in Manhattan accounting for half of the amount.
> Right now, I guess that there are at least a dozen buildings in the
> core area that are being converted from manufacturing to commer-
> cial space, ending their lives as garment factories and being reborn
> as offices and shops.
>
> Poor immigrant families have been priced out and displaced to
> other areas; and more and more better-to-do Asians, and even some
> of the non-Chinese artists and Wall Street Yuppies have started
> to purchase converted condominiums in Chinatown at the average
> price of $150,000. The community has been gentrified; it has be-
> come a place for the wealthy, rather than just a poor immigrant
> ghetto.[35]

Real estate transactions in Chinatown yielded tremendous profit for
investors and landowners during the late 1970s and the early 1980s. Residential rents increased by 200 to 300 percent within a short period of
time. Illegal "key money," a lump sum renters were required to pay to
obtain housing, brought additional profit to investors.[36] Mr. Lu, when
I interviewed him, had lived and worked in Chinatown for over twenty
years. He was also shocked by the extremely large profits owners could
make by converting a building from residential to commercial use. Here
is an example he gave:

> Some lucky owners can make a lot of money through conversion. For
> example, before conversion of a five-story building on Canal Street,
> the ground floor was an electronics store, the second to the third
> floors used to be garment shops, and the top two floors housed about

eight families. From what I know, the first four floors have been converted to commercial space. Instead of collecting rents from two garment shops and a store, the owner now has twelve commercial tenants, each paying at least eighteen hundred dollars a month, plus the key money. Key money is illegal and everybody knows it, but no one can do anything about it. In the 1970s, key money ranged from five hundred to two thousand dollars. Now it is usually ten times the rent.[37]

The most serious threat to Chinatown residents originating from the land development and speculation is tenant harassment and eviction. According to Mr. Mui, an activist from Asian-Americans for Equality, Chinatown tenants have recently started to file legal complaints and lawsuits against their landlords for the leaky ceilings, peeling plaster, and poor security in their buildings and for excessive rent increases. Mr. Mui said:

> The Chinese immigrants are usually very tolerant and they know little about their rights as tenants. They do not want any trouble; they do not want to have anything to do with a lawsuit. If they did, it would mean they were very serious.
>
> For example, in 1984 twenty-two tenants of two tenements on Henry Street in Chinatown filed a legal complaint against their landlords for excessive rent increases. Most of these tenants were longtime residents who had been working in Chinatown. They suspected that the increases were a prelude to getting them out and getting in those with more money to spend on rent. Among them, there was a Mrs. Wong, a sixty-six-year-old garment worker who had lived there for almost forty years. She said she would have no place else to go and that this had been her home.
>
> Mrs. Wong's landlord, Mr. Sung, won the endorsement of the Chinatown Planning Council for a plan to rehabilitate his Henry Street building in 1982. After making some improvements—new storm windows, light fixtures, an intercom system, and a coat of paint—the landlord received an approval for rent increases of up to 30 percent. The new rent for eighty-eight-year-old Mr. Yuen, another longtime resident, who lived alone in one room there, was $200.68, from $77.44. Mr. Yuen's social security check could barely cover the increased rent.
>
> The tenants decided to pay the old rents while they challenged the

increases. However, the landlord, Mr. Sung, simply put the building up for sale. The tenants did not win the case.

There have been cases that tenants have won. When tenants saw their landlord fined and thrown out of the Rent Stabilization Association, and the building reverted to rent control, they felt they could do something to protect themselves.

In the past few years, we have received a lot of phone complaints from tenants against their landlords. Most of the time, they come to us for advice; they want us to help them settle the problems without going to court. Some of the landlords take advantage of the legal ignorance of the Chinese immigrants. Our goal is to educate them and help them stand up and confront their landlords for tenant harassment and eviction.[38]

I find, in short, that the cost of property, particularly renovated space, in the core Chinatown area has now become so high that there is little affordable fringe housing left there. What is operative is not simply the gentrification trend that has created greater demand for space throughout Manhattan but also a specific change in Chinatown. Chinatown used to be a residential enclave, based on a social structure of sojourning. Now the enclave has increasingly become a center for economic development. Whether they are priced out or pushed out of Chinatown, recent immigrants are adapting to this transformation.

Family and Kinship Ties as Determinants

In the previous statistical analyses, I found that family situation variables—being married and having children—were significant predictors of living outside the enclave, but none of the immigration variables had any significant effects. These findings imply that it is perhaps not necessary for a recent immigrant to live in Chinatown first and then move on to better neighborhoods as time goes by, as was posited by the traditional succession model of ethnic assimilation. Immigrants could simply bypass Chinatown to find their first settlement area elsewhere. Apparently, what is missing in the logistic analyses is the effect of family ties and networks, which are directly related to immigration in determining where one lives.

The reason the Chinese have concentrated in large metropolitan coastal cities such as San Francisco, Los Angeles, and New York is connected with the history of Chinese immigration. The Chinese came to wherever their predecessors were. As discussed in the earlier chapters, more than 80 percent of the Chinese quota immigrants came to the

United States under relative-preference categories, and less than 20 percent came under occupational-preference categories; the spouse of a U.S. citizen is not subject to the quota system. More than 90 percent of the Chinese immigrants came to join their families and relatives. This same family networking has significantly shaped the settlement patterns of the new wave of Chinese immigrants.

Whenever I asked, "Why did you come to settle in New York?" the immediate response was usually "Because my relatives are here." Mr. Lee recalled the first few months after his family of six came to New York:

> My wife and I and our four children, the oldest being fifteen years old, immigrated in 1979 from Taishan. My sister-in-law, Ah Ling, who is a naturalized U.S. citizen, helped us out.
>
> When we were about to leave China, my country folks asked me where in America I would go. I told them New York. They wondered why not San Francisco. All I could tell them was because Ah Ling was there and she was the only one who would receive us in the U.S. Actually, I (like my country folks) knew nothing else other than San Francisco and New York, where most of the relatives lived.
>
> When we arrived at JFK International Airport in New York, Ah Ling and her husband came to pick us up. She said, "You have to live with us for the time being. I hope you don't mind." I was only grateful. How could I possibly resist such a generous offer?
>
> Ah Ling's family lived in a small two-bedroom apartment in Jackson Heights, Queens. They had three kids similar to the age of mine. They gave us a bedroom and the eleven of us all crammed in this small apartment with three of the older kids sleeping on the living room floor at night.

Mr. Lee shares the first experience of many Chinese immigrants. He was certain that for almost all immigrant Chinese, where they lived depended on where the relatives who got them here lived. He continued,

> We did not have a choice but listened to whatever Ah Ling had to say. We did not have any money; we did not know anybody else; we did not speak a single word of English; and everything here was so foreign to us that we were basically scared.
>
> I knew that a lot of immigrant families had to go through this. I did the same thing to my own brother's family when I got them out a couple of years ago. I had to put them up in my apartment for half a

year. This is a tradition that has been going on for a long time; it is a family obligation which you are not supposed to avoid.[39]

Mr. Lee has never lived in Chinatown, simply because his relatives did not live there.

Another family, which has always been in Chinatown since immigration, told the other side of the story. Mrs. Chen, who came from Zhongshan to join her husband, has lived in Chinatown since 1980. Her husband, Mr. Chen, immigrated in 1969 as a refugee from Hong Kong. He was originally smuggled into Hong Kong from Zhongshan during the Chinese Cultural Revolution and then came to the United States at the age of eighteen. With little education, no English-language ability, and few relatives here, he had to turn to Chinatown for support. He first worked in a restaurant as a dishwasher. He learned how to cook while working close to the cooks, and currently he cooks for one of the Chinatown restaurants. He shared a unit (one room with a small kitchen and a bathroom) with three other bachelor coworkers in one of the bachelors' quarters in Chinatown. Like many of the bachelors, he had to go home to find a wife. When Mrs. Chen came, they managed to rent the whole unit in the bachelors' quarter when Chen's three roommates volunteered to move out. Mr. Chen had to pay five hundred dollars to each of his roommates for moving expenses, in the common practice of Chinatown. The rent itself was low, only seventy-five dollars, because the apartment was rent controlled, but the Chens had to pay eight hundred dollars in "key money" every two years to renew the lease. Mrs. Chen now has two children, and she and her husband and children still live in the apartment in Chinatown. When asked whether the family had considered moving, she replied:

> Not at the moment. Maybe when the kids grow older, we would move into a bigger apartment somewhere. Living in Chinatown is just so convenient. We don't have to spend time on the subway train; my husband and I only walk a few blocks to work. It is also safer. My husband gets off work at 11:00 P.M. with cash wages in his pocket. Riding on a subway train at night is not very safe; besides, it is time-consuming. Also, I can leave my kids next door at my neighbors'. If you lived elsewhere, even if there were other Chinese around, you could not possibly find a baby-sitter so close by, and you would have to hurry off every day in the morning to send your kids to the baby-sitter and then catch the subway train to work, or you couldn't work at all. Moreover, I don't have to pack my refrigerator; I can bring

in fresh vegetables and food everyday after work. I feel life is much easier when you are close to an environment similar to the one you grew up in.[40]

Mrs. Chen came right to Chinatown. She did not make her own residential choice; she lived in Chinatown because her husband was there. Now she has gotten so used to Chinatown's conveniences that she can tolerate the extreme crowdedness and poor housing. She and her family may live there for a long time, until her children grow older or the crowdedness becomes unbearable.

Mrs. Chen's case has one thing in common with Mr. Lee's. Both came to join their relatives and settled wherever their relatives were. In the Old Chinatown area, as the growth of the Chinese population far exceeds the scale of residential expansion, the level of segregation has increased along with the density level. In other parts of the city, family chain networks have directed immigrants into neighborhoods where a considerable number of Chinese families have already concentrated, thus establishing new enclaves and resegregating the group. In other words, other areas have developed Chinese populations, in part from the outward movement of people from Chinatown and in part through family networks of new immigrants.

The Impact of an Ethnic Housing Market

A growing ethnic housing market also functions to help immigrants overcome the language barrier in their effort to find affordable housing. This pattern, in turn, may help to account for the unexpectedly high level of residential segregation. The basic concern of the Chinese immigrants is housing, for both practical and cultural reasons. Practically speaking, they need a decent place to live. Culturally speaking, the Chinese have always had a craving for land. The dearest wish of early sojourners was to save enough money so that they could buy land at home, because they saw land as something they could pass on to the next generation. Now Chinese immigrants are no longer going back to China, but this craving has grown even stronger; their ultimate goal is to own a piece of property in the United States on which their families can live. It seems that many Chinese immigrants are working hard in order to move to self-employment, but in reality, not every immigrant Chinese has actually ended up running his or her own business. For many, the American dream is, perhaps, to own a house. Success in the United States has been measured not so much by what one does as by how much property one owns. Since the majority of the immigrant Chinese speak very little English, have limited contact with the outside society, and have no knowledge of the larger housing market, they have to depend on the ethnic market to satisfy their housing demands. If they decide to hunt for housing by themselves, they usually check the Chinese newspaper ads put up mostly by Chinese landlords and call around accordingly. If the landlord who answers the call happens to be a non-Chinese, they often just hang up, because they can speak only Chinese. Immigrants also depend on the Chinese-run banks and real estate agencies.

Chinese immigrants, because they lack a credit history, lack English-language ability, and lack stable incomes, have more difficulty than native Americans in obtaining loans from mainstream banks. They go to Chinese banks for credit whenever necessary. Generally, however, they try not to borrow. Traditionally, the concept of credit is totally foreign to most Chinese immigrants. If one does not have money, one should not be tempted to buy; borrowing should be resorted to only in extreme emergencies. Many families postpone buying until they have saved enough to cover the entire cost. They scrimp and economize, putting aside a large proportion of their income for this goal.[41] More recently, some families have begun to borrow money from the banks, but only when they realize that their mortgage interest can be deducted from income taxes.

Real estate agencies help immigrant Chinese both in purchasing houses and in renting apartments. Many Chinese immigrants depend on these Chinese-run agencies. Even if they search for housing by themselves in order to save some money, they are still confined to the ethnic housing market, and they often end up spending more money and more time on worse housing. "It is a pain and time-consuming to look for a suitable apartment all by yourself," said Mr. Lee when he talked about his experience of house hunting, and many new immigrant families would echo his statement. "After my wife and I both got a job," he continued,

> we decided to look for an apartment by ourselves. We picked up a Chinese newspaper in Chinatown, and started making phone calls at night. If the landlord was not a Chinese, I would hang up on him, because I could not talk in English. Most of the available units rented out by Chinese owners seemed to be in convenient locations because the owners themselves lived in the same house. But when you actually went there to see the unit, it might not be the one you wanted. Those houses look pretty nice from outside, but from inside many units we could afford were not in very good shape. The owners did not seem to do much to maintain their rental units, let alone reno-

vate them. Housing was in such great demand that those landlords did not have to worry about whether their units could be rented out or not. Most of the time, it was the landlord who chose his tenants rather than the other way around.

We had looked at five or six houses before we decided on one in a neighborhood a few blocks from my sister-in-law's in Jackson Heights. We did not dare to move far, since we barely knew anybody here. It took us three weekends just to look from one house to another. Some people would simply pay a hundred-dollar fee and leave the whole thing to the real estate agency. I would have done so if I had anticipated the hectic experience.[42]

Real estate agents and brokers have played an important role in guiding residential choices. They are also able to make good profits in their business simply by increasing the number of clients who are recent immigrants so desperately in need of housing but with so little knowledge about the general housing market. The real estate agencies, with the support of ethnic financial capital from abroad, often manage to buy into low-income minority neighborhoods where old owners are in a hurry to sell their properties for cash to invest in their homes elsewhere. In such cases, the agents and brokers are able to obtain the houses at a lower price and then turn around and immediately sell the same houses to immigrant Chinese families, usually without any repairs or improvement, at higher prices—ranging from 25 percent to 50 percent higher than the take-over prices. The new owners live on one or two floors and rent the rest out, again without much repair work, to other Chinese immigrant families.

Heavy demand from immigrant Chinese for affordable housing in New York City has stimulated investment in outlying neighborhoods in Queens and Brooklyn. The active functioning of the enclave housing market, combined with ethnicity and the economic ties to Chinatown, has shaped the residential patterns of New York City's Chinese. However, the dispersion of the Chinese and the resulting neighborhood take-over tend to occur in poorer and less desirable areas and hence tend to displace low-income minority groups and threaten the white working class of the city. As a result, incidents of overt conflict have become more frequent. For example, a Chinese family that bought a house on an all-white working-class block in Prospect Park, Brooklyn, and brought along with them two Chinese families as tenants, repeatedly experienced racial attacks on their property and cars from some of their neighbors.[43] Moreover, even if they have enough money, the Chinese are still blocked by redlining from buying into more favorable middle-class neighborhoods.

Even assuming that the effect of discriminatory redlining and ignorance of the larger society is zero, the ethnic housing market is able to operate in such a way that it effectively maneuvers the residential movement of the Chinese. Consequently, new satellite Chinese enclaves have been produced in new locations in Queens and Brooklyn. The rise of these new enclaves provides evidence of resegregation for the Chinese, who have supposedly escaped Chinatown. Ms. Liang, for example, who is an immigrant herself and runs a real estate agency in Flushing, commented: "Our customers are exclusively Chinese, most of whom are immigrants and speak very little English. They want to buy or rent a house, but they don't know how and where. They come to us, and we provide them with all the necessary information and help in every step to their satisfaction. We deal with our customers in Chinese and in ways that they are familiar with."[44]

The kinship network, which helps immigrants overcome the language barrier in their effort to find affordable housing outside Chinatown, may also help to account for the unexpectedly high level of residential segregation for the Chinese.[45] The family network affects residential mobility. Immigrant Chinese who fulfill their strong desire to own a piece of property in the United States on which their families can live achieve a sense of social mobility even if they do not rise in the occupational ladder. Sixty-seven-year-old Mr. Cheung, who had just retired from his restaurant job, explained this in an interview at his own home in Jackson Heights, Queens:

> I immigrated with my family in 1965 from Hong Kong. I worked in a restaurant for twenty-three years. The whole family—my wife and I, and six kids—used to cram into a small two-room apartment in Chinatown. Both my wife and I worked right away, and three years later, my two elder daughters worked to help bring in income. We worked hard and lived on a very tight budget with a goal of buying our own home. In 1984 we purchased this three-story house. Now my wife and I with our two youngest children live on the second floor; the first and the third floor are rented out to two immigrant families who recently arrived from Guangdong. Only since then have I started to think of retiring, because I finally have something that can be left for my children.[46]

Housing is an immediate concern for recent Chinese immigrants. Those who immigrate with a lot of money, especially those from Hong

Kong, Taiwan, and Southeast Asia, want to purchase their own housing. Those who come without money need to rent a place first. Mrs. Lai said:

> My husband and I want to buy our own home somewhere in the city. We both feel that if we have a job, work hard, and live on a frugal budget, we can save money to invest in housing. For us, buying a home is a more secure and practical investment than starting up a small business. Not everybody is successful in business.
>
> My family of six, including my parents-in-law, who also work, now live in a three-bedroom apartment in Sunset Park, Brooklyn. We pay $650 rent. With four workers in the household, it is not difficult to pool money to purchase a house.[47]

The real estate agent Ms. Liang added: "Because rents are so high, immigrants who have been here for a while would rather buy their own housing. Housing investment is based on longtime savings and a family effort for most of the people. With three or four working people in a household and a frugal lifestyle, it is not difficult to save the amount needed to pay the down payment, and they can rent part of the house out to get money to pay off their mortgage."[48] Almost all my informants, particularly those who work in the enclave, shared Mr. Cheung's, Mrs. Lai's, and Ms. Liang's idea about housing. Even if their earnings may not be transferred into higher occupational status, they can be converted into residential gains. This strategy implies a collective effort. It is a family strategy, distinct from the generally assumed path of socioeconomic mobility.

The settlement patterns for New York's Chinese also suggest a voluntary process. Originally Chinatown was established as a means of self-defense against the hostile environment with which immigrant Chinese were confronted. Later it developed into voluntary segregation in order to preserve group solidarity for mutual help and for linguistic and cultural security.[49] Today, the voluntary aspect of segregation has become more persistent as the amount of hostility generally faced by the group has decreased. Also, the preference of immigrant Chinese for proximity and accessibility to the economic enclave largely determines their residential choices. Again, informant interviews offered some interpretation:

> Chinese immigrants have some essential preferences concerning where they would like to live. First, the location has to be convenient—near the subway lines, for many of the immigrants work in Chinatown and the subway is their only means of transportation.

Second, the neighborhood has to be safe with a good mix of ethnic groups. The Chinese prefer to live in a neighborhood with at least a Chinese family, some Asians, and maybe some Hispanics. People used to joke that the Chinese had a herd instinct; they were inclined to herd around their own folks. They don't want to be the first one to move into a non-Chinese neighborhood, but as soon as one makes such a move, others will follow. There is rarely such a thing as just one Chinese family in a neighborhood. They feel more comfortable living with other Chinese, or with people who share at least some Oriental culture. Also, Asians are believed to be less crime-prone.[50]

Today, New York City's Chinese continue to cluster on the Lower East Side of Manhattan. Those who disperse mainly concentrate in Flushing, Elmhurst, Corona, Jackson Heights, Astoria, and Rego Park in Queens; Borough Park, Flatbush, Bay Ridge, Park Slope, Midwood, Sheepshead Bay, and Sunset Park in Brooklyn.[51] Many immigrant families in outlying areas may be wealthier than those who live in Chinatown; however, there are also a large number of poor immigrant families who simply bypass Chinatown to settle elsewhere. These immigrants show a tendency toward resegregation or self-segregation in certain neighborhoods. Some of them share exactly the same characteristics as the Chinatown residents and suffer similar immigrant disadvantages. This finding suggests that, on the one hand, ethnicity, or race, is perhaps more salient than class in the residential choices of immigrant Chinese, and on the other hand, current residential patterns outside Chinatown, determined largely by ethnic segmentation of the housing market, prevent the Chinese from gaining familiarity and knowledge of the larger society, thus reinforcing resegregation in satellite Chinatowns.

Conclusion

The Chinese in New York are concentrated in Manhattan, Queens, and Brooklyn, and they are more highly segregated than one might have anticipated from the research literature. For the Chinese, decentralization is strongly associated with less segregation from non-Hispanic whites. This finding supports a key prediction of assimilation theory. But segregation from other Asian subgroups is lowest in Manhattan and highest in the outer boroughs. This discrepancy serves as a reminder that there is no necessary link between such abstract categories as "centralization" and "segregation," or "suburbanization" and "assimilation." One needs considerable additional information: Where were the areas of initial settlement? How distinctive were these areas? Under what conditions in the housing market did immigrants resettle? What is the economic basis of the ethnic group, and how do labor-market factors affect residential location? Chinatown is an important point of orientation for the Chinese, and for many whose jobs are tied to the ethnic economy it serves as an anchor for residential choices.

The residential patterns of Chinese in New York are related to socioeconomic status—a pattern that both the assimilation and enclave models agree upon. That is, the Chinese are more likely to live outside of Manhattan and outside the city itself if they have higher socioeconomic status and if their family situation (marital status and presence of children) promotes it. Field interviews confirm that for many Chinese the purchase of a home in the neighborhoods of Queens or Brooklyn is perceived as a prime achievement and a symbol of success in life. Residential mobility, in many cases, is an expression of socioeconomic mobility.

However, residential decentralization may not serve as a good indicator of cultural assimilation into mainstream society for the Chinese, because recent Chinese immigrants are just as likely as the native-born to live in outer boroughs or suburban areas, even though English-language ability does make a difference. An important factor to take into account is the social organization of the Chinese community, which I have examined in terms of ties to the enclave, kinship networks, and the ethnic housing market. Whether one lives in Manhattan (more convenient) or in the outer boroughs or even in the suburban areas outside New York City (less expensive but accessible by subway or train), the tie to the enclave is persistent. Chinese families maintain links to the enclave even while enjoying upward social mobility and even when they live outside of Chinatown. Moreover, for immigrants, the key question is where their relatives live, and this preference is clearly reflected in the lack of association of citizenship and year of immigration with place of residence. Chinese immigrant families in New York express a strong inclination to live close to other Chinese, and they build their own ethnic community in the new neighborhoods they move to. Beyond the family network, there is also a formal real estate market organized through Chinese realtors, which tends to reinforce tendencies toward clustering in certain neighborhoods. For these reasons, immigrants simply do not participate widely in the open housing market. The set of market conditions that has traditionally operated to restrict such persons to the deteriorated, old, and dense housing stock of the inner city does not apply to them, and at the same time, housing prices in the core area have tended to force them out.

These findings may have implications for the future evolution of settlement patterns. Given cultural preferences and the strength of an ethnic and kinship-based real estate market, it is not likely that location outside of Chinatown will long remain associated with markedly lower segregation. Also, in the case of New York's Chinese, residential segregation results in large part from voluntary choices and may not cause any disadvantages. The enclave economy and segmented housing market provide the Chinese with a positive mode of incorporation distinct from assimilation into the larger society. This pattern is consistent with what is known about the operation of the enclave labor market discussed in the earlier chapters. But the Chinese pay a price: Wages in the enclave industries are low; housing prices in the Chinese market are high; and extended families live for long periods in crowded quarters.

9

Conclusion:

Rising Out of Chinatown

This book tells the story of immigrant Chinese entering the United States in the past two decades and their daily struggle to gain social positions in American society. It is about how Chinatown is understood by immigrant Chinese as a positive means of adaptation to their new country. In the preceding chapters, I have analyzed and synthesized a great deal of information from the U.S. census, various published sources, and my fieldwork data, bringing them to bear on both theoretical and practical issues involving the mode of adaptation of immigrant Chinese in the United States. I argue that the enclave works to channel its group members into the larger society instead of setting barriers to immigrant incorporation.

Chinatown and Assimilation of the Chinese

Upon arrival in the United States, the social and economic behavior of immigrant Chinese is largely defined by culture and ethnicity, but their experience is often judged by American standards. When Chinatown produces effects that are at odds with the values and norms of the larger society, the image is often negative. However, from the perspective of immigrant Chinese, Chinatown has shown its great potential in helping to ease the transition to their new country and to facilitate their social mobility in American society. Community networks and social capital serve as major resources for achieving their socioeconomic goals. In the cultural environment of Chinatown immigrants can conduct their daily lives in their own language, following their own customs and rituals without fear and intimidation. Immigrants depend on this distinct ethnic identity, which they trust because it is familiar. They share the work ethic of Chinatown, the standard of value that keeps their hopes and dreams alive. For many immigrants of various socioeconomic backgrounds, Chinatown is a chance to rise out of poverty,[1] to gain entrance to the mainstream society, and to stand up as Chinese-Americans.

The Chinese are not innately unassimilable. In the past, the sojourning Chinese perceived their stay as the best option for achieving socio-economic status in China. This sojourning mentality—to stay and make enough money to go back to China—led them into a particular mode of adaptation that separated them from society. They came when the United States was badly in need of cheap labor to exploit the undeveloped West and to build the transcontinental railroad. Compared to the politically strong native working class, they accepted worse jobs at lower pay in the open labor market in the hope that they could save money to return home. Unfortunately, after most of the mines were exhausted and the transcontinental railroad completed, they found that they had not saved enough money and wanted to stay longer to work. Yet, the depressed labor-market conditions and their willingness to work for wages that whites considered unfair increasingly threatened the employment opportunities and ideology of the American white working class, which eventually rose up against Chinese laborers and pushed for legal exclusion. As a direct response to the structural barriers—social and labor-market discrimination and other immigrant disadvantages—Chinese laborers were forced into Chinatowns, where they found economic niches in which they could continue to pursue their sojourning goals. Old Chinatown in New York City was not unique. Like other immigrant enclaves, it served as a defense and survival strategy for immigrants in their receiving country. What was unique about the sojourning immigrants was that they never really attempted to incorporate into the United States.

Unlike their predecessors, recent immigrant Chinese have given up the sojourning mentality and have been inspired and motivated to integrate into American society. However, initial immigrant disadvantages and structural barriers—lack of English-language ability, marketable skills, and knowledge of the larger society; presumed racism and intimidation; urban industrial transition in the larger economy—still effectively limit their options of integration upon arrival in the United States. By way of Chinatown, the majority of the recent immigrant Chinese have been able to mobilize ethnic resources to build an alternative path that can speed up the integration process and lead to eventual success in their new country.

How does Chinatown incorporate its group members into the larger society? Today's Chinatown is no longer an isolated, self-contained immigrant community like the prewar U.S. Chinatowns. The enclave economy has developed a structural duality, an interaction between the protected sector and the export sector, which has slowly become incorporated into a particular segment constituent of the U.S. economy. Chinatown's enclave economy thrives under three major conditions: a large immigrant population, a steady and constant influx of physical capital, and a close-knit network of ethnic relations.

New York City has been the second largest receiving city for immigrant Chinese since the turn of the century, though the Chinese population there increased substantially only after 1965. Why should immigrant Chinese be concentrated in New York City or other large U.S. cities? It is generally presumed that job opportunities offered by large cities are the magnet drawing immigrants. However, in contemporary American cities, where large-scale industrial transition has occurred, many jobs that used to fit the needs and skills of new migrants, that is, blue-collar manufacturing jobs, have declined significantly, causing a high rate of joblessness.[2] Nevertheless, many immigrants still tend to cluster in big cities. They do so not merely because of jobs offered by the larger labor market (about which they may not know anything) but because of preexisting community and family networks, which create jobs for them and provide them with necessary help and support. In New York City's Chinatown, recent immigration has supplied the enclave with a large pool of cheap labor and also with a group of well-qualified and ambitious entrepreneurially minded immigrants. The immigrant Chinese, meanwhile, form a considerable group of ethnic consumers, large enough to support the enclave protected sector.

The resulting ethnic labor and consumer markets have transformed the economic structure of Chinatown. On the one hand, the demand for goods and services that are not easily accessible in the larger society gives rise to a larger and more diversified protected sector supplying basic as well as luxury goods and services. On the other hand, the large pool of surplus immigrant labor makes it possible for the enclave to develop an export sector that can successfully compete with the larger economy and generate income to reinvest in the enclave. Consequently, the enclave protected sector and the export sector not only depend upon each other but also develop linkages and increase the interface with the larger economy. In this way, the enclave no longer serves only the simple survival needs of the immigrants but is itself incorporated into the larger economy as a distinct segment.

Chinatown's post-1965 development has also been fueled by a significant influx of foreign capital. The fear of the uncertain political future in Southeast Asia, Taiwan, and Hong Kong has caused a large capital outflow from that region to the United States, a more secure site for investment. Foreign money does not come only from the rich, though some of the large corporations and businesses have indeed shifted part of their operations to the United States. It also comes from middle-class professionals and small businessmen, who have transferred their capital or savings as the first step in leaving their homeland. With a sufficiently large amount of foreign capital flowing into and circulating in Chinatown, combined with income generated from the enclave export sector, the enclave is able to grow beyond the low-end industries into a more diversified economy.

Furthermore, the development of the enclave economy relies, to a great extent, on the role of community and networks of kinship and family relations. The family and kinship connections affect such business operations as marketing, financing, investment, and employment. Both enclave entrepreneurs and workers are bound by and benefit from ethnic solidarity—mutual obligations, trust, and loyalty—which constitutes a form of social capital absent beyond the enclave boundaries. In Chinatown, the economic behavior of enclave participants is not purely self-interested, nor is it based on strict calculation in dollars. However, it is rational. It is embedded in an ongoing structure of social relations. Ethnic entrepreneurs depend on a motivated, reliable, and exploitable labor force to survive in the highly competitive business environment. In return, they create job opportunities serving the short-term goals of ethnic members who must choose between low wages and joblessness.

What is good about the enclave? With the existence of a diversified economy, immigrant Chinese are provided with security of employment, shelter against overt or covert ethnic discrimination, and for some, opportunities for upward mobility. There are jobs in Chinatown that are immediately available for even the most recent arrivals. Many of these jobs are characterized by low wages, long hours, and poor working conditions, which seem highly exploitative from the mainstream standpoint. However, for many immigrant workers, accepting the low-paid menial jobs provided by the enclave is an expected part of their time-honored path toward upward social mobility of the family. After immigration, they set themselves a specific goal—to succeed in America socioeconomically. In Chinese culture, failure is not tolerated; it is considered shameful to be on welfare and not to work. The work ethic of immigrant Chinese is built on a value standard from the Chinese culture and not on the one from the dominant culture. Therefore, substandard wages, which are much higher than wages in China as calculated by immigrant Chinese, are regarded as better than no wages at all. Also, immigrant Chinese are used to working long hours before immigration. If they can earn more by working longer, they prefer to do so. This by no means suggests that immigrant Chinese willingly accept menial jobs, low wages, and long working hours. Rather, they perceive them as a shortcut to their long-term goal, which is to benefit not themselves but their children.

The other reason why immigrant workers prefer working in the enclave is that they perceive certain benefits that compensate for the disadvantages. First, a close-knit employment network based on the family, kinship, and community agencies effectively reduces the hassles and time involving in looking for a job. Many jobs in Chinatown do not have to be advertised, for entrepreneurs depend on the employment network to recruit workers. Those who are uneducated, unskilled, and without English-language ability cannot possibly have a job outside of Chinatown. Some may venture outside, but the limited jobs available to them pay the minimum wage and call for a standard five-day work schedule. Take-home pay is often less than it is within the enclave. For those immigrant Chinese who are well educated and skilled, but without sufficient English-language ability, the enclave has certain higher-ranking service-oriented jobs, particularly those in the protected sector, that enable them to avoid menial jobs. It is evident that enclave participation by male immigrant workers can bring significant income and occupational returns on human capital, similar to the returns gained in the larger economy.

Women workers, however, have not been able to achieve as much as their male counterparts in Chinatown. The conditions of the enclave have not led to economic independence for women. They are still expected, and they themselves expect, to continue to perform their multiple roles as wives, as mothers, and as wage workers. Yet, their behavior must be understood in the context of Chinese culture, which gives priority not to individual achievement but to the welfare of the family and the community as a whole. Many immigrant Chinese women have adopted a short-term orientation toward work: their purpose is not to develop careers but to contribute immediately to the household income for the benefit of the whole family. Women are most concerned about job security and the ability to augment family income, and they are less worried about being paid unfairly. In the enclave they are supplied with the kinds of jobs that fit in with their short-term purposes. As a result, what women workers have lost for themselves as individuals actually has turned out to be a substantial gain for their families. Their enclave participation is necessary for the family to achieve its economic goals.

Chinatown also functions as a shelter against the assignment of inferior social status to members of ethnic minorities. Within the enclave, racial/ethnic tensions are minimal, but outside it immigrant workers have to overcome presumed racism. In Chinatown the culture instills pride and confidence in individuals, thus building and strengthening ethnic identity and solidarity. In turn, workers are better able to understand their current situation as necessary and meaningful.

Chinatown fosters the development of ethnic businesses and a path on which immigrants can proceed toward self-employment. Enclave employment serves as an effective means of training and capital accumulation, which ambitious immigrants can use to start up their own businesses. Self-employment is perhaps the most significant indicator of economic success in Chinatown, and the enclave has generated many opportunities for business development and expansion not only in the protected sector but also in the export sector (for example, the garment industry). While some medium-scale or large-scale ethnic corporations emerge to replace smaller operations, most of the ethnic firms still remain small and family-run without any, or with only a few, non-Chinese employees. Despite the sometimes cutthroat competition among the self-employed and the hard work and long hours required of most enclave entrepreneurs, immigrants almost uniformly perceive self-employment as the best path to their economic goals, though only a few are very successful. The availability of a reliable, low-wage ethnic labor force represents an inevitable condition for the survival and success of many enclave small businesses. Self-employment enables ambitious immigrants to move ahead, but it also creates jobs for the majority of immigrant Chinese, who would otherwise be jobless in the larger labor market. In this sense, both entrepreneurs and workers gain economic benefits from the development of the enclave economy.

Does the enclave limit the residential mobility of the Chinese? To a certain extent, yes. Immigrant Chinese have been able to convert economic gains into residential ones through enclave participation. However, they tend to develop intangible ties to Chinatown, which, in turn, influence their residential patterns. Today, although many immigrant Chinese are still concentrated in New York City's Chinatown, the enclave is no longer the only point of entry for newcomers to America; some of the newer arrivals have, in fact, bypassed Chinatown to settle elsewhere in the city. Chinatown is simply not large enough to accommodate all new arrivals. Immigrant Chinese families have started to disperse to the outer boroughs of the city, forming new, smaller residential enclaves in Queens and Brooklyn. But even here they remain at least moderately segregated.

The factors that influence the residential patterns of immigrant Chinese are not merely socioeconomic ones; family and kinship networks, economic ties to the enclave economy, and the functions of an existing ethnic housing market all play important roles in determining where people live. Immigrant Chinese prefer to live close to their own people. Adaptation is not a matter of simply moving from the ethnic community into a mixed community. Ethnic members who are able to move out still rely heavily on ethnic bonds. Residential dispersion indicates that, on the one hand, today's immigrant Chinese are more adaptable than their predecessors to environments outside Chinatown and, on the other hand, that they are better able to convert economic gains into residential ones by moving into neighborhoods with more desirable characteristics than Chinatown. In New York City, however, the residential mobility of the Chinese is limited by place of work. Immigrant families move only as far as the outer boroughs, usually not out of the city altogether. They prefer to live close to where they work. Moreover, moving into mixed neighborhoods does not eliminate the possibility of ethnic resegregation. Chinese in the outer boroughs of the city are still highly segregated from the majority group.

I believe that English-language ability, cultural factors, and systematic discrimination still remain significant hindrances to the residential integration of immigrant Chinese. Yet, second-generation Chinese are on their way up in the larger society. As immigrants improve their language skills, gradually learn to accept or tolerate the cultural values of the dominant group, and are themselves accepted by the dominant group, they may have a better chance of residential assimilation.

In sum, three major outcomes can be derived from participating in Chinatown. The first one is spatial decentralization from the enclave. Many Chinese are able to convert economic gains into residential ones either by obtaining housing in desirable, middle-class, and mostly white neighborhoods or by succeeding to and renovating poor and run-down neighborhoods in outer boroughs of New York City and its suburbs. But spatial detachment from the enclave does not necessarily mean that group members are cut off from it. The effects of residential choice are twofold: First, moving out into mixed, middle-class neighborhoods smooths the path for the second-generation Chinese to assimilate into the American society; second, ethnic succession in poor neighborhoods has effectively prevented those neighborhoods from further decay.[3] Many Chinese immigrant families who have bought into poor neighborhoods have started to revitalize and upgrade their new properties.

The second outcome is structural assimilation. Spatial assimilation provides opportunities for structural assimilation. Part of the income generated from enclave employment is reinvested in the replenishment of labor. More relevant is the human-capital investment for the second generation. With socioeconomic achievement and spatial assimilation, immigrant children are incorporated into better public schools in more desirable districts. They are pushed harder by their immigrant parents and culture to excel in school. Consequently, many have moved straight into the middle-class.

The third outcome is the creation of an entrepreneurial culture.[4] Ethnic group members are not born entrepreneurs, nor are they especially and innately good at doing business. It is from their particular immigrant experience in a new country that they develop an entrepreneurial culture, which reinforces the values of hard work, frugality, future orientation, and delayed gratification. The entrepreneurial culture keeps alive a sense of identity, pride, self-esteem, and group solidarity, which feeds back to the building of social capital and further consolidates the structure of the enclave.

Chinatown creates a situation whereby ethnic employers use ethnic resources and family ties in the process of social advancement, and ethnic employees are given employment opportunities that they would otherwise be deprived of because of lack of suitable jobs in the larger labor market, poor language ability, and low educational qualifications. Therefore, participating in the enclave does not necessarily block immigrants from moving up socioeconomically in the larger society. Many successful immigrant Chinese have, in fact, risen out of the enclave. In the 1980s, they have levels of educational attainment and median household income higher than the national average. But Chinatown persists.

Theoretical and Practical Implications

This study of New York City's Chinatown tests hypotheses offered by the assimilation, the ethnic-cultural and the enclave-economy models. The assimilationist model assumes that the United States is a "melting pot," and that the only opportunity for success lies in the larger society. If immigrants hold on to their own culture, language, and values, they will always remain foreign and irrelevant. Moreover, the model assumes fair and natural competition in a labor market where jobs at different skill levels are evenly distributed in the larger economic structure. Immigrants who have fewer skills and human-capital credentials are generally competing at the lower end of the job hierarchy. As immigrant group members gradually establish themselves in the larger society through socioeconomic attainment, they tend to leave behind their less successful co-ethnics, move out of the enclave, and eventually assimilate into the dominant society. Consequently, the enclave remains a homogeneous urban ghetto, experiencing constant decline and, possibly, eventual extinction. In other words, the enclave is nothing more than a springboard, and assimilation is nothing more than acceptance of and identification with mainstream middle-class values and standards.

The experience of New York's Chinese shows that the "melting pot" works only in certain respects.[5] Immigrant Chinese continue to work hard and save in order to escape Chinatown and to buy into suburban middle-class neighborhoods. As time goes by, immigrant Chinese are gradually assimilating into the larger society. Many of the second-generation Chinese have successfully done so through formal social and economic institutions. They have excelled in schools and disproportionately won high-ranking professional jobs in the larger economy. In recent years, they have been celebrated as a "model minority."

What is missing from this account, however, is the narrow and rugged path leading the Chinese to where they are today in America. The success of the Chinese has been built on a collective effort of the family and community that overcomes many obstacles along the way. The Chinese are not as ready as expected to give up their culture, language, and values. The majority of them take pride in being Chinese. Even those who have a good command of English speak Chinese at home. They require their children to speak Chinese and to learn Chinese moral teaching, fearing that otherwise their children might become too "Americanized." They hold on to their traditional dietary habits. They maintain their own pattern of savings and consumption. Some of the more successful immigrant Chinese, who own homes outside of Chinatown and in suburban areas and are supporting children in college, still work for low wages in restaurants and garment shops.

Is this assimilation? Certainly, but not in the expected form. What about Chinatown? According to the predictions of the assimilation model, if many successful immigrant Chinese move out of Chinatown and they are constantly succeeded by poor and new immigrants, Chinatown will have a tendency to decline. This is what is happening to many inner-city black neighborhoods which have experienced a constant decline and social dislocation as their more successful members move away and integrate into the middle-class.[6] Urban blacks have not only been blocked by barriers associated with their slave legacy and inferior social status but have also been deprived of the cultural endowment and social capital that have helped many non-European immigrant groups to succeed. In recent years, studies have found that only a small number of blacks were able to move up by way of education and other social institutions in the larger society.[7] The social mobility and spatial assimilation of this small black middle-class have been accompanied by the social dislocation and economic deprivation of a substantial segment of the black population, resulting in ghettoization and the formation of an urban underclass. The urban underclass, despite government policies including public assistance, affirmative action, civil rights legislation, urban development, and neighborhood renovation programs, continues to deteriorate.[8]

Chinatown presents the opposite case. It has been growing and expanding in new directions, showing no signs of decline. Instead of allowing a slow and painful degeneration, immigrant Chinese have developed their enclave to provide opportunities for their own economic advancement, bypassing the step-by-step rise from the bottom and the acceptance of an inferior social status.

These contrasting outcomes in Chinatown are not unique to the Chinese. The Koreans, one of the most recent and fastest growing Asian immigrant groups, have succeeded in monopolizing New York City's neighborhood grocery trade. Although most of them are well educated and well-to-do, many do not know English and are disadvantaged at first. But their already established middle-class status before immigration and their sense of pride do not allow them to accept low-paid, menial jobs at the bottom of the larger economy. By mobilizing their ethnic resources, they rise up as entrepreneurs, building an enclave economy that transcends geographical boundaries. Today, the Koreans own and operate most of the corner grocery stores all over the city, particularly in low-income neighborhoods. Yet, they are not concentrated residentially in those poor neighborhoods.[9]

The Dominican immigrants in New York City, who were once described as a typical low-wage labor inflow because of their low levels of education and tenuous legal status, have begun to rise out of the dead-end jobs at the lower end of the occupational spectrum in the larger economy via their own ethnic enclave. Studies have found that the Dominican community in Washington Heights not only sustains an expanding ethnic enclave economy but has also developed and expanded businesses back in the Dominican Republic.[10] Many Dominican immigrants still remain poor by American standards, but they work hard to live up to their own expectations.

The Cuban immigrants, another often-cited success story, began their process of assimilation as refugees.[11] Unlike other immigrant groups, their refugee status qualified them to obtain government assistance in job training and employment. The government efforts to direct them away from Little Havana in Miami and disperse them into different jobs in the larger labor market, mostly in the larger secondary labor market, have not had much impact. Successful and rich Cuban immigrants have succeeded through self-employment in the enclave economy rather than from wage jobs in the larger secondary economy. Evidence from Miami's Cuban enclave has shown that immigrant Cubans who are employed in the enclave have occupations that correspond more closely to their educational attainment and earnings that correspond more closely to their occupational status than those who are employed in the larger secondary economy.[12] The enclave provides a greater probability of self-employment, an alternative path to success without going through the process by which immigrants enter the labor market from the bottom and then gradually move up, and also affords the social capital to help immigrants surmount obstacles to economic advancement.

The assimilation model does not seem to encompass these non-European immigrant groups, nor is it able to explain the urban ghetto phenomenon. Obviously, departure from the enclave is closely associated with higher socioeconomic achievement for immigrants groups, but the higher socioeconomic status of a particular immigrant group may not necessarily lead to abandonment of the original enclave. Successful Chinese, Koreans, and Dominicans do not tend to live in Chinatown, Koreatown, and the Dominican community in New York City. Cuban entrepreneurs and better-off workers tend to obtain homes in suburban Miami. But these ethnic out-migrants do not discard their community. Their fortunes and an important part of their lives are still tied to the enclave.

To what extent do the mobility patterns of some immigrant groups avoid the disadvantages faced by other minority groups, particularly blacks? The ethnic-cultural model stresses the importance of ethnic solidarity in the process of immigrant adaptation. It implies diversity among various immigrant groups in their particular mode of adaptation to the new country. It maintains that the initial immigrant disadvantages do produce a significant effect on segregation of ethnic enclaves, precisely by supporting the vitality of a distinctive culture, which, in turn, functions routinely as a source of employment, social support, and social adaptation in a familiar and dependable environment and smooths the path of eventual incorporation. Although, over time, immigrants and their descendants may move to newer and better neighborhoods, the original area of settlement often remains a symbol of a common ethnic identity.

The ethnic-cultural model does not deny the possibility of eventual assimilation; it only applauds the importance of the cultural traits and ethnic networks of immigrants in helping them negotiate the specific situation into which they immigrate. However, this model emphasizes only preexisting patterns of culture and ethnicity and takes for granted the positive aspects of these patterns. It ignores such major questions as how those patterns are maintained and work to the advantage of some groups but are systematically destroyed and function to enforce the inferiority of others.

The enclave-economy model incorporates a cultural component, but it is clearly focused on the structural conditions that give rise to the observed differences in circumstances and behavior of various immigrant groups. Certain immigrant groups are structurally denied equal access to the larger economy, presumably because they are newer entrants to the labor force and have less experience, poorer skills, and perhaps less education.

New York City's Chinese immigrants, like other immigrants from Asia, the Caribbean, and Latin America, are handicapped by the lack of English-language ability. Many of them are educated, at various levels, and have labor-market skills, but their education and skills are not easily transferable. Further, they lack information about the larger labor market. In terms of individual human-capital credentials, they start from a position, similar to, if not worse than, that of the urban underclass. If they were competing with the native working class in the same labor market, as is often presumed, they would either outcompete the natives by accepting low wages in the larger secondary economy or be driven out of the labor market altogether by the unions and the politically strong native working class, just as their predecessors were a century ago. But most of the disadvantaged immigrant Chinese are not in the larger labor market, simply because there are not enough jobs there.

Urban industrial transition has taken away many blue-collar, manufacturing jobs from New York City. In the 1970s the city lost more than 170,000 jobs in blue-collar occupations while gaining 260,000 information-intensive occupations.[13] The urban working class was particularly hard hit, and many native workers were left jobless. During this decade, immigrants were pouring into New York in large numbers. The Chinese population alone increased by 80 percent. Without an enclave economy to accommodate the influx of immigrant labor, the disadvantaged Chinese immigrants would simply have been jobless as well.

In mobilizing ethnic resources, the export sector of Chinatown's enclave-economy is able to pull back some of the manufacturing jobs that have been pushed out of the city because of the globalization and reorganization of the capitalist economy. Hence, Chinatown opens up a structure of job opportunities that fits in with the needs and values of immigrant Chinese, who try hard to assimilate into American society.

Considered on the basis of the norms and values of the outsiders, this sector of the enclave economy seems extremely exploitative. It is true that its survival depends on the availability of cheap immigrant labor, for none of the native workers is likely to be interested in the jobs it offered. (The high cost of labor is one of the major factors in shrinking the manufacturing sector in cities.) Also, cheap labor removes a significant stimulus toward technological innovation. The labor-intensive enterprises depend on the continued input of immigrant labor to stay competitive in the long run. In the short run, recruitment for low-wage jobs gives a great advantage to individual immigrants and ethnic companies, but movement into these sectors may be unhelpful for economic integration of the enclave economy. Certain kinds of jobs will continue to be labeled as immigrants' jobs and will be shunned even more by the native work force. Thus, the economic enclave, though able to adapt to structural changes and new situations in the larger economy, will never be able to be equated with, or incorporated into, the primary sector. Therefore, Chinatown does not match the expectations of the larger society. However, this reality is understood and accepted by immigrant Chinese as a necessary means through which they can achieve their goals. Without this ethnic consensus, the economic enclave could not possibly thrive.

In the foreseeable future, Chinese immigration will continue to affect the enclave. Chinatown will continue to serve as an alternative path to integration for newer immigrants. The positive side of the future of Chinatown is its unexpectedly strong economic development since 1965. Its thriving economy and the increasing vitality and heterogeneity of its changing population strengthen the position of Chinatown as one of the most dynamic immigrant enclaves in New York City. On the negative side, the best-known problems associated with the disadvantaged status of immigrants are still present. Chinatown will continue to serve as an initial immigrant settlement center, and low-wage and labor-intensive jobs will still dominate the enclave labor market. But this economic structure does not necessarily reduce the significance of Chinatown's success.

The experience of the Chinese enclave economy may have some bearing on solutions to the position of the urban underclass. First, it shows that economic integration of a minority group does not necessarily follow a unilateral path. There is no doubt that education is important for individuals of any disadvantaged group to rise out of poverty. However, within a racially defined hierarchy in the larger society, certain elements of social life and public policy systematically discourage minority members from going through the formal channels of social mobility. If the chance of social mobility depended merely on performance in school and minority members saw that many of their group members were in the top-ranking occupations that define success, their aspirations and motivation would be greatly increased. Otherwise, they would be easily alienated. Many school dropouts in central cities are the ones who cannot meaningfully relate their future to what they are currently trying to do.

Second, it is important to dispel the notion that the enclave represents a dead end for its group members. In the cities, minority entrepreneurship is one of the few opportunities left for minority groups. More important, self-employment is a shortcut to overcome discrimination and accumulate resources for human-capital investment. In the case of the Chinese, Japanese, and Koreans (as well as some of the earlier immigrant groups, for example, the German and Russian Jews), economic resources accumulated from self-employment of first-generation immigrants are reinvested in the second generation to secure the best education possible. There is also evidence that children of black entrepreneurs have a better chance of going to college and thus have a higher rate of college graduation than the rest of the group.[14] Ethnic entrepreneurs are structurally linked to their community even though they may be living elsewhere. This connection effectively prevents ethnic resources from draining out of the community.

Third, certain aspects of culture and ethnicity sustain a sense of identity, community, and self-esteem. Ethnic solidarity endows group members with resources that compensate for their disadvantages as minorities. Social capital, such as family and kinship networks, loyalty, mutual trust and obligation, facilitates entrepreneurial success. As ethnic businesses succeed, they generate jobs and set up role models for other group members. More important, they show co-ethnics that they can rise out of their own enclave on their own terms, regardless of negative stereotypes and cultural prejudices prevalent in the mainstream. In many cases, minority groups have goals that are compatible with those of the mainstream; yet the means of achieving these goals may vary according to the group's specific cultural values. For example, the wealthy entrepreneurial Chinese and low-wage enclave workers both push their children very hard to excel in school. The high value placed on education in this culture (like that of the mainstream) affects the social mobility of the second-generation. Further, it is important to create a repertoire of bicultural skills that combine the best of what the mainstream and group cultures have to offer.[15]

Chinatown is, no doubt, a success. Yet, this very success is posing challenges that will confront the community in the future. Some might wonder if immigration slowed down, whether Chinatown's enclave economy might decline and eventually vanish. This is unlikely. The zero-growth scenario cannot be assumed to reflect real world behavior. Further, the internal development of the economic enclave is influenced by the larger economic structure of the United States, and thus, Chinatown's future does not rest solely upon immigration. Whatever else can be said about Chinatown in the next ten or twenty years, one thing is certain: the influence of the enclave economy on immigrant Chinese will continue to be pervasive. No single economic structure survives forever, but the economic enclave need not decline with the slowdown of the immigration on which it was built, as long as new ventures emerge to take the place of old ones. The measure of an ethnic community, like that of a person, is not whether it lives forever but what it contributes for the time it exists and the renewal it generates before and upon its death.

Still, the enclave-economy model has been posited so recently that it has yet to be carefully studied. Therefore, any results require cautious interpretation and their generalizability is limited. The results of this study do not suggest a total rejection of the assimilation model. It is possible that a longer time perspective will provide different conclusions. High-volume Chinese immigration began only after changes in immigration law in 1965, barely fifteen years before the census on which my statistical analysis is based. Although other researchers have also applied the model to Hispanic and Asian minorities with high proportions of immigrants, the assimilation model relies on changes across generations which I may not have perceived. It remains an open question whether the structural conditions that sustain the enclave economy in the 1980s will persist into the next century, and what effects they will have for the children and grandchildren of today's Chinese-Americans.

Notes

Chapter 1

1. This is a popular kind of Cantonese appetizer. The words *dim sum* in Cantonese literally mean a little bit of the heart.

2. S. Lieberson 1980, *A Piece of the Pie*, p. 290.

3. M. Freeman 1983, "The Labor Market for Immigrants in New York City"; R. Waldinger 1986b, "Immigrant Enterprises."

4. E. W. Burgess 1923, "The Growth of the City"; S. Lieberson 1963, *Ethnic Patterns in American Cities*; R. Hodge and P. Hodge 1965, "Occupational Assimilation as a Competitive Process"; R. E. Park and E. W. Burgess 1967, *The City*.

5. O. Handlin 1951, *The Uprooted*; W. L. Yancey, E. P. Ericksen, and R. N. Juliani 1976, "Emergent Ethnicity"; H. J. Gans 1979, "Symbolic Ethnicity"; R. D. Alba 1985b, *Italian Americans*.

6. H. J. Gans 1962, *The Urban Villagers*; Alba 1985a, "The Twilight of Ethnicity among Americans of European Ancestry," and 1985b.

7. Gans 1962; G. Suttles 1972, *The Social Construction of Communities*; A. Hunter 1974, *Symbolic Communities*; W. Peterson and M. Novak 1982, *Concepts of Ethnicity*; C. S. Fischer 1984, *The Urban Experience*.

8. M. M. Gordon 1964, *Assimilation in American Life*; G. Suttles 1968, *The Social Order of the Slum*.

9. R. Waldinger 1987, "Beyond Nostalgia."

10. I. H. Light 1972, *Ethnic Enterprises in America*, and 1984, "Immigrant and Ethnic Enterprise in North America"; I. Kim 1981, *New Urban Immigrants*; Waldinger 1986b; H. Aldrich and C. Zimmer 1989, "Continuities in the Study of Ecological Succession."

11. Light 1984, pp. 201–202.

12. E. Bonacich and J. M. Modell 1980, *The Economic Basis of Ethnic Solidarity*; J. G. Reitz 1980, *The Survival of Ethnic Groups*; Light 1984, p. 207; M. Semyonov 1981, "The Effect of Community on Status Attainment."

13. A. Portes and R. L. Bach 1980, "Immigrant Earnings," and 1985, *The Latin Journey*; K. L. Wilson and A. Portes 1980, "Immigrant Enclaves"; K. L. Wilson and W. A. Martin 1982, "Ethnic Enclaves"; A. Portes and A. Stepick 1985, "Unwelcome Immigrants"; A. Portes and R. D. Manning 1986, "The Immigrant Enclave"; A. Portes and L. Jensen 1987, "What's an Ethnic Enclave?"

14. Wilson and Portes 1980, p. 313.

15. Portes and Bach 1985, p. 347.

16. Quoted by J. Kifner 1991, "Immigrant Waves from Asia Bring an Underworld Ashore."

17. P. Kwong 1987, *The New Chinatown*, pp. 6, 79.

18. W. J. Wilson 1987, *The Truly Disadvantaged*; L. Wacquant and W. J. Wilson 1989, "The Cost of Racial and Class Exclusion in the Inner City."

19. B. L. Sung 1967, *The Story of the Chinese in America*; S. C. Miller 1969, *The Unwelcome Immigrants*; V. Nee and B. de B. Nee 1973, *Longtime Californ'*; C. Kuo 1977, *Social and Political Change in New York's Chinatown*; B. P. Wong 1979, *A Chinese American Community*.

20. Kwong 1987.

21. A. Portes 1981, "Modes of Structural Incorporation and Present Theories of Immigration," p. 291.

22. Portes and Jensen 1987, p. 769; see also Wilson and Martin 1982; Portes and Manning 1986.

23. Portes and Bach 1985, pp. 204–205.

24. Key Publications 1988, *Chinese Business Guide and Directory for Metropolitan New York and Boston*.

25. M. Granovetter 1985, "Economic Action and Social Structure," pp. 481–510.

26. A. Portes and L. E. Guarnizo 1991, "Tropical Capitalists."

27. J. S. Coleman 1988, "Social Capital in the Creation of Human Capital"; B. P. Wong 1988, *Patronage, Brokerage, Entrepreneurship, and the Chinese Community of New York*, p. 115.

28. Portes and Bach 1985.

29. Ibid., pp. 3–7.

30. A. Portes and R. G. Rumbaut 1990, *Immigrant America*, p. 85.

Chapter 2

1. R. H. Conwell 1871, *Why and How*; M. R. Coolidge 1909, *Chinese Immigration*; R. H. Dillon 1962, *The Hatchet Men*; G. Barth 1964, *Bitter Strength*; S. M. Lyman 1974, *Chinese Americans*; G. F. Seward 1970, *Chinese Immigration*; A. Saxton 1971, *The Indispensable Enemy*; V. Nee and B. de B. Nee 1973, *Longtime Californ'*; D. L. McKee 1977, *Chinese Exclusion versus the Open Door Policy*; S. Aubits 1988 "Tracing Early Chinese Immigration into the United States"; R. Daniels 1988, *Asian America*.

2. According to legend, the Chinese were descendants of the dragon.

3. B. L. Sung 1967, *The Story of the Chinese in America*; A. Ugalde, F. D. Bean, and G. Cardenas 1979, "International Migration from the Dominican Republic"; M. Weiner 1987, "International Emigration and the Third World"; A. Portes and R. G. Rumbaut 1990, *Immigrant America*, pp. 10–12.

4. B. L. Sung 1967, p. 10; P. Kwong 1979, *Chinatown, New York*.

5. The Opium War (1838–1842) between China and Great Britain ended by the Treaty of Nanking, signed on August 29, 1842. The Treaty of Nanking ended

the Chinese merchants' monopoly, establishing five treaty ports where foreigners could live and work outside of Chinese legal jurisdiction. See R. L. McCunn 1979, *An Illustrated History of the Chinese in America*, pp. 12–17.

6. M. Banno 1964, *China and the West*, pp. 2–3.

7. J. Chen 1980, *The Chinese of America*, pp. 3–6.

8. Barth 1964, p. 50; Conwell 1871, pp. 82–93; Coolidge 1909, p. 19.

9. Banno 1964, p. 128.

10. Personal interview, November 1988.

11. Barth 1964; S. Chan 1986, *This Bitter-sweet Soil*.

12. E. Bonacich 1984a, "Asian Labor in the Development of California and Hawaii," p. 140.

13. Kwong 1979, p. 20.

14. Barth 1964; Chan 1986.

15. Barth 1964; McCunn 1979, p. 22.

16. Coolidge 1909, p. 17.

17. Barth 1964, p. 62.

18. Saxton 1971; Chan 1986.

19. C. P. Siu 1987, *The Chinese Laundryman*, p. 4.

20. Chen 1980, p. 21.

21. Nee and Nee 1973, p. 33.

22. Coolidge 1909, p. 37; Chen 1980, p. 48.

23. D. Chu and S. Chu 1967, *Passage to the Golden Gate*, pp. 50–77.

24. Kwong 1979, p. 23; Chan 1986.

25. McCunn 1979, p. 75.

26. Ibid., pp. 70–82; S. C. Miller 1969, *The Unwelcome Immigrants*; Saxton 1971.

27. Saxton 1971.

28. Kwong 1979, p. 24.

29. Bonacich 1984a, p. 131.

30. Coolidge 1909, p. 119.

31. Chinese Exclusion Act, May 6, 1882, chap. 126, *United States Statutes at Large*, vol. 22, pp. 59–61.

32. R. D. McKenzie 1927, *Oriental Exclusion*.

33. "An Act to Prohibit the Coming of Chinese Laborers to the United States," September 13, 1888, public law 1015, *United States Statutes at Large*, vol. 25, pp. 476–479, 504. On October 1, 1888, a supplement to the Chinese Exclusion Act of 1882 was passed by the Congress prohibiting the return of Chinese laborers to the United States. See public law 1064, *United States Statutes at Large*, vol. 25, p. 504.

34. McCunn 1979, p. 87.

35. Extension of the Chinese Exclusion Act of 1882, passed by the Congress on May 5, 1892. See public law 60, *United States Statutes at Large*, vol. 27, pp. 25–26.

36. On March 3, 1901, an act supplementary to the 1882 Chinese Exclusion Act granted the right to the U.S. district attorney to issue warrants of arrest for any unlawful Chinese persons. See public law 845, *United States Statutes at Large*,

vol. 31, p. 1093. In the following year, April 29, 1902, Chinese exclusion was extended to island territories of the United States. See public law 641, *United States Statutes at Large*, vol. 32, pp. 176–177.

37. Nee and Nee 1973, p. 56.
38. Saxton 1971; Nee and Nee 1973, p. 55; McCunn 1979, p. 79.
39. Nee and Nee 1973, pp. 62–63. See also McCunn 1979, p. 88; Siu 1987, pp. 196–197.
40. Personal interview, May 1988.
41. Nee and Nee 1973.
42. *New York Times*, June 7, 1868; Miller 1969, p. 171.
43. D. Y. Yuan 1963, "Voluntary Segregation," pp. 258–259; C. Kuo 1977, *Social and Political Change in New York's Chinatown*.
44. Yuan 1963.
45. B. P. Wong 1988, *Patronage, Brokerage, Entrepreneurship, and the Chinese Community of New York*, pp. 30–31.
46. Siu 1987.
47. Chen 1980, p. 198.
48. Wong 1988, p. 81.
49. "An Act to Repeal the Chinese Exclusion Act," passed on December 17, 1943, repealed most of the discriminatory legislation against the Chinese. See public law 344, *United States Statutes at Large*, vol. 57, pp. 600–601. The War Brides Act, passed on December 28, 1945, allowed wives of members of the American armed forces to enter the United States. The following year fiancés of American soldiers were allowed to immigrate. Public law 271, *United States Statutes at Large*, vol. 59, pt. II, p. 659.
50. Personal interview, October 1988.
51. S. H. Tsai 1986, *The Chinese Experience in America*, p. 120.

Chapter 3

1. Public law 236, *United States Statutes at Large*, vol. 79, pp. 911–922.
2. *Washington Post*, July 23, 1988, p. A1.
3. B. L. Sung 1987, *The Adjustment Experience of Chinese Immigrant Children in New York City*, p. 22.
4. The Immigration Act of 1990, signed by President Bush on November 29, 1990, public law 101–649, printed by Bureau of International Labor Affairs, U.S. Department of Labor, Washington, D.C., p. 5.
5. A. Portes and R. G. Rumbaut 1990, *Immigrant America*, p. 85.
6. Sung 1987, p. 22.
7. M. J. Piore 1986, "The Shifting Grounds for Immigration," p. 24.
8. R. Bach 1986, "Immigration," p. 147.
9. R. T. Averitt 1968, *The Dual Economy*; J. K. Galbraith 1971, *The New Industrial State*; D. Gordon 1972, *Theories of Poverty and Underemployment*; R. C. Edwards 1975, "The Social Relations of Production in the Firm and Labor Market Structure"; E. M. Beck, P. M. Horan, and C. M. Tolbert 1978, "Stratification in a Dual Economy"; C. M. Tolbert, P. M. Horan, and E. M. Beck 1980, "The Structure of Economic Segmentation"; R. M. Hauser 1980, "On Stratification

in a Dual Economy"; R. Houston and R. L. Kaufman 1982, "Economic Dualism"; M. Wallace and A. L. Kalleberg 1982, "Economic Organization of Firms and Labor Market Consequences."

10. Piore 1980, "The Technological Foundations of Dualism and Discontinuity."

11. Piore 1986, p. 24.

12. S. C. Miller 1969, *The Unwelcome Immigrants*; Kwong 1979, *Chinatown, New York*; A. Portes and R. L. Bach 1985, *The Latin Journey*; A. Portes and A. Stepick 1985, "Unwelcome Immigrants."

13. R. K. Miller 1982, "Patterns of Employment Difficulty among European Immigrant Industrial Workers during the Great Depression"; J. D. Kasarda 1983, "Entry-Level Jobs, Mobility, and Urban Minority Unemployment"; T. Bailey and R. Waldinger 1984, "A Skills Mismatch in New York's Labor Market?"; G. Tyler 1987, "A Tale of Three Cities"; S. Sassen-Koob 1987, "Growth and Informalization at the Core," and 1988, *The Mobility of Labor and Capital*.

14. Piore 1979, *Birds of Passage*.

15. A. Portes 1976, "Determinants of the Brain Drain"; P. Meadows 1980, "Immigration Theory"; A. Portes 1989a, *Unauthorized Immigration and Immigration Reform*; A. R. Zolberg 1989, "The Next Waves"; Portes and Rumbaut 1990. See also G. J. Borjas 1990, *Friends or Strangers*.

16. Borjas 1990, p. 7.

17. T. L. Parcel 1979, "Race, Regional Markets, and Earnings," and 1982, "Development and Functioning of the American Urban Export Sector"; T. Muller and T. Espenshade 1985, *The Fourth Wave*; J. D. Heinberg, J. K. Harris, and R. L. York 1989, "The Process of Exempt Immediate Relative Immigration to the United States"; D. G. Papademetriou et al. 1989, "The Effects of Immigration on the U.S. Economy and Labor Market"; G. J. Borjas 1989, "Economic Theory and International Migration," and 1990, pp. 190–191; D. G. Papademetriou 1990, "Contending Approaches to Reforming the U.S. Legal Immigration System," p. 8.

18. Bach 1986, p. 148.

19. V. M. Briggs 1975, "Mexican Workers in the United States Labor Market."

20. K. L. Wilson and A. Portes 1980, "Immigrant Enclaves"; I. Light 1984, "Immigrant and Ethnic Enterprise in North America"; M. Zhou and J. R. Logan 1989, "Returns on Human Capital in Ethnic Enclaves."

21. Papademetriou 1990, p. 12.

22. Borjas 1990, p. 177.

23. H. M. Choldin 1973, "Kinship Networks in the Migration Process"; S. M. Nishi 1979, "The New Wave of Asian Americans"; M. G. Wong 1986, "Post-1965 Asian Immigrants"; Sung 1987; Portes and Rumbaut 1990.

24. Sung 1987, pp. 18–19.

25. Heinberg, Harris, and York 1989, pp. 844–846.

26. Personal interview, September 1988.

27. Personal interview, September 1988.

28. Personal interview, January 1989.

29. Public law 99-639, *United States Statutes at Large*, vol. 100, pp. 3537–3544.

30. Papademetriou 1990, p. 12.

31. M. Tienda and R. Angel 1982, "Headship and Household Composition among Blacks, Hispanics, and Other Whites"; Perez 1986, "Immigrant Economic Adjustment and Family Organization."

32. The Great Proletarian Cultural Revolution (1966–1976) was launched by Mao Tse-tung's government to attack revisionists at a time when the United States was escalating its aggression in Vietnam. It first attempted to purge revisionists and bourgeois agents inside the party and later spread throughout China, particularly in the cities. There, workers, intellectuals, and students were engulfed in "great revolutionary storms and waves," a process of "struggle-criticism-transformation" on three levels: an extreme intense struggle to "seize power" at all levels of government; a nationwide campaign against the "four olds" (old ideas, old culture, old customs, and old habits); and a drive for a united leadership by the army, the working class, and the revolutionary masses. The Chinese government later termed the revolution a national "political disaster." See C. Kung 1975, "Cultural Revolution in Modern Chinese History."

33. The Chinese government restrictions designed to control students studying abroad change constantly, swinging back and forth according to the changing political winds. The restrictions I outline here came into effect from 1987 to 1991.

34. Portes and Rumbaut 1990, pp. 11–12.

35. Sung 1987, p. 27.

36. I. Kim 1987, "The Koreans," p. 223.

37. SSBC 1986, *Statistical Yearbook of China*, pp. 576, 40.

38. Ibid., p. 582.

39. Personal interview, September 1988.

40. Personal interview, April 1988.

41. Sung 1987, p. 15.

42. Personal interview, September 1988.

43. For detailed accounts, see N. Cheng 1987, *Life and Death in Shanghai*.

44. Personal interview, September 1988.

45. F. Strebeigh 1989, "Training China's New Elite," p. 89; Z. Deng 1991, "China's Brain Drain Problem," p. 9.

46. The British won the Opium War in 1842 and received the island of Hong Kong as part of the Treaty of Nanking. In 1860 Britain gained control of the Kowloon Peninsula as part of a settlement of further trade disputes with China. In 1898 China leased the New Territories to Britain for 99 years. Under a 1984 agreement between China and Britain, control of Hong Kong (Hong Kong Island, Kowloon, the New Territories, and the related islands) is scheduled to be transferred to China in 1997.

47. *World Journal*, August 18, 1990.

48. *Financial Times*, June 12, 1990.

49. The old Chinese proverb is "Fallen leaves return to their roots." It means that one should always retire and die on the soil of one's birth. It connotes a strong nostalgia and an ethnocentric norm in the Chinese culture.

Chapter 4

1. *Boston Globe,* July 28, 1988.
2. *Financial Times,* May 8, 1990. US$1 was approximately equivalent to HK$7.8.
3. *Wall Street Journal,* March 30, 1988.
4. *Wall Street Journal,* January 8, 1988.
5. *Financial Times,* May 17, 1990.
6. In China peasants in rural areas were not salaried workers and were thus not incorporated into the country's occupational structure. Thus they were likely to report that they did not have an occupation before emigration.
7. B. L. Sung 1976, *A Survey of Chinese-American Manpower and Employment,* p. 4.
8. A. Portes and R. G. Rumbaut 1990, *Immigrant America,* p. 48.
9. ILGWU 1983, *The Chinatown Garment Industry Study,* p. i.
10. J. D. Kasarda 1983, "Entry-Level Jobs, Mobility, and Urban Minority Unemployment," p. 23; J. D. Kasarda 1989, "Urban Industrial Transition and the Underclass."
11. *New York Times,* December 29, 1981; *Crain's New York Business,* May 18, 1987.
12. *New York Times,* June 27, 1985, IV.
13. *New York Times,* August 8, 1988.

Chapter 5

1. P. C. Siu 1987, *The Chinese Laundryman,* p. 120.
2. B. P. Wong 1979, *A Chinese American Community,* p. 74.
3. Key Publications, 1988, *Chinese Business Guide and Directory for Metropolitan New York and Boston.*
4. U.S. Bureau of the Census 1987, *Survey of Minority-Owned Business Enterprises.*
5. P. Kwong 1987, *The New Chinatown,* p. 26; M. Zhou and J. R. Logan 1989, "Returns on Human Capital in Ethnic Enclaves," p. 812.
6. *People's Daily* (Overseas edition), December 17, 1988.
7. *Bu Gao Ban* (Summer 1984): 3.
8. S. Sassen-Koob 1989, "New York City's Informal Economy"; R. Waldinger 1986a, *Through the Eye of the Needle.*
9. ILGWU 1983, *The Chinatown Garment Industry Study,* p. 41.
10. P. Kwong 1987, p. 31.
11. ILGWU 1983.
12. Personal interview, April 1988.
13. ILGWU 1983, p. 59.
14. Personal interview, April 1988.
15. Kwong 1987, p. 32.
16. ILGWU 1983, p. 81.
17. Personal interview, September 1988.
18. NYCREC 1988, *Manhattan Real Estate Transactions.*

19. E. Tobier 1979, "The New Face of Chinatown"; J. Wang 1979, "Behind the Boom."

20. *New York Times*, September 20, 1981.

21. Ibid., December 25, 1986.

22. *New York Newsday*, March 2, 1987, III:8.

23. I. H. Light 1972, *Ethnic Enterprises in America*.

24. Personal interview, May 1988.

25. *World Journal*, January 13, 1989, p. 24.

26. Light 1972; R. Waldinger 1986c, "Changing Ladders and Musical Chairs"; H. Aldrich and R. Waldinger 1990, "Ethnicity and Entrepreneurship."

27. Light 1972; H. Aldrich and J. Carter 1985, "Ethnic Residential Concentration and the Protected Market Hypothesis"; P. G. Min 1988, *Ethnic Business Enterprise*; M.D.R. Evans 1989, "Immigrant Entrepreneurship"; Aldrich and Waldinger 1990.

28. M. Semyonov 1988, "Bi-ethnic Labor Markets, Mono-ethnic Labor Markets, and Socioeconomic Inequality."

29. Aldrich and Waldinger 1990.

30. Wong 1979, p. 74.

31. Sassen-Koob 1989, p. 67.

32. E. Bonacich 1972, "A Theory of Ethnic Antagonism"; Lieberson 1980, *A Piece of the Pie*; S. Spilerman "Careers, Labor Market Structure, and Socioeconomic Achievement"; Waldinger 1977, 1986a, and 1986b, "Immigrant Enterprises"; Semyonov 1988.

33. Waldinger 1986a.

34. Bonacich 1973, "A Theory of Middleman Minorities"; D. Mar 1984, *Chinese Immigrants and the Ethnic Labor Market*; J. M. Sanders and V. Nee 1987, "Limits of Ethnic Solidarity in the Enclave Economy"; Aldrich and Waldinger 1990.

35. T. Shibutani and K. M. Kwan 1965, *Ethnic Stratification*; A. Saxton 1971, *The Indispensable Enemy*; A. Portes and R. L. Bach 1985, *The Latin Journey*.

36. Mar 1984; Sanders and Nee 1987.

37. Portes and Bach 1985, pp. 19–20.

Chapter 6

1. J. M. Sanders and V. Nee 1987, "Limits of Ethnic Solidarity in the Enclave Economy"; A. Portes and L. Jensen 1987, "What's an Ethnic Enclave?" M. Zhou and J. R. Logan 1989, "Returns on Human Capital in Ethnic Enclaves."

2. K. L. Wilson and A. Portes 1980, "Immigrant Enclaves"; A. Portes and R. L. Bach 1985, *The Latin Journey*.

3. Sanders and Nee 1987.

4. In a footnote, Sanders and Nee (1987, p. 756) reported that when the enclave was defined as Dade County, there was a modest return on education for enclave workers.

5. Portes and Jensen 1987.

6. K. L. Wilson and W. A. Martin 1982, "Ethnic Enclaves"; A. Portes and R. D. Manning 1986, "The Immigrant Enclave"; Portes and Jensen 1987.

7. Portes and Jensen 1987, p. 768.

8. Sanders and Nee (1987, p. 751) compensated for this possibility by including a variable in their equations, ETHNIC, which represented the percentage of Chinese and Cuban residents in the city, town, or county in which the respondent lived.

9. Key Publications 1988, *Chinese Business Guide and Directory for Metropolitan New York and Boston.*

10. The enclave industries include the 1980 PUMS standard industry codes 132 to 152, 500 to 532, 540 to 542, 550 to 571, 580 to 691, 771 to 780, and 812 to 830. The nonenclave industries include all the other industrial codes except 900 to 992 (public administration and experienced unemployed not classified by industry).

11. Personal interview, September 1988.

12. Including all foreign-born workers between twenty-five and sixty-four years of age who worked at least 160 hours and earned a minimum of five hundred dollars in 1979. By age twenty-five, most of them would have finished school, and by age sixty-five, most would have retired. The hour and wage limits were set to exclude part-time and seasonal workers. See M. Zhou 1989, *The Enclave Economy and Immigrant Incorporation in New York City's Chinatown.*

13. B. R. Chiswick 1977, "Sons of Immigrants," 1980, "Immigrant Earnings Patterns by Sex, Race, and Ethnic Groupings," and 1983, "An Analysis of the Earnings and Employment of Asian-American Men."

14. Personal interview, May 1988.

15. The data for the analyses of this section were extracted from the 5 percent Public Use Microdata Sample of the Census of Population and Housing (1980). The sample was limited to male immigrant Chinese, aged twenty-five to sixty-four, who worked at least 160 hours and earned a minimum of five hundred dollars in 1979 (in order to deemphasize immigrants who might be regarded as only occasional workers). Persons in the sample were categorized as employees or entrepreneurs. Public-sector employees were excluded from the analysis. Sampling selection bias was tested and found to be minimum (see R. A. Berk 1983, "An Introduction to Sample Selection Bias in Sociological Data"). I included only counties in New York City and other counties adjacent to New York City in New York and New Jersey, referring to the area of analysis as the New York metropolitan area. These counties were Bronx, Kings, Nassau, New York, Queens, Richmond, Rockland, Suffolk, and Westchester in New York and Bergen, Essex, Hudson, Mercer, Middlesex, Monmouth, Morris, Passaic, Somerset, and Union in New Jersey (The 1980 PUMS standard county group codes: 34001 to 34035, 34049, 34050, 36036 to 36044). Note: This sample is different from the one used by Zhou and Logan (1989), which included all counties of New York State and some counties of New Jersey adjacent to New York City. See Zhou 1989, chap. 4; Zhou and Logan 1989.

16. M. Zhou 1989, p. 103. F-tests of the significance of differences in coefficients between different pairs of subsamples showed that the equations for employees and entrepreneurs were significantly different, whether inside or outside the enclave defined by place of residence and by industry, which means that the two should be analyzed separately.

17. NORC 1988, *General Social Surveys*. See P. Blau and O. D. Duncan 1967, *The American Occupational Structure*; O. D. Duncan 1977a, "A Socioeconomic Index for All Occupations," and 1977b, "Properties and Characteristics of the Socioeconomic Index." Studies have provided ample evidence that the occupational ranking is fairly stable over time and is cross-national, see A. Portes and R. L. Bach 1985, *The Latin Journey*, p. 227.

18. The operationalization of the independent variables is as follows: (1) labor-market experience was calculated from a person's age, not counting the years in which the person was in school and the years before school; the squared term was included to measure nonlinearity (but its inclusion and exclusion did not affect the estimates of coefficients for other independent variables in this case); (2) education was represented by three variables showing the number of years up to or above a given threshold: elementary education (a maximum of ten years), high school education (with a minimum of zero and maximum of four years), and college education (with a minimum of zero and maximum of eight years); (3) English, U.S. citizenship, and marital status were dummy variables; (4) years of immigration were represented by three dummy variables with pre-1965 immigration as the omitted variable; (5) occupation was represented by four dummy variables with executive-managerial occupation as the omitted variable.

19. See Zhou and Logan 1989, pp. 813–815, whose analyses were based on a slightly different sample (including counties in upstate New York), but the effect of college education on earnings was similar.

20. Sanders and Nee (1987) similarly found that English-language ability was a significant predictor of earnings for both Cuban and Chinese employees who lived within the enclave. For detailed accounts, see Zhou and Logan 1989, pp. 813–815; Zhou 1989, pp. 103–105.

21. For details, see Zhou 1989, pp. 106–109.

22. Personal interview, May 1988.

23. Personal interview, May 1988.

24. Personal interview, February 1989.

25. Personal interview, May 1988.

26. Field records collected by author, September 1988.

27. Personal interview, December 1988.

28. Personal interview, May 1988.

29. Personal interview, December 1988.

30. Personal interview, December 1988.

31. Personal interview, April 1988.

32. NYS-IATFIA 1988, *Workplace Discrimination under the Immigration Reform and Control Act of 1986*.

33. Personal interview, April 1988.

34. Personal interview, May 1988.

35. P. Li 1977, "Occupational Achievement and Kinship Assistance among Chinese Immigrants in Chicago"; M. Semyonov and A. Tyree 1981, "Community Segregation and the Costs of Ethnic Subordination"; W. M. Hurh and K. C. Kim 1984, *Korean Immigrants in America*; D. Mar 1984, *Chinese Immigrants and the Ethnic Labor Market*; Sanders and Nee 1987, p. 764.

Chapter 7

1. E. Bonacich, I. Light, and C. C. Wong 1977, "Koreans in Small Business"; L. Perez 1986, "Immigrant Economic Adjustment and Family Organization"; E. Bonacich and I. Light, 1988, *Immigrant Entrepreneurs*; A. Portes and L. Jensen 1989, "The Enclave and the Entrants"; M. Zhou and J. R. Logan 1989, "Returns on Human Capital in Ethnic Enclaves"; A. Portes and R. G. Rumbaut 1990, *Immigrant America.*

2. Bonacich, Light and Wong 1977; A. Phizacklea 1983, *One-Way Ticket*; E. Bonacich 1984b, "United States Capitalist Development."

3. Perez 1986; D. W. Haines 1986, "Vietnamese Refugee Women in the U.S. Labor Force"; Zhou and Logan 1989; Portes and Jensen 1989; Portes and Rumbaut 1990.

4. L. Kung 1983, *Factory Women in Taiwan*, p. 7; J. W. Salaff 1981, *Working Daughters of Hong Kong.*

5. Personal interview, September 1987. See also I. Tinker 1978, "Women in Developing Societies."

6. Under the new immigration law, children under twenty-one can immigrate with their parents; and unmarried adult children can come after their immigrant parents acquire a green card (legal alien residency), usually in about two years.

7. Personal interview, September 1987.

8. Personal interview, April 1988.

9. Many inexperienced workers can make only around three dollars per hour.

10. NYCDCP 1986, *Asians in New York City*, p. 7.

11. "Key money" is a lump sum collected in advance by the landlord upon renting an apartment. For residential units, the key money was usually ten times as much as the rent and ranged from $800 to $5,000. For commercial space, it could be as high as $20,000. Though illegal, the practice was widespread in Chinatown. Because most of Chinatown's rental apartment units were rent controlled, landlords could not raise the rent substantially unless they were able to drive the old tenants out. See also Kwong 1987, *The New Chinatown*, p. 51.

12. Personal interview, May 1988.

13. Compare E. Glenn 1983, "Split Household, Small Producer, and Dual Wage Earner."

14. Multivariate regression models of returns on human capital for female immigrant Chinese workers had the same set of independent variables as those for men discussed in Chapter 6, adding only one dummy variable—fertility—to control for the effect of having children. The analyses were based on the same data set as that for men. The garment industry included the 1980 PUMS standard industry codes 132–152. For more details, see Zhou and Logan 1989, pp. 815–18; Zhou 1989, *The Enclave Economy and Immigrant Incorporation in New York City's Chinatown*, pp. 149–52.

15. See Zhou 1989, pp. 152–153.

16. NORC 1988, *General Social Surveys.*

17. ILGWU 1983, *The Chinatown Garment Industry Study*, pp. 43, 49; T. Bailey and R. Waldinger 1987, *A Human Resource Development Strategy for the New York City Garment Industry*; R. Waldinger 1990, *Tattered and Torn.*

18. ILGWU 1983, p. 44.

19. Stone 1983, "Motherhood and Waged Work," p. 46; F. D. Blau and M. A. Ferber 1986, *The Economics of Women, Men, and Work*, p. 164.

20. Phizacklea 1983, p. 2.

21. Ibid., p. 5.

22. ILGWU 1983, p. 34; S. Sassen-Koob 1984, "Notes on the Incorporation of Third World Women into Wage Labor through Immigration and Off-shore Production"; E. Weiner and H. Green 1984, "A Stitch in Our Times."

23. Personal interview, May 1988.

24. Personal interview, May 1988.

25. Personal interview, January 1989.

26. B. L. Sung 1987, *The Adjustment Experience of Chinese Immigrant Children in New York City*, p. 86.

27. *New York Times* October 19, 1979, II; and April 25, 1981.

28. *New York Times* May 5, 1981.

29. Personal interview, April 1988.

30. J. Huber and G. Spitze 1983, *Sex Stratification*, p. 166.

31. R. Kahn-Hut, A. K. Daniels, and R. Colvard 1982, *Women and Work*, p. 4.

32. Glenn 1983; Perez 1986.

Chapter 8

1. O. D. Duncan and B. Duncan 1955, "A Methodological Analysis of Segregation Indices"; O. D. Duncan and S. Lieberson 1959, "Ethnic Segregation and Assimilation"; A. M. Guest and J. A. Weed 1976, "Ethnic Residential Segregation"; S. Lieberson 1980, *A Piece of the Pie*; D. S. Massey and B. P. Mullan 1984, "Processes of Hispanic and Black Spatial Assimilation"; D. S. Massey and N. A. Denton 1985, "Spatial Assimilation as a Socioeconomic Outcome," 1987, "Trends in the Residential Segregation of Blacks, Hispanics, and Asians," and 1988, "Suburbanization and Segregation in U.S. Metropolitan Areas."

2. B. P. Wong 1979, *A Chinese American Community*, p. 16; P. Jackson 1983, "Ethnic Turf."

3. This is defined analytically by fourteen census tracts of the *U.S. Census of Population*, including neighborhoods where the Chinese have begun to concentrate.

4. C. Kuo 1977, *Social and Political Change in New York's Chinatown*; E. A. Gargan 1981, "New Money, People, and Ideas Alter Chinatown of Tradition."

5. P. Kwong 1987, *The New Chinatown*, p. 51.

6. Personal interview, December 1988.

7. Ibid.

8. Lieberson 1980, p. 290.

9. H. Gans 1962, *The Urban Villagers*; R. D. Alba 1985b, *Italian Americans*.

10. Massey and Denton 1987.

11. R. D. Alba and J. R. Logan 1991, "Variations on Two Themes."

12. A. Portes and R. L. Bach 1985, *The Latin Journey*.

13. A. Portes and L. Jensen 1987, "What's an Ethnic Enclave?" p. 768.

14. Counties included in this analysis are Bronx, Kings, Nassau, New York,

Queens, Rockland, Suffolk, and Westchester of New York State and Bergen, Essex, Hudson, Mercer, Middlesex, Monmouth, Morris, Passaic, Somerset, and Union of New Jersey. For detailed accounts of these analyses, see M. Zhou 1989, *The Enclave Economy and Immigrant Incorporation in New York City's Chinatown*, chap. 6; M. Zhou and J. R. Logan 1991, "In and Out of Chinatown."

15. The analysis of the degree of segregation of the Chinese from other groups was based on the census-tract-level data (Summary Tape File 3A—STF3 —of the 1980 *Census of Population and Housing*). The analysis is limited to tracts with a total population (of all races) of over fifty in the area. For the calculation of the index of dissimilarity, see Lieberson 1980, p. 254. Also see C. R. Cortese, R. F. Falk, and J. K. Cohen 1976, "Further Consideration of the Methodological Analysis of Segregation Indices."

16. For detailed analysis, see Zhou and Logan 1991. The determinants of place of residence for individual Chinese household heads use the 1980 PUMS data. In order to avoid double counting within the same household, the logistical models are based on samples limited to householders twenty-five years of age or older. This choice also has a substantive justification, inasmuch as location decisions are made by households, not individuals. More than three-fourths of the householders were immigrants.

The logit equation is as follows:

$$R = a + b_1 X_1 + b_2 X_2 + b_3 X_3 + b_4 X_4 + b_5 X_5 + b_6 X_6 + b_7 X_7 + b_8 X_8 + b_9 X_9 + b_{10} X_{10} + b_{11} X_{11} + b_{12} X_{12}$$

R is the log odds of place of residence. In its most common form, logit regression predicts a dependent variable with only two categories. Both R_1 (the odds of living outside New York City versus living within the city) and R_2 (the odds of living in the outer boroughs versus living in Manhattan) are predicted by the same set of variables: X_1—years of education completed by the household head; X_2—median household income; X_3—occupational prestige of the household head; X_4—sectoral employment; X_5—English-language ability; X_6—U.S. citizenship; X_7—U.S. birth; X_8—immigration before 1965; X_9—immigration between 1965 and 1974; X_{10}—age; X_{11}—marital status; X_{12}—presence of children under seventeen; and e—residual. For details about interpretation of the logit models, see R. D. Alba 1986, "Interpreting the Parameters of Log-Linear Models."

17. NORC 1988. According to the 1970 NORC occupational prestige scale, a two-digit number is assigned to each respondent's occupational category to create a new variable.

18. M. Zhou and J. R. Logan 1989, "Returns on Human Capital in Ethnic Enclaves." For non-Hispanic whites, this variable indicates employment in the so-defined enclave industries.

19. I looked at the characteristics of neighborhoods into which the Chinese tend to move through the 1980 census tract data (STF3). Also see Zhou 1989.

20. N. Kantrowitz 1973, *Ethnic and Racial Segregation in the New York Metropolis*; Massey and Denton 1988. Also see Zhou and Logan 1991.

21. Kwong 1987; B. P. Wong 1988, *Patronage, Brokerage, Entrepreneurship, and the Chinese Community of New York*; Zhou 1989.

22. M. Sakong 1990, *Rethinking the Impact of the Enclave*, p. 84.

23. I. Kim 1987, "The Koreans," p. 229; E. P. Kraly 1987, "U.S. Immigration Policy and the Immigrant Populations of New York," p. 68.
24. Kraly 1987.
25. For detailed analysis, see Zhou and Logan 1991.
26. Residence 1975 by residence 1980 by years of immigration, using variables MIG75 (residence in 1975: state-county recode) and IMMIGR (years of immigration) in the 1980 PUMS data. See Zhou and Logan 1991.
27. J. R. Logan and L. B. Stearns 1981, "Suburban Racial Segregation as a Non-ecological Process"; J. R. Logan and M. Schneider 1984, "Racial Segregation and Racial Change in American Suburbs"; Massey and Denton 1988.
28. Zhou 1989, pp. 174–177.
29. Massey and Denton 1987, p. 817.
30. Telephone interview, January 1989.
31. Personal interview, January 1989.
32. Gargan 1981; A. Scardino 1986, "Commercial Rents in Chinatown Soar as Hong Kong Exodus Grows"; Kwong 1987, pp. 44–45.
33. J. Wang 1979, "Behind the Boom"; Kwong 1987, pp. 43–53; Zhou 1989, pp. 59–60.
34. Kwong 1987, p. 51.
35. Personal interview, May 1988.
36. Kwong 1987, pp. 50–51.
37. Personal interview, September 1988.
38. Personal interview, May 1988.
39. Personal interview, December 1988.
40. Personal interview, January 1989.
41. B. L. Sung 1987, *The Adjustment Experience of Chinese Immigrant Children in New York City*, p. 119.
42. Personal interview, December 1988.
43. Personal interview with Mr. Zhou, a tenant, December 1988.
44. Personal interview, September 1988.
45. D. Y. Yuan 1963, "Voluntary Segregation," p. 260.
46. Personal interview, September 1988.
47. Personal interview, September 1988.
48. Personal interview, September 1988.
49. Yuan 1963, p. 260; C. Loo and D. Mar 1982, "Desired Residential Mobility in a Low Income Ethnic Community," p. 103.
50. Personal interview with Ms. Liang, September 1988.
51. NYCDCP 1986, *Asians in New York City*, p. 7.

Chapter 9

1. G. Kinkead 1991, "A Report at Large: Chinatown," p. 46.
2. W. J. Wilson 1987, *The Truly Disadvantaged*; W. H. Frey and A. Speare 1988, *Regional and Metropolitan Growth and Decline in the United States*; J. D. Kasarda 1989, "Urban Industrial Transition and the Underclass."
3. L. Winnick 1990, *New People in Old Neighborhoods*.

4. R. E. Friedman 1986, "Entrepreneurial Renewal in the Industrial City"; H. Aldrich and R. Waldinger 1990, "Ethnicity and Entrepreneurship."

5. Also see C. Hirchman 1983, "America's Melting Pot Reconsidered"; M. Langberg and R. Farley 1985, "Residential Segregation of Asians in 1980"; M. Tienda and D. Lii 1987, "Minority Concentration and Earning Inequalities"; R. M. Jiobu 1988, *Ethnicity and Assimilation*; R. Wilson 1988, "Is the American Dream Still Deferred?"

6. W. J. Wilson 1987; C. Jencks and P. E. Peterson 1991, *The Urban Underclass*.

7. Wilson 1987.

8. Kasarda 1989, p. 27.

9. I. Kim 1981, *New Urban Immigrants*; M. Sakong 1990, *Rethinking the Impact of the Enclave*.

10. A. Portes 1987, "The Social Origins of the Cuban Enclave Economy of Miami"; A. Portes and L. E. Guarnizo 1991, "Tropical Capitalists".

11. K. L. Wilson and A. Portes 1980, "Immigrant Enclaves."

12. Ibid., p. 313.

13. Kasarda 1989, pp. 28–29.

14. J. S. Butler 1991, *Entrepreneurship and Self-Help among Black Americans*.

15. J. D. Greenstone 1991, "Culture, Rationality, and the Underclass," p. 407.

References

Alba, Richard D. 1986. "Interpreting the Parameters of Log-Linear Models." *Sociological Methods and Research* 16 (1): 45–77.

———. 1985a. "The Twilight of Ethnicity among Americans of European Ancestry: The Case of Italians." *Ethnic and Racial Studies* 8 (1): 134–158.

———. 1985b. *Italian Americans: Into the Twilight of Ethnicity*. Englewood Cliffs, N.J.: Prentice-Hall.

Alba, Richard D., and John R. Logan. 1991. "Variations on Two Themes: Racial and Ethnic Patterns in the Attainment of Suburban Residence." *Demography* 28 (3): 431–453.

Aldrich, Howard, and John Carter. 1985. "Ethnic Residential Concentration and the Protected Market Hypothesis." *Social Forces* 63: 996–1009.

Aldrich, Howard, and Roger Waldinger. 1990. "Ethnicity and Entrepreneurship." *Annual Review of Sociology* 16: 111–135.

Aldrich, Howard, and Catherine Zimmer. 1989. "Continuities in the Study of Ecological Succession: Asian Businesses in Three English Cities." *Social Forces* 67: 920–944.

Aubits, Shawn. 1988. "Tracing Early Chinese Immigration into the United States: The Use of I.N.S. Documents." *Amerasia Journal* 14 (2): 37–46.

Averitt, Robert T. 1968. *The Dual Economy: The Dynamics of American Industry Structure*. New York: Norton.

Bach, Robert L. 1986. "Immigration: Issues of Ethnicity, Class, and Public Policy in the United States." *Annals of the American Academy of Political and Social Sciences* 485 (May): 139–152.

Bailey, Thomas, and Roger Waldinger. 1987. *A Human Resource Development Strategy for the New York City Garment Industry*. A report prepared for the Garment Industry Development Corporation.

———. 1984. "A Skills Mismatch in New York's Labor Market?" *New York Affairs* 8 (3): 3–18.

Banno, Masatak. 1964. *China and the West, 1858–1861*. Cambridge: Cambridge University Press.

Barth, Gunther. 1964. *Bitter Strength: A History of the Chinese in the United States, 1850–1870*. Cambridge: Harvard University Press.

Beck, E. M., Patrick M. Horan, and Charles M. Tolbert II. 1978. "Stratification in a Dual Economy: A Sectoral Model of Earnings Determination." *American Sociological Review* 43: 704–720.

Berk, Richard A. 1983. "An Introduction to Sample Selection Bias in Sociological Data." *American Sociological Review* 48: 386–398.

Blau, Francine D., and Marianne A. Ferber. 1986. *The Economics of Women, Men, and Work*. Englewood Cliffs, N.J.: Prentice-Hall.

Blau, Peter, and Otis Dudley Duncan. 1967. *The American Occupational Structure*. New York: Free Press.

Bonacich, Edna. 1984a. "Asian Labor in the Development of California and Hawaii." In Lucie Cheng and Edna Bonacich, eds., *Labor Immigration under Capitalism: Asian Workers in the United States before World War II*. Berkeley: University of California Press. Pp. 130–185.

———. 1984b. "United States Capitalist Development: A Background to Asian Immigration." In Lucie Cheng and Edna Bonacich, eds., *Labor Immigration under Capitalism: Asian Workers in the United States before World War II*. Berkeley: University of California Press. Pp. 79–129.

———. 1973. "A Theory of Middleman Minorities." *American Sociological Review* 38: 583–594.

———. 1972. "A Theory of Ethnic Antagonism: The Split Labor Market." *American Sociological Review* 37: 547–59.

Bonacich, Edna, and Ivan Light. 1988. *Immigrant Entrepreneurs: Koreans in Los Angeles, 1965–1982*. Berkeley: University of California Press.

Bonacich, Edna, Ivan Light, and Charles Choy Wong. 1977. "Koreans in Small Business." *Society* 14: 54–59.

Bonacich, Edna, and John M. Modell. 1980. *The Economic Basis of Ethnic Solidarity: Small Business in the Japanese Community*. Berkeley: University of California Press.

Borjas, George J. 1990. *Friends or Strangers: The Impact of Immigrants on the U.S. Economy*. New York: Basic Books.

———. 1989. "Economic Theory and International Migration." *International Migration Review* 23 (3): 457–85.

Briggs, Vernon M. 1975. "Mexican Workers in the United States Labor Market: A Contemporary Dilemma." *International Labor Review* 112 (November): 351–368.

Bu Gao Ban. Newsletter of the New York Chinatown History Project, 1984–1989.

Burgess, Ernest W. 1923. "The Growth of the City: An Introduction to a Research Project." In *Proceedings of the American Sociological Society*. Vol. 18. Chicago: University of Chicago Press. Pp. 57–85.

Butler, John S. 1991. *Entrepreneurship and Self-Help among Black Americans: A Reconsideration of Race and Economics*. New York: State University of New York Press.

Chan, Sucheng. 1986. *This Bitter-sweet Soil: The Chinese in California Agriculture, 1860–1910*. Berkeley: University of California Press.

Chen, Jack. 1980. *The Chinese of America*. San Francisco: Harper and Row.

Cheng, Lucie, and Edna Bonacich, eds. 1984. *Labor Immigration under Capital-*

ism: Asian Workers in the United States before World War II. Berkeley: University of California Press.

Cheng, Nien. 1987. *Life and Death in Shanghai*. New York: Grove Press.

Chiswick, Barry R. 1983. "An Analysis of the Earnings and Employment of Asian-American Men." *Journal of Labor Economics* 1 (2): 197–214.

———. 1980. "Immigrant Earnings Patterns by Sex, Race, and Ethnic Groupings." *Monthly Labor Review* 103 (October): 22–25.

———. 1977. "Sons of Immigrants: Are They at an Earnings Disadvantage?" *American Economic Review* 7 (Supplement): 376–380.

Choldin, Harvey M. 1973. "Kinship Networks in the Migration Process." *International Migration Review* 7 (Summer): 163–175.

Chu, Daniel, and Samuel Chu. 1967. *Passage to the Golden Gate: A History of the Chinese in America to 1910*. New York: Zenith Books.

Cobas, José A. 1985. "A New Test and Extension of Propositions from the Bonacich Syntheses." *Social Forces* 64: 432–441.

Coleman, James S. 1988. "Social Capital in the Creation of Human Capital." *American Journal of Sociology* 94 (Supplement): S95–120.

Conwell, Russell H. 1871. *Why and How: Why the Chinese Emigrate and the Means They Adopt for the Purpose of Reaching America*. Boston: Lee and Shepard.

Coolidge, Mary Roberts. 1909. *Chinese Immigration*. New York: Henry Holt.

Cortese, Charles, R. Frank Falk, and Jack K. Cohen. 1976. "Further Considerations of the Methodological Analysis of Segregation Indices." *American Sociological Review* 41: 630–637.

Daniels, Roger. 1988. *Asian America: Chinese and Japanese in the United States since 1850*. Seattle: University of Washington Press.

Davis, Kingsley, and Wilbert E. Moore. 1945. "Some Principles of Stratification." *American Sociological Review* 10: 242–247.

Deng, Zhiduan. 1991. "China's Brain Drain Problem: Causes, Consequences, and Policy Options." *Papers of the Center for Modern China* 11: 1–46.

Dillon, Richard H. 1962. *The Hatchet Men: The Story of the Tong Wars in San Francisco's Chinatown*. New York: Coward-McCann.

Duncan, Otis Dudley. 1977a. "A Socioeconomic Index for All Occupations." In Albert J. Reiss, Otis Dudley Duncan, Paul K. Hatt, and Cecil C. North, eds. *Occupation and Social Status*. New York: Arno Press. Pp. 109–138.

———. 1977b. "Properties and Characteristics of the Socioeconomic Index." In Albert J. Reiss, Otis Dudley Duncan, Paul K. Hatt and Cecil C. North, eds. *Occupation and Social Status*. New York: Arno Press. Pp. 139–161.

Duncan, Otis Dudley, and Beverly Duncan. 1955. "A Methodological Analysis of Segregation Indices." *American Sociological Review* 20: 210–217.

Duncan, Otis Dudley, and Stanley Lieberson. 1959. "Ethnic Segregation and Assimilation." *American Journal of Sociology* 64: 364–374.

Edwards, Richard C. 1975. "The Social Relations of Production in the Firm and Labor Market Structure." In Richard C. Edwards, Michael Reich, and David M. Gordon, eds., *Labor Market Segmentation*. Lexington, Mass.: D.C. Heath. Pp. 3–26.

England, Paula. 1982. "Assessing Trends in Occupational Sex Segregation,

1900–1976." In Ivar Berg, ed., *Sociological Perspectives on Labor Markets*. New York: Academic Press. Pp. 273–295.

Evans, M.D.R. 1989. "Immigrant Entrepreneurship: Effects of Ethnic Market Size and Isolated Labor Pool." *American Sociological Review* 54: 950–962.

Fischer, Claude S. 1984. *The Urban Experience*. 2d ed. New York: Harcourt Brace Jovanovich.

Freeman, Marcia. 1983. "The Labor Market for Immigrants in New York City." *New York Affairs* 7 (4): 94–111.

Frey, William H., and Aldon Speare, Jr. 1988. *Regional and Metropolitan Growth and Decline in the United States*. New York: Russell Sage Foundation.

Friedman, Robert E. 1986. "Entrepreneurial Renewal in the Industrial City." *Annals of the American Academy of Political and Social Sciences* 488 (November): 35–44.

Galbraith, John K. 1971. *The New Industrial State*. New York: Mentor.

Gans, Herbert. 1979. "Symbolic Ethnicity: The Future of Ethnic Groups and Cultures in America." *Ethnic and Racial Studies* 2: 1–20.

———. 1962. *The Urban Villagers: Group and Class in the Life of Italian-Americans*. New York: Free Press.

Gargan, Edward A. 1981. "New Money, People, and Ideas Alter Chinatown of Tradition." *New York Times*, December 28, 1:1.

Glazer, Nathan, and Daniel P. Moynihan. 1970. *Beyond the Melting Pot: The Negroes, Puerto Ricans, Jews, Italians, and Irish of New York City*. Cambridge, Mass.: MIT Press.

Glenn, Evelyn. 1983. "Split Household, Small Producer, and Dual Wage Earner: An Analysis of Chinese-American Family Strategies." *Journal of Marriage and the Family* 45: 35–46.

Gordon, David M. 1972. *Theories of Poverty and Underemployment: Orthodox, Radical, and Dual Labor Market Perspectives*. Lexington, Mass.: D. C. Heath.

Gordon, Milton M. 1964. *Assimilation in American Life: The Role of Race, Religion, and National Origins*. New York: Oxford University Press.

Granovetter, Mark. 1985. "Economic Action and Social Structure: The Problem of Embeddedness." *American Journal of Sociology* 91: 481–510.

Greenstone, J. David. 1991. "Culture, Rationality, and the Underclass." In Christopher Jencks and Paul E. Peterson, eds. *The Urban Underclass*. Washington, D.C.: Brookings Institution. Pp. 399–408.

Guest, Avery M., and James A. Weed. 1976. "Ethnic Residential Segregation: Patterns of Change." *American Journal of Sociology* 81: 1088–1111.

Haines, David W. 1986. "Vietnamese Refugee Women in the U.S. Labor Force: Continuity or Change?" In Rita James Simon and Caroline B. Brettell, eds., *International Migration: The Female Experience*. New Jersey: Rowman and Allanheld. Pp. 62–75.

Handlin, Oscar. 1951. *The Uprooted: The Epic Story of the Great Migrations That Made the American People*. Boston: Little, Brown.

Hauser, Robert M. 1980. "On Stratification in a Dual Economy: A Comment on Beck, Horan, and Tolbert, 1978." *American Sociological Review* 45: 702–712.

Heinberg, John D., Jeffrey K. Harris, and Robert L. York. 1989. "The Process of Exempt Immediate Relative Immigration to the United States." *International Migration Review*. 23 (4): 839–855.

Hirschman, Charles. 1983. "America's Melting Pot Reconsidered." *Annual Review of Sociology* 9: 397–423.

Hodge, Robert W., and Patricia Hodge. 1965. "Occupational Assimilation as a Competitive Process." *American Journal of Sociology* 71: 249–264.

Houston, Randy, and Robert L. Kaufman. 1982. "Economic Dualism: A Critical Review." *American Sociological Review* 47: 727–739.

Hsia, Hayjia. 1988. *Asian Americans in Higher Education and at Work*. Hillsdale, N.J.: Lawrence Erlbaum Associates.

Huber, Joan, and Glenna Spitze. 1983. *Sex Stratification: Children, Housework, and Jobs*. New York: Academic Press.

Hunter, Albert. 1974. *Symbolic Communities: The Persistence and Change of Chicago's Local Communities*. Chicago: University of Chicago Press.

Hurh, Won Moo, and Kwang Chung Kim. 1984. *Korean Immigrants in America: A Structural Analysis of Ethnic Confinement and Adhesive Adaptation*. Rutherford, N.J.: Fairleigh Dickinson University Press.

ILGWU (International Ladies' Garment Workers' Union, Local 23–25) and the New York Skirt and Sportswear Association. 1983. *The Chinatown Garment Industry Study*. New York: Abeles, Schwartz, Haeckel & Silverblatt.

INS Statistical Yearbook. 1950 to 1988. *Statistical Yearbook of the Immigration and Naturalization Service*. U.S. Department of Justice.

Jackson, Peter. 1983. "Ethnic Turf: Competition on the Canal Street Divide." *New York Affairs* 7 (4): 149–158.

Jencks, Christopher, and Paul E. Peterson, eds. 1991. *The Urban Underclass*. Washington, D.C.: Brookings Institution.

Jiobu, Robert M. 1988. *Ethnicity and Assimilation: Blacks, Chinese, Filipinos, Japanese, Koreans, Mexicans, Vietnamese, and Whites*. Albany: State University of New York Press.

Kahn-Hut, Rachel, Arlene Kaplan Daniels, and Richard Colvard. 1982. *Women and Work: Problems and Perspectives*. New York: Oxford University Press.

Kantrowitz, Nathan. 1973. *Ethnic and Racial Segregation in the New York Metropolis*. New York: Praeger.

Kasarda, John D. 1989. "Urban Industrial Transition and the Underclass." *Annals of the American Academy of Political and Social Science* 501: 26–47.

———. 1983. "Entry-Level Jobs, Mobility, and Urban Minority Unemployment." *Urban Affairs Quarterly* 19 (1): 21–40.

Key Publications. 1988. *Chinese Business Guide and Directory for Metropolitan New York and Boston, 1988*.

Kifner, John. 1991. "Immigrant Waves from Asia Bring an Underworld Ashore." *New York Times*, January 6, p. 1.

Kim, Illsoo. 1987. "The Koreans: Small Business in an Urban Frontier." In Nancy Foner, ed., *New Immigrants in New York*. New York: Columbia University Press. Pp. 219–242.

———. 1981. *New Urban Immigrants: The Korean Community in New York*. Princeton: Princeton University Press.

Kinkead, Gwen. 1991. "A Report at Large: Chinatown." *The New Yorker*, June 16, pp. 45–83.

Kraly, Ellen Percy. 1987. "U.S. Immigration Policy and the Immigrant Populations of New York." In Nancy Foner, ed. *New Immigrants in New York*. New York: Columbia University Press. Pp. 35–78.

Kung, Chung-wu, 1975. "Cultural Revolution in Modern Chinese History." In Victor Nee and James Peck, eds., *China's Uninterrupted Revolution, from 1840 to the Present*. New York: Pantheon Books. Pp. 218–321.

Kung, Lydia. 1983. *Factory Women in Taiwan*. Studies in Cultural Anthropology. Ann Arbor, Mich.: UMI Research Press.

Kuo, Chia-ling. 1977. *Social and Political Change in New York's Chinatown: The Role of Voluntary Associations*. New York: Praeger.

Kwong, Peter. 1987. *The New Chinatown*. New York: Hill and Wang.

———. 1979. *Chinatown, New York: Labor and Politics, 1930–1950*. New York: Monthly Review Press.

Langberg, Mark, and Reynolds Farley. 1985. "Residential Segregation of Asians in 1980." *Sociology and Social Research* 69: 51–61.

Li, Peter. 1977. "Occupational Achievement and Kinship Assistance among Chinese Immigrants in Chicago." *Sociological Quarterly* 18: 478–489.

Lieberson, Stanley. 1980. *A Piece of the Pie*. Berkeley: University of California Press.

———. 1963. *Ethnic Patterns in American Cities*. New York: Free Press.

Lieberson, Stanley, and D. K. Carter. 1982. "Temporal Changes and Urban Differences in Residential Segregation: A Reconsideration." *American Journal of Sociology* 89: 296–310.

Lieberson, Stanley, and Mary C. Waters. 1986. "Ethnic Groups in Flux: The Changing Ethnic Responses of American Whites." *Annals of the American Academy of Political and Social Sciences* 487 (September): 79–91.

Light, Ivan H. 1984. "Immigrant and Ethnic Enterprise in North America." *Ethnic and Racial Studies* 7, (2): 195–216.

———. 1972. *Ethnic Enterprises in America: Business Welfare among Chinese, Japanese, and Blacks*. Berkeley: University of California Press.

Light, Ivan H., and Charles Choy Wong. 1975. "Protest or Work: Dilemmas of the Tourist Industry in American Chinatowns." *American Journal of Sociology* 80: 1342–1368.

Lindstrom-Best, Varpu. 1988. *Defiant Sisters: A Social History of Finnish Immigrant Women in Canada*. Toronto: Multicultural History Society of Ontario.

Logan, John R., and Mark Schneider. 1984. "Racial Segregation and Racial Change in American Suburbs, 1970–1980." *American Journal of Sociology* 89: 875–888.

Logan, John R., and Linda B. Stearns. 1981. "Suburban Racial Segregation as a Non-ecological Process." *Social Forces* 60: 61–73.

Loo, Chalsa, and Don Mar. 1982. "Desired Residential Mobility in a Low Income Ethnic Community: A Case Study of Chinatown." *Journal of Social Issues* 38 (3): 95–106.

Lyman, Stanford M. 1986. *Chinatown and Little Tokyo: Power, Conflict, and Com-*

munity among Chinese and Japanese Immigrants in America. Millwood, N.Y.: Associated Faculty Press.

———. 1974. *Chinese Americans.* New York: Random House.

MacDonald, J. S., and L. D. MacDonald. 1964. "Chain Migration, Ethnic Neighborhood Formation, and Social Networks." *Milbank Memorial Fund Quarterly* 42: 82–91.

Mar, Don. 1984. *Chinese Immigrants and the Ethnic Labor Market.* Ph.D diss., University of California, Berkeley.

Massey, Douglas S., and Nancy A. Denton. 1988. "Suburbanization and Segregation in U.S. Metropolitan Areas." *American Journal of Sociology* 94: 592–626.

———. 1987. "Trends in the Residential Segregation of Blacks, Hispanics, and Asians, 1970–1980." *American Sociological Review* 52: 802–825.

———. 1985. "Spatial Assimilation as a Socioeconomic Outcome." *American Sociological Review* 50: 94–105.

Massey, Douglas S., and Brendan P. Mullan. 1984. "Processes of Hispanic and Black Spatial Assimilation." *American Journal of Sociology* 89: 836–73.

McCunn, Ruthanne Lum. 1979. *An Illustrated History of the Chinese in America.* San Francisco: Design Enterprises of San Francisco.

McKee, Delber L. 1977. *Chinese Exclusion versus the Open Door Policy, 1900–1906: Clashes over China Policy in the Roosevelt Era.* Detroit: Wayne State University Press.

McKenzie, Roderick D. 1927. *Oriental Exclusion.* New York: American Group Institute of Pacific Relations.

Meadows, Paul. 1980. "Immigration Theory: A Review of Thematic Strategies." In Roy Simon Bryce-Laporte, ed., *Sourcebook on the New Immigration.* New Brunswick, N.J.: Transaction Books. Pp. 397–411.

Miller, Robert K. 1982. "Patterns of Employment Difficulty among European Immigrant Industrial Workers during the Great Depression: Local Opportunity and Cultural Heritage." In Ivar Berg, ed., *Sociological Perspectives on Labor Markets.* New York: Academic Press. Pp. 297–325.

Miller, Stuart Creighton. 1969. *The Unwelcome Immigrants: The American Image of the Chinese, 1785–1882.* Berkeley: University of California Press.

Min, P. G. 1988. *Ethnic Business Enterprise: Korean Small Business in Atlanta.* New York: AMS Press.

Mincer, Jacob. 1974. *Schooling and Experience.* New York: National Bureau of Economic Research.

Muller, Thomas, and Thomas J. Espenshade. 1985. *The Fourth Wave: California's Newest Immigrants.* Washington, D.C.: Urban Institutes.

Nee, Victor, and Brett de Bary Nee. 1973. *Longtime Californ': A Study of an American Chinatown.* Stanford: Stanford University Press.

Nee, Victor, and Jimy M. Sanders. 1987. "On Testing the Enclave-Economy Hypothesis." *American Sociological Review* 52: 771–73.

———. 1985. "The Road to Parity: Determinants of the Socio-economic Achievements of Asian Americans." *Ethnic and Racial Studies* 8: 75–93.

Nishi, Setsuko Matsunaga. 1979. "The New Wave of Asian Americans." *New York Affairs* 5 (3): 82–86.

NORC (National Opinion Research Center, University of Chicago). 1988. *General Social Surveys, 1972–1988: Cumulative Codebook.* Produced as part of the National Data Program for the Social Sciences, July.

NYCDCP (New York City Department of City Planning). 1986. *Asians in New York City: A Demographic Summary.* Prepared for the Mayor's Task Force on the Year 2000: Asian-American Issues, by Office of Immigrant Affairs and Population Analysis Division.

———. 1979. *Manhattan Bridge Area Study: Chinatown.*

———. 1976. *Chinatown Street Revitalization.*

NYCREC (New York City Real Estate Corporation). 1988. *Manhattan Real Estate Transactions, 1988.*

NYS-IATFIA (New York State Inter-Agency Task Force on Immigration Affairs). 1988. *Workplace Discrimination under the Immigration Reform and Control Act of 1986: A Study of Impacts on New Yorkers.*

Papademetriou, Demetrios G. 1990. "Contending Approaches to Reforming the U.S. Legal Immigration System." Paper prepared for the NYU/Rockefeller Foundation Conference on Migration, Ethnicity, and the City, the Arden Homestead, New York. November 2–4.

Papademetriou, Demetrios G., et al. 1989. "The Effects of Immigration on the U.S. Economy and Labor Market." U.S. Department of Labor, International Labor Affairs Bureau, October.

Parcel, Toby L. 1982. "The Development and Functioning of the American Urban Export Sector, 1947–1972." In Ivar Berg, ed., *Sociological Perspectives on Labor Markets.* New York: Academic Press. Pp. 187–217.

———. 1979. "Race, Regional Labor Markets, and Earnings." *American Sociological Review* 44: 262–279.

Park, Robert E., and Ernest W. Burgess. 1967. *The City.* Chicago: University of Chicago Press.

Patel, Dinker I. 1988. "Asian Americans: A Growing Force." *Journal of State Government* (Council of State Governments) 61 (2): 71–76.

Perez, Lisandro. 1986. "Immigrant Economic Adjustment and Family Organization: The Cuban Success Story Reexamined." *International Migration Review* 20 (1): 4–20.

Petersen, William, and Michael Novak. 1982. *Concepts of Ethnicity.* Cambridge: Belknap Press of Harvard University Press.

Phizacklea, Annie, ed. 1983. *One-Way Ticket: Migration and Female Labor.* London: Routledge and Kegan Paul.

Piore, Michael J. 1986. "The Shifting Grounds for Immigration." *Annals of the American Academy of Social Sciences* 485: 23–33.

———. 1980. "The Technological Foundations of Dualism and Discontinuity." In Suzanne Berger and Michael J. Piore, eds., *Dualism and Discontinuity in Industrial Society.* Cambridge: Cambridge University Press. Pp. 55–81.

———. 1979. *Birds of Passage: Migrant Labor and Industrial Societies.* Cambridge: Cambridge University Press.

Portes, Alejandro. 1989a. *Unauthorized Immigration and Immigration Reform:*

Present Trends and Prospects. Washington, D.C.: Commission for the Study of International Migration and Cooperative Economic Development.

————. 1989b. "Latin American Urbanization during the Years of Crisis." *Latin American Research Review* 24: 7–44.

————. 1987. "The Social Origins of the Cuban Enclave Economy of Miami." *Sociological Perspectives* 30 (October): 340–372.

————. 1981. "Modes of Structural Incorporation and Present Theories of Immigration." In Mary M. Kritz, Charles B. Keely, and Sylvano M. Tomasi, eds., *Global Trends in Migration*. Staten Island, N.Y.: CMS Press. Pp. 279–297.

————. 1976. "Determinants of the Brain Drain." *International Migration Review* 10 (4): 489–508.

Portes, Alejandro, and Robert L. Bach. 1985. *The Latin Journey: Cuban and Mexican Immigrants in the United States*. Berkeley: University of California Press.

————. 1980. "Immigrant Earnings: Cuban and Mexican Immigrants in the United States." *International Migration Review* 14 (3): 315–41.

Portes, Alejandro, Manuel Castells, and Lauren A. Benton, eds. 1989. *The Informal Economy: Studies in Advanced and Less Developed Countries*. Baltimore: Johns Hopkins University Press.

Portes, Alejandro, Juan M. Clark, and Robert L. Bach. 1977. "The New Wave: A Statistical Profile of Recent Cuban Exiles in the United States." *Cuban Studies* 7: 1–32.

Portes, Alejandro, and Luis E. Guarnizo. 1991. "Tropical Capitalists: U.S.-Bound Immigration and Small-Enterprise Development in the Dominican Republic." In S. Diaz-Briquets and S. Weinstraub, eds., *Migration, Remittances, and Small Business Development*. Boulder, Colo.: Westview Press. Pp. 101–131.

Portes, Alejandro, and Leif Jensen. 1989. "The Enclave and the Entrants: Patterns of Ethnic Enterprise in Miami before and after Mariel." *American Sociological Review* 54: 929–949.

————. 1987. "What's an Ethnic Enclave? The Case for Conceptual Clarity." *American Sociological Review* 52: 768–771.

Portes, Alejandro, and Robert D. Manning. 1986. "The Immigrant Enclave: Theory and Empirical Examples." In Susan Olzak and Joame Nagel, eds., *Comparative Ethnic Relations*. New York: Academic Press. Pp. 47–68.

Portes, Alejandro, and Rubén G. Rumbaut. 1990. *Immigrant America: A Portrait*. Berkeley: University of California Press.

Portes, Alejandro, and Alex Stepick. 1985. "Unwelcome Immigrants: The Labor Market Experience of 1980 (Mariel) Cuban and Haitian Refugees in South Florida." *American Sociological Review* 50: 493–514.

Reitz, Jeffrey G. 1980. *The Survival of Ethnic Groups*. Toronto: McGraw-Hill.

Richmond, Anthony H. 1988. *Immigration and Ethnic Conflict*. New York: St. Martin's Press.

Rosenberg, Carolyn. 1981. "The Liability of Ethnicity in Israel." *Social Forces* 59: 667–686.

Rosenberg, Samuel. 1980. "Male Occupational Standing and the Dual Labor Market." *Industrial Relations* 19: 34–49.

Sakong, Myungduk. 1990. *Rethinking the Impact of the Enclave: A Comparative Analysis of Korean Americans' Economic and Residential Adaptation.* Ph.D. Diss., State University of New York at Albany.

Salaff, Janet W. 1981. *Working Daughters of Hong Kong: Filial Piety or Power in the Family?* London: Cambridge University Press.

Sanders, Jimy M., and Victor Nee. 1987. "Limits of Ethnic Solidarity in the Enclave Economy." *American Sociological Review* 52: 745–767.

SAPB (Sino-American Publicity Bureau). 1958. *1957–58 Chinese Directory of Eastern Cities.*

Sassen-Koob, Saskia. 1989. "New York City's Informal Economy." In Alejandro Portes, Manuel Castells, and Lauren A. Benton, eds., *The Informal Economy: Studies in Advanced and Less Developed Countries.* Baltimore: Johns Hopkins University Press. Pp. 60–77.

————. 1988. *The Mobility of Labor and Capital: A Study in International Investment and Labor Flow.* New York: Cambridge University Press.

————. 1987. "Growth and Informalization at the Core: A Preliminary Report on New York City." In Michael P. Smith and Joe R. Feagin, eds., *The Capital City: Global Restructuring and Community Politics.* New York: Basil Blackwell. Pp. 138–154.

————. 1984. "Notes on the Incorporation of Third World Women into Wage Labor through Immigration and Off-shore Production." *International Migration Review* 18 (4): 1144–1167.

Saxton, Alexander. 1971. *The Indispensable Enemy: Labor and the Anti-Chinese Movement in California.* Berkeley: University of California Press.

Scardino, Albert. 1986. "Commercial Rents in Chinatown Soar as Hong Kong Exodus Grows." *New York Times*, December 25.

Semyonov, Moshe. 1988. "Bi-ethnic Labor Markets, Mono-ethnic Labor Markets, and Socioeconomic Inequality." *American Sociological Review* 53: 256–266.

————. 1981. "The Effect of Community on Status Attainment." *Sociological Quarterly* 22: 359–72.

Semyonov, Moshe, and Andrea Tyree. 1981. "Community Segregation and the Costs of Ethnic Subordination." *Social Forces* 59: 649–66.

Seward, George F. 1970. *Chinese Immigration: Its Social and Economic Aspects.* New York: Arno Press and the *New York Times.*

Shibutani, Tamotsu, and Kian M. Kwan. 1965. *Ethnic Stratification: A Comparative Approach.* New York: Macmillan.

Siu, Paul C. 1987. *The Chinese Laundryman: A Study of Social Isolation.* New York: New York University Press.

Sorensen, Aage B., and Arne L. Kalleberg. 1982. "An Outline of a Theory of the Matching of Persons to Jobs." In Ivar Berg, ed., *Sociological Perspectives on Labor Markets.* New York: Academic Press. Pp. 49–74.

Spilerman, Seymour. 1977. "Careers, Labor Market Structure, and Socioeconomic Achievement." *American Journal of Sociology* 83: 551–93.

Spilerman, Seymour, and Jack Jabib. 1976. "Development Towns in Israel:

The Role of Community in Creating Ethnic Disparities in Labor Force Characteristics." *American Journal of Sociology* 81: 781–812.

SSBC (State Statistical Bureau, China). 1986. *Statistical Yearbook of China, 1986*. Oxford: Oxford University Press.

Stolzenberg, Ross M. 1975. "Occupations, Labor Markets, and the Process of Wage Attainment." *American Sociological Review* 40: 645–665.

Stone, Karen. 1983. "Motherhood and Waged Work: West Indian, Asian, and White Mothers Compared." In Annie Phizacklea, ed., *One-Way Ticket: Migration and Female Labor*. London: Routledge and Kegan Paul. Pp. 33–52.

Stonequist, Everett V. 1961. *The Marginal Man: A Study in Personality and Culture Conflict*. New York: Russell and Russell.

Strebeigh, Fred. 1989. "Training China's New Elite." *The Atlantic Monthly* (April), p. 74.

Sung, Betty Lee. 1987. *The Adjustment Experience of Chinese Immigrant Children in New York City*. New York: Center for Migration Studies.

———. 1978. *Chinese Population in Lower Manhattan*. A report prepared for the Employment and Training Administration, U.S. Department of Labor.

———. 1976. *A Survey of Chinese-American Manpower and Employment*. New York: Praeger.

———. 1974. *Racial and Ethnic Group Population by Census Tracts: The SMSA of New York City, 1970*. New York: Department of Asian Studies, City University of New York.

———. 1967. *The Story of the Chinese in America*. New York: Collier Books.

Suttles, Gerald. 1972. *The Social Construction of Communities*. Chicago: University of Chicago Press.

———. 1968. *The Social Order of the Slum: Ethnicity and Territory in the Inner City*. Chicago: University of Chicago Press.

Tienda, Marta, and Ronald Angel. 1982, "Headship and Household Composition among Blacks, Hispanics, and Other Whites." *Social Forces* 61: 508–529.

Tienda, Marta, and Ding-Tzann Lii. 1987. "Minority Concentration and Earning Inequalities: Blacks, Hispanics, and Asians Compared." *American Journal of Sociology* 93: 141–165.

Tinker, Irene. 1978. "Women in Developing Societies: Economic Independence Is Not Enough." In Jane R. Chapman, ed., *Economic Independence for Women: The Foundation for Equal Rights*. Beverly Hills: Sage. Pp. 113–135.

Tobier, Emanuel. 1979. "The New Face of Chinatown." *New York Affairs* 5 (3): 66–76.

Tolbert, Charles M., II, Patrick M. Horan and E. M. Beck. 1980. "The Structure of Economic Segmentation: A Dual Economic Approach." *American Journal of Sociology* 85: 1095–1116.

Tomasi, Lydio F. 1990. *In Defense of the Alien. Proceedings of the 1989 Annual National Legal Conference on Immigration and Refugee Policy*. Vol. 12.

Trent, Katherine, and Richard D. Alba. 1988. "Population." In Gerald Benjamin and Charles Brecher, eds., *The Two New Yorks: State-City Relations in the Changing Federal System*. New York: Russell Sage Foundation. Pp. 81–105.

Tsai, Shih-shan Henry. 1986. *The Chinese Experience in America*. Bloomington: Indiana University Press.

Tyler, Gus. 1987. "A Tale of Three Cities: Upper Economy, Lower and Under." *Dissent* (Fall): 463–470.

Ugalde, Antonio, Frank D. Bean, and Gilbert Cardenas. 1979. "International Migration from the Dominican Republic: Findings from a National Survey." *International Migration Review* 13 (2): 235–254.

U.S. Bureau of the Census, Washington, D.C.: Department of Commerce. *Census of Population*. 1910–1980.

——. *Census of Population and Housing*. 1980.

——. *Census of Population and Housing*. 1970.

——. *Census of Population and Housing*. Census Tracts, 1980.

——. *Census of Population and Housing*. Census Tracts, 1970.

——. *Census of Population and Housing*. 1980 PUMS.

——. *Census of Population and Housing*. 1980 STF3A.

——. *Socioeconomic Characteristics of the U.S. Foreign-Born Population Detailed in Census Bureau Tabulations*, 1984.

——. *Survey of Minority-Owned Business Enterprises: Asian Americans, American Indians, and Others* (1972, 1977, 1982, and 1987).

USCCR (U.S. Commission on Civil Rights). 1988. *The Economic Status of Americans of Asian Descent*. June. Washington, D.C.: Government Printing Office.

United States Statutes at Large. Various years. Washington, D.C.: Government Printing Office.

Wachter, Michael L. 1974. "Primary and Secondary Labor Markets: A Critique of the Dual Approach." *Brookings Paper on Economic Activity* 3: 637–80.

Wacquant, Loïc J. D., and William J. Wilson 1989, "The Cost of Racial and Class Exclusion in the Inner City." *Annals of the American Academy of Political and Social Science* 501: 8–25.

Waldinger, Roger. 1990. *Tattered and Torn: The Garment Industry Hangs On*. Prepared for the Manhattan Institute.

——. 1987. "Beyond Nostalgia: The Old Neighborhood Revisited." *New York Affairs* 10 (1): 1–12.

——. 1986a. *Through the Eye of the Needle: Immigrants and Enterprise in New York's Garment Trades*. New York: New York University Press.

——. 1986b. "Immigrant Enterprises: A Critique and Reformulation." *Theory and Society* 15 (1–2): 249–285.

——. 1986c. "Changing Ladders and Musical Chairs: Ethnicity and Opportunity in Post-industrial New York." *Politics and Society* 15: 369–401.

Wallace, Michael, and Arne L. Kalleberg, 1982. "Economic Organization of Firms and Labor Market Consequences: Toward a Specification of Dual Economy Theory." In Ivar Berg, ed., *Sociological Perspectives on Labor Markets*. New York: Academic Press. Pp. 77–117.

Wang, John. 1979. "Behind the Boom: Power and Economics in Chinatown." *New York Affairs* 5 (3): 77–81.

Weiner, Myron. 1987. "International Emigration and the Third World." In William Alonso, ed., *Population in an Interacting World*. Cambridge: Harvard University Press. Pp. 173–200.

Weiner, Elizabeth, and Hardy Green. 1984. "A Stitch in Our Times: New York's Hispanic Garment Workers in 1980s." In Joan M. Jensen and Sue

Davidson, eds., *A Needle, a Bobbin, a Strike: Women Needleworkers in America.* Philadelphia: Temple University Press. Pp. 278–296.

Wilson, Carol Green. 1931. *Chinatown Quest: The Life Adventures of Donaldina Cameron.* Stanford: Stanford University Press.

Wilson, Kenneth L., and W. Allen Martin. 1982. "Ethnic Enclaves: A Comparison of the Cuban and Black Economies in Miami." *American Journal of Sociology* 88: 135–160.

Wilson, Kenneth L., and Alejandro Portes. 1980. "Immigrant Enclaves: An Analysis of the Labor Market Experiences of Cubans in Miami." *American Journal of Sociology* 86: 305–319.

Wilson, Roger. 1988. "Is the American Dream Still Deferred?" *Journal of State Government* (Council of State Governments) 61 (2): 81–86.

Wilson, William J. 1991. "Public Policy Research and the Truly Disadvantaged." In Christopher Jencks and Paul E. Peterson, eds., *The Urban Underclass.* Washington, D.C.: Brookings Institution. Pp. 460–481.

———. 1987. *The Truly Disadvantaged: The Inner City, the Underclass, and Public Policy.* Chicago: University of Chicago Press.

Winnick, Louis. 1990. *New People in Old Neighborhoods: The Role of New Immigrants in Rejuvenating New York's Communities.* New York: Russell Sage.

Wong, Bernard P. 1988. *Patronage, Brokerage, Entrepreneurship, and the Chinese Community of New York.* New York: AMS Press.

———. 1979. *A Chinese American Community: Ethnicity and Survival Strategies.* Singapore: Chopmen Enterprises.

Wong, Morrison G. 1986. "Post-1965 Asian Immigrants: Where Do They Come from, Where Are They Now, and Where Are They Going?" *Annals of the American Academy of Political and Social Sciences* 487 (September): 150–168.

Yancey, William L., Eugene P. Ericksen, and Richard N. Juliani. 1976. "Emergent Ethnicity: A Review and Reformulation." *American Sociological Review* 41: 391–403.

Yuan, D. Y. 1963. "Voluntary Segregation: A Study of New Chinatown." *Phylon* 24 (3): 255–268.

Zhou, Min. 1989. *The Enclave Economy and Immigrant Incorporation in New York City's Chinatown.* Ph.D. diss., State University of New York at Albany.

Zhou, Min, and John R. Logan. 1991. "In and out of Chinatown: Residential Mobility and Segregation of New York City's Chinese." *Social Forces* 70 (2):

———. 1989. "Returns on Human Capital in Ethnic Enclaves: New York City's Chinatown." *American Sociological Review* 54: 809–820.

Zolberg, Aristide R. 1989. "The Next Waves: Migration Theory for a Changing World." *International Migration Review* 23 (3): 403–430.

Index

"Salad-bowl" thesis, 3
San Francisco, 24, 122; Chinese concentration in, 208; earthquake, 32
Sanders, Jimy M., 120–121, 137
Sandwich Islands, 21
Second-generation Chinese, 128–130,
133, 225
Segregation: of Asians, 192, 202–203;
of blacks, 203; of Chinese, 1–2, 14,
90, 193, 229; of Chinese from other
ethnic groups, 194–196; ethnic, 33,
150, 185, 203 (*see also* Index of dis-
similarity; Logit model); findings of
residential, 194–196; of Hispanics,
193, 203; involuntary, 33, 39; resi-
dential, 192, 202, 211, 214; voluntary,
33, 39, 215, 218
Self-confidence, 9
Self-employment, 12, 88, 96, 165, 211,
224, 229, 232; as indication of social
mobility, 138–140
Self-esteem, 9, 232
Self-exploitation, 12
Self-isolation, 40
Self-protection, 31, 89
Self-sacrifice, 9, 20
Self-segregation, 216
Semynov, Moshe, 111
Settlement, 16
Settlers, 36–37
Sex, ix, 79–80; ratio, 37–38, 80, 159
Shaanxi, 60
Shandong, 60
Shanghai, 20, 59, 60, 66, 72
Shanxi, 60
Siam, 21
Sichuan, 60
Sino-American Publicity Bureau (SAPB),
95
Sino-American relations, 107
Slums, 10
Social capital, 12, 15, 115, 219, 222,
226, 229, 232
Social dislocation, 1, 228
Social status, 228
Socioeconomic achievement, xvii, 67,
140, 226, 227; and aspirations, 165;

and potential, xvii, xviii; and status,
192, 194, 196, 199, 220, 229; and
status of Chinese immigrant women,
162. *See also* Achievement; Assimilation
Socioeconomic hierarchy, xvii; and
institutions, 10
Sociological inquiry, xiii
Sojourners, 32, 35, 40, 69, 88, 211
Sojourning, 18, 93, 208, 220; character
of early Chinese immigration, 16, 25;
goals of, 25, 31, 39, 220
Solidarity, 3, 215; communal, 3; ethnic,
xvii, 10, 117, 148, 150, 151, 224, 229
South America, 21; immigrants from,
41
South China Sea, 19
Southeast Asia, 21; garment industry
in, 175; Hong Kong exodus to, 66;
immigrants from, 41, 42, 215; politi-
cal uncertainty and instability in, 49,
86, 221
Southern Overseas Chinese Journal, 57
Spaniards, 21
Spitze, Glenna, xxiii
Subordinate position of women, 153,
154, 175. *See also* Chinese women
Substandard working conditions, 180–
181
Suburbanization, 85, 192, 202, 217
Sung, Betty Lee, xxiii, 187
Survey Research of Hong Kong, 72
Swanstrom, Todd, xxiii

Taishan (Toishan), xxi, 25, 32; and
Taishanese, 69
Taiwan, x; exodus from, 74; fear of
Communist take-over in, 74; foreign
reserves in, 73; garment industry
in, 175; Guomindang Nationalist
government of, 55, 63, 64, 73, 74;
immigrants from, 41–43, 48, 59, 63,
73–75, 76, 77, 79, 99, 104, 153, 159–
160, 215; martial law in, 74; political
uncertainty and instability in, 49, 86,
205; population of, 74; return visits
to, 107; Taipei, 74